Useful Expressions and Vocabulary for English Composition

K. C. Chen • T. M. Cheung

Greenwood Press

GREENWOOD PRESS
47 Pokfulam Road, 8/F., Hong Kong.
Tel: (852) 2546 8212, 2547 7041
Email: gwpress@ctimail.com
Web site: www.green-woodpress.com

2nd Revised Edition 2008
    Reprinted 2009

ISBN: 978-962-279-261-6

PRINTED IN HONG KONG

Preface to the 2nd revised edition

This book has been very popular as a reference for English composition for over ten years.

This edition has been thoroughly revised and enlarged with the addition of five new topics.

The main purpose of this book is to help Hong Kong students master English composition. The wide range of relevant vocabulary and useful expressions, on a number of common topics, give students a practical guide for writing compositions. On average, there are 40 complete sentences, 20 phrases and a list of 55 words for each of the 69 topics listed.

The three sections in each topic are briefly described as follows:

In the first part, the complete sentences are suggestions that may be used as content in a particular topic. These sentences, as far as possible, are written in a logical sequence so as to represent a development of ideas. They are by no means exhaustive, but they do provide a suitable framework which could be filled with other relevant material. Apart from providing ideas, these sentences also show the correct use of common words and expressions for particular contexts.

The second part consists of a number of phrases relevant to the topic. Students are advised to make good use of these phrases, and to consult a good English dictionary when in doubt as to their proper use.

The third part is a carefully prepared list of words related to the topic. They are mostly useful and relevant nouns, although appropriate adjectives and verbs have also been included. In most topics, the vocabulary is listed in such a way that nouns come first, followed by adjectives and verbs.

In all three parts, the Chinese translation is given to facilitate better understanding and provide a quick reference. On some topics, special effort has been made to incorporate information and vocabulary that reflect the latest developments.

On the whole, this book should be a valuable source of reference for those learning to write English compositions. Students can derive maximum benefit they study the content seriously and also use it in English conversation.

It is the sincere intention of the authors to help students master the English structure and usage so that they can write accurate English compositions with little difficulty. Therefore, any helpful comments and suggestions that lead to the improvement of this book will be very much appreciated.

July, 2008

The Authors

Contents

Accident

Sentences

1. In a big city, there are traffic accidents every day and there is no exception in Hong Kong.

   大城市每天都會發生交通意外，香港亦不例外。

2. The basic cause for traffic accidents is careless driving but sometimes the accidents are caused by the tiredness of the driver.

   交通意外的基本原因是不小心駕駛，但有時也會因司機困倦所致。

3. Traffic accidents bring about casualties and traffic congestions.

   交通意外會造成傷亡，引致交通擠塞。

4. Pedestrians do not cross the road along the zebra crossing.

   行人不沿斑馬線橫過馬路。

5. Jumping the red traffic light causes the traffic accident.

   汽車衝紅燈造成交通意外。

6. The youth was knocked down by a car.

   那個青年被汽車撞倒。

7. The spot was crowded with many passers-by.

   很多路人在現場圍觀。

8. The policeman was directing the traffic.

   一個警員在指揮車輛行駛。

9. The police dispersed the on-lookers.

   警員驅散圍觀者。

10. Reporters took pictures on the spot and gathered information.

    記者在現場拍照及蒐集資料。

11. The injured were hurriedly rushed to hospital for treatment.

    傷者被迅速地送往醫院接受治療。

12. The traffic soon returned to normal.

    交通不久回復正常。

13. The sports-car came round the corner.

    那輛跑車從街角駛來。

14. I heard a car screeching.

    我聽到一輛汽車發出尖叫聲。

15. The victim was lying unconscious in a pool of blood.

受害者躺在血泊中，不省人事。

16. The driver dialled 999.

司機打 999 報警。

17. Traffic came to a standstill and many vehicles were held up.

交通停頓，使很多車輛不能前進。

18. A policeman was accusing the driver of careless driving.

一個警員控告那司機不小心駕駛。

19. The police persuaded the crowd to disperse.

警員勸喻羣眾散去。

20. A policeman jotted down the details of the accident.

一個警員記下意外詳情。

21. The pedestrian was also to blame.

那個行人也應受譴責。

22. The driver was travelling too fast.

司機當時超速駕駛。

23. Two cars had a head-on collision.

兩輛汽車迎頭相撞。

24. The underlying cause of the accident was careless driving.

這宗意外的基本原因是不小心駕駛。

25. Four people were involved in this accident.

這宗意外牽涉到四個人。

26. A queue of cars quickly formed.

一條車龍很快形成。

27. The accident caused serious traffic congestion.

這宗意外引致嚴重的交通擠塞。

28. The lorry stopped unexpectedly.

貨車突然停下來。

29. The driver took the risk of overtaking the bus.

那個司機冒險超越巴士。

30. The lorry ran into the back of a private car.

貨車撞向一輛汽車的後面。

31. The driver was putting his foot on the accelerator.

司機當時正踏着加速器。

32. The black car bumped into the double-decker in front.

黑色汽車猛烈地撞中前面的雙層巴士。

33. The man was covered with bruises.

男人滿身傷痕。

34. Many on-lookers uttered a sigh.

很多旁觀者發出歎息聲。

35. What a terrifying experience it was!

多麼可怕的經驗啊！

36. The driver paid for the damage. 司機賠償損失。

37. Some on-lookers appeared to be grieved. 一些旁觀者露出哀傷的神情。

 **Phrases**

1. a speeding car 一輛疾駛的汽車

2. a screeching sound of brakes 制動器發出的尖叫聲

3. apathetic on-lookers 漠不關心的旁觀者

4. negligence and carelessness 疏忽大意

5. deaths and injuries 傷亡

6. fitting and wearing of seat belts 安裝及佩戴安全帶

7. driving under the influence of alcohol 醉酒駕駛

8. serious congestion problem 嚴重的擠塞問題

9. maintaining traffic flow 維持交通流量

10. to identify accident causes 確定意外成因

11. accident prevention measures 預防意外的措施

12. disobeying traffic signals 違反交通信號的規定

13. driving too close 跟車太貼

14. a set of improvement measures 一系列的改善措施

15. safe and sound 安全無恙

16. to cherish life 愛惜生命

17. driving exceeds the speed limit 超速駕駛

18. brake failure 汽車控制失靈

19. to change lane (overtaking) 切線（爬頭）

20. a chain of car collisions 連環撞車

21. dangerous driving 危險駕駛

22. no entry 禁止駛入

23. illegal car race   非法賽車

24. no thorough road   此路不通

 # Vocabulary

1.	eye-witness	目擊證人	23. squash	壓碎
2.	passers-by	路人	24. lorry	貨車
3.	victim	受害者	25. number plate	號碼牌
4.	scene/spot	出事地點	26. licence number	車牌號碼
5.	blood	血	27. headlights	車頭燈
6.	ambulance	救護車	28. bumper	車前緩衝器
7.	ambulancemen	救護人員	29. steering wheel	駕駛軚盤
8.	stretcher	擔架	30. brake	制動器
9.	first aid	急救	31. bang	砰的一聲
10.	traffic policemen	交通警員	32. windscreen	擋風玻璃
11.	investigate	調查	33. boot	車尾箱
12.	witness (v.)	目睹	34. tyre	車胎
13.	crash	撞擊	35. bruise	傷痕
14.	co-operate	合作	36. bleed	流血
15.	civic-minded	有公民意識	37. rear-seat passengers	後座乘客
16.	reporter	記者	38. passenger casualties	乘客的傷亡
17.	comment	評論		
18.	headline	報紙標題	39. public awareness	公眾意識
19.	fault	過失		
20.	carelessness	不小心	40. accident black spots	交通黑點
21.	unconscious	昏迷		
22.	fatal	致命的	41. close circuit television	閉路電視

42.	road safety compaigns	交通安全運動	46.	news report	新聞報導

42. road safety compaigns　交通安全運動

43. road safety patrol teams　交通安全隊

44. survivors　生還者

45. official report　官方報告

46. news report　新聞報導

47. the screening breath test　酒精測試（吹波仔）

48. 3rd party insurance　第三者保險

49. passing place　黃色方格

Advertisement

Sentences

1. The survival of the newspaper depends mainly on the revenue from advertisements.　報章主要倚靠廣告費的收入而生存。

2. The revenue from selling the newspaper may not be able to cover the paper and printing cost.　報費的收入未必能支付紙張和印刷的費用。

3. Using e-mail to send advertisements saves time and the cost is low.　利用電郵發出廣告，既快捷，成本又低。

4. Too many e-mail advertisements result in a flood of rubbish mail.　太多的電郵廣告造成垃圾郵件泛濫。

5. Many commercial organizations use e-mail to send advertisements. There are also companies which specially send fax advertisements.　很多商業機構利用電郵發出廣告。有些公司也專門替人發放傳真廣告。

6. Some small restaurants employ workers to distribute fliers in the street.　有些小餐廳僱人在街頭派發傳單。

7. There are advertisements on the body of the bus and tram and also at the stations.　巴士及電車車身印有廣告，車站也有。

8. There are also television advertisements on the bus.　巴士上亦有電視廣告。

9. Mobile phones also receive commodity promotion advertisements.

手提電話亦收到推銷商品的廣告。

10. Most of advertisements we see every day are about property selling and body trimming.

我們日常看到的廣告以售樓及纖體為多。

11. Through advertising, businessmen announce the sale of some new products.

商人通過廣告來推銷新產品。

12. Advertising can often help to sell more goods.

廣告通常能幫助銷售更多的貨品。

13. Advertising can also make one's wants known.

廣告亦能告知別人自己所需。

14. The message is usually expressed through the mass media.

訊息通常是透過大眾傳播媒介傳達。

15. We can insert an advertisement in the newspaper.

我們可以在報章上刊登廣告。

16. Indeed, many people in Hong Kong make use of the services provided by the Classified Advertisement of the newspaper.

事實上，很多香港人利用報章的分類小廣告所提供的服務。

17. New products or services must be widely publicized.

新產品或服務必須廣為宣傳。

18. Advertising is an art of persuading people into buying something.

廣告是說服他人購買物品的藝術。

19. Successful advertising can often bring about an increase in sales, production, employment and income.

成功的廣告通常能導致銷售、生產、就業和收入的增加。

20. On the other hand, advertising increases the cost and selling price of goods.

另一方面，刊登廣告增加產品的成本及售價。

21. The goods advertised can usually be known by more people.

刊登廣告的商品通常能被較多人熟悉。

22. However, the good points of a product are sometimes exaggerated.

然而，一種商品的優點有時會被誇大。

23. It stimulates more spending.

它刺激更多的消費。

24. In a highly competitive commercial society, advertising has almost become a must.

在一個高度競爭的商業社會裏，刊登廣告幾乎是必要的。

25. Advertisements aim at appealing to more customers.

廣告的目的是吸引更多的顧客。

26. Advertising on television is a powerful instrument of sales.

電視廣告是有力的銷售工具。

27. Under the influence of commercial advertising, people may easily be made to pursue material comfort.

人們受到商業廣告的影響，會容易追求物質享受。

28. Advertising provides more employment opportunities because it has become a thriving industry in itself.

廣告提供更多的就業機會，因為它本身已成為一種發展蓬勃的工業。

29. It adds colour to life.

它使生活增添色彩。

30. New products are usually introduced to potential customers through advertising.

新產品通常是通過廣告介紹給未來的顧客的。

31. However, it often spreads a sense of enjoyment.

然而，它時常散播一種追求享受的意識。

32. The style of advertising has made remarkable progress.

廣告的形式已有顯著的進步。

33. Advertising can popularize new products.

廣告能推廣新產品。

34. Advertising is necessary to make the goods known.

若要商品被人認識，刊登廣告是必須的。

35. Good quality and reasonable price are always the best advertisement.

最佳的廣告總是良好的品質及合理的價格。

36. It is largely through the medium of advertising that buyers and sellers get in touch with one another.

買賣雙方得以互相接觸，大部分有賴於廣告這個媒介。

37. The hypnotising effects of advertising cannot be underestimated.

我們不能低估廣告的催眠效果。

38. Many young people are unaware of the harmful effects that advertising may have on them.

很多年青人不察覺廣告對他們可能造成的壞影響。

39. Many advertisements influence people into believing the concept of value being publicized.

很多廣告引誘人們相信它們所宣揚的價值觀。

40. Some advertisements spread unhealthy thoughts.

有些廣告散播不健康的思想。

Phrases

1.	standard of living	生活水準
2.	modern commercial art	現代化的商業藝術
3.	sign-boards hanging in front of every shop	每間商店門前所懸掛的招牌
4.	a new brand	新牌子
5.	a new product	新產品
6.	striking advertisements	吸引人的廣告
7.	the credulous public	輕易相信事物的大眾
8.	epigrammatic phrases	精警的片語
9.	the highly complex modern life	高度複雜的現代生活
10.	catchy and arresting	吸引人的
11.	prospective customers	將來的顧客
12.	irresistible appeal	不能抗拒的吸引力
13.	particular brand of articles	特別牌子的貨品
14.	famous brand name	名牌子
15.	in order to attract more customers	以廣招徠
16.	widely publicized	廣泛的宣傳
17.	enormous advertising fees	巨大的廣告費
18.	luxurious consumer goods	奢侈的消費品
19.	cigarettes and wines	煙酒
20.	whisky and brandy	威士忌及白蘭地酒
21.	sports wear and shoes	運動服裝及鞋
22.	exaggerated phrasing	誇張的語句
23.	regardless of the quality	不理會品質
24.	a symbol of good taste	良好品味的象徵
25.	a symbol of status	地位的象徵

26. a big bargain sale   大平賣

27. advertising blitz   廣告攻勢

28. to place advertisements in newspapers   在報章刊登廣告

29. to make a small profit to enable a big sale   薄利多銷

30. the right of the consumers   消費者權益

31. minimum charge   最低消費

 ## Vocabulary

1.	newspapers	報章	19. slogan	口號
2.	television screen	電視熒光幕	20. reaction	反應
3.	radio	電台	21. brand-new	簇新的
4.	cinema	電影院	22. fascinating	迷人的
5.	posters	海報	23. effective	有效的
6.	neon-signs	霓虹光管招牌	24. irresistible	不能抗拒的
7.	magazines	雜誌	25. misleading	誤導的
8.	brand name	牌子名	26. disgusting	厭惡的
9.	transactions	交易	27. announce	宣佈
10.	mass media	大眾傳播媒介	28. promote	推廣
11.	commodity	商品	29. persuade	說服
12.	customers	顧客	30. exaggerate	誇大
13.	design	設計	31. deceive	欺騙
14.	technique	技術	32. influence	影響
15.	sign-boards	招牌	33. pervade	滲透
16.	commercials	商業廣告	34. registered trade marks	註冊商標
17.	revenue	收入	35. direct marketing	直銷
18.	symbol	象徵		

36.	gags	橋段
37.	catchword	標語
38.	logo	標誌
39.	shoddy goods	劣貨
40.	billboard	廣告牌
41.	coupon	代用券
42.	cost of production	生產成本
43.	cost of sales	銷貨成本
44.	advertising agencies	廣告代理商
45.	lucky draws	幸運抽獎
46.	free gifts	贈品
47.	electric goods	電器產品
48.	classified advertisement	分類小廣告
49.	advertising company	廣告公司
50.	movie advertisement	電影廣告
51.	advertising film	廣告片
52.	mobile advertisement	流動廣告
53.	sandwich man	三文治式廣告人
54.	promotion price	推廣價
55.	Consumer Council	消費者委員會
56.	complimentary ticket	贈券
57.	on-line shopping	網上購物

At the Airport

 ## Sentences

1. Electronic screens are installed everywhere at the airport to show arrival and departure status of the aeroplanes.

    機場到處都裝有電子熒幕，顯示班機的升降情況。

2. Free wheelchair services are provided to facilitate the sick and disabled.

    機場提供免費輪椅服務，方便病人和傷健人士。

3. Before entering the restricted area, passengers must pass the strict security check.

乘客進入禁區前，必須通過嚴密的安全檢查。

4. Online booking air tickets is convenient and fast.

在網上預定機票，方便快捷。

5. For the long distance flight, economic class passengers can carry 2 bags of checked baggage.

每位長途客機的經濟艙位乘客可攜帶兩件限定重量的寄艙行李。

6. Cabin baggage cannot exceed the set measurement and weight limit.

手提行李箱不能超出限定的大小及重量。

7. Many passengers select an isle seat because it is convenient to go in and out.

很多乘客選擇機艙的路口位，以便出入。

8. For short distance flights, only soft drinks but not meals are provided.

短程班機不供應餐膳，只提供飲品。

9. Please buckle your safety belt tight.

請扣緊安全帶。

10. Smoking is prohibited in the compartment.

機艙內全面禁煙。

11. Electronic devices such as mobile phones and notebook computers should be switched off when the plane is taking off or landing.

飛機升降時，乘客不能使用電子用具，如手機、手提電腦。

12. Supersonic jumbo jets have replaced the old propeller aeroplanes.

超音速珍寶噴射機已取代了舊式螺旋槳飛機。

13. Many aeroplanes can be seen busily landing and taking off at the airport.

在機場內，我們可以看到很多飛機正在繁忙地升降。

14. It provides round the clock service.

它提供二十四小時服務。

15. Parking space is limited.

泊車空間有限。

16. The airport is equipped with modern facilities.

機場擁有現代化的設施。

17. Radio and radar navigation facilities are widely used.

無線電及雷達導航設施被廣泛應用。

18. The newly introduced measures are very efficient in clearing passengers.

新措施對疏導旅客十分有效率。

19. Night landings and take-offs are very common.

飛機在晚上升降是十分常見的。

20. Chek Lap Kok Airport is comparable to any modern airport in the world.

赤鱲角機場可媲美世界上任何一個現代化機場。

21. Hong Kong is on the international air route.

香港位於國際航線之上。

22. Many passengers stop over at the airport.

很多乘客在機場停留。

23. There are several hundred flights to and from Hong Kong every week.

每個星期有數百班機進出香港。

24. Passengers have to book their seats three days in advance.

乘客須於三天前預訂座位。

25. Many people go to the airport to see their relatives and friends off.

很多人去機場送別親友。

26. They wave good-bye to their relatives and friends.

他們向親友揮手道別。

27. Aeroplanes land by remote control.

飛機靠遙控降落。

28. Passengers have to check in at the counter.

乘客須在櫃台前辦理登機手續。

29. They put the luggage on the scale.

他們把行李過磅。

30. Passengers board the plane in an orderly manner.

乘客有秩序地登機。

31. The aeroplane takes off gradually.

飛機徐徐起飛。

32. It arrives on time at the destination.

它準時到達目的地。

33. It makes a perfect landing.

它的降落很完美。

34. Advanced electronic equipment can be seen everywhere at the airport.

先進的電子設備在機場內隨處可見。

35. Radio communication facilities have been widely used.

無線電通訊設施已被廣泛應用。

36. Every day there are a large number of in-coming and out-going flights.

每天都有為數眾多的入境及離境班機。

37. Expansion is necessary to cope with the increasing demand.

為了應付需求的增長，擴展是必須的。

38. There is a busy and hectic scene at the airport.

機場內一片繁忙的景象。

39. Some tourists are inquiring about bookings of hotel rooms.

有些遊客正在查詢酒店訂房的事宜。

40. Many people are transit passengers.	很多人是過境旅客。
41. Some people are on a business trip.	有些人作業務旅行。
42. We wait for the plane to land on the ground.	我們等候飛機着陸。
43. Passengers walk up the gangway into the plane.	乘客登上梯級進入飛機內。
44. The aeroplane takes off in ten minutes.	飛機在十分鐘後起飛。

 ## Phrases

1.	landing safely	安全着陸
2.	on time	準時
3.	stand-by	候補機位
4.	low-priced air ticket	廉價機票
5.	turbulent air current	不穩定氣流
6.	hours of operations	運作時間
7.	heavy passenger traffic	繁忙的客運
8.	frequency of flights	飛機班次的密度
9.	scheduled passenger and cargo services	定期的客貨運服務
10.	wide-bodied aircraft	廣體客機
11.	air traffic control	航空交通管制
12.	computerized allocation	電腦編配
13.	spacious environment	寬敞的環境
14.	check in	辦理登機手續

 ## Vocabulary

1.	passenger terminal	客運大樓	3.	luggage/ baggage	行李
2.	shopping arcade	購物商場	4.	control tower	控制塔

5.	aircraft runway	飛機跑道	31.	lounge	休憩室
6.	airline companies	航空公司	32.	television screen	電視熒光幕
7.	safety-belts	安全帶	33.	airport cafeteria	機場餐廳
8.	cargoes	貨物	34.	duty	關稅
9.	air freight	航空貨運	35.	journey	旅程
10.	computerization	電腦化	36.	suitcase	小行囊
11.	radar	雷達	37.	travel documents	旅遊證件
12.	visibility	能見度	38.	chop	印鑑
13.	Boeing 747 jets	波音七四七噴射機	39.	procedure	程序
14.	Jumbo jets	珍寶噴射機	40.	airfield	機場
15.	gangway	座間通道	41.	Chek Lap Kok	赤鱲角
16.	first class	頭等艙位	42.	Lantau Island	大嶼山
17.	business class	商務客位	43.	air traffic control centre	空中交通控制中心
18.	economy class	經濟艙位	44.	radio	無線電
19.	flight number	航班號碼	45.	passengers	乘客
20.	counter	櫃台	46.	announcer	廣播員
21.	scale	磅	47.	porter	挑夫
22.	return ticket	雙程機票	48.	ground staff	地勤人員
23.	information desk	詢問處	49.	air-hostess	空中小姐
24.	arrival gate	入閘	50.	crew	機上全體職員
25.	departure gate	出閘	51.	immigration officers	人民入境事務官員
26.	customs	海關	52.	pilot	機師
27.	arrival hall	候機室	53.	engineers	工程師
28.	departure hall	送機室	54.	customs officers	海關官員
29.	sofa	沙發椅			
30.	rest room	休息室			

55.	stewardess	女侍應生
56.	automatic	自動化的
57.	fasten	繫牢
58.	declare	申報
59.	check	核對
60.	announce	宣佈
61.	inspect	檢查
62.	the VIP Suite	機場貴賓室
63.	baggage handling hall	行李處理大堂
64.	multi-storey car park	多層停車場
65.	contingency plan	應變計劃
66.	Airport Express	機場快線
67.	City Flyer	城巴機場快線
68.	conveyor	輸送帶
69.	helicopter	直升機
70.	quarantine	檢疫
71.	contraband	違禁品
72.	hijack	劫機
73.	air bus	空中巴士
74.	smoking room	吸煙室

75.	body temperature checking device	體溫檢查儀
76.	window seat	窗口位
77.	aisle seat	路口位
78.	direct flight	直航
79.	transfer	轉機
80.	command pilot	機長
81.	international airport	國際機場
82.	domestic airport	內陸機場
83.	electronic air ticket	電子機票
84.	boarding pass	登機證
85.	delay	延遲
86.	special plane	專機
87.	connect flight	接駁班機
88.	flight time	飛行時間
89.	online booking	網上訂位
90.	advance booking	預訂
91.	moving belt	運輸帶
92.	special bus	特別巴士

Autumn

Sentences

1.	Autumn is a season of harvest.	秋天是收穫的季節。
2.	Farmers are busy reaping the fruits of their labour.	農夫們正忙於收割他們勤勞所得的成果。
3.	The breeze refreshes us.	微風使我們精神為之一振。
4.	Many young people go for a picnic in the countryside.	很多年青人到郊外旅行。
5.	Flowers, grass and trees can be seen everywhere.	花草樹木隨處可見。
6.	Old people romp round the park in the morning.	清晨時分，老年人在公園的四週漫步。
7.	They smile sweetly.	他們展現出甜美的微笑。
8.	It is beyond their happiness.	他們感到極其快樂。
9.	The brightly decorated flower square is especially attractive.	那繽紛的花圃分外迷人。
10.	The cool, dry climate in autumn makes it the best season for picnics.	涼快而乾燥的天氣使秋天成為郊遊的最佳季節。
11.	The weather is neither too hot nor too cold.	天氣從不太熱，也不太冷。
12.	Days are getting shorter and the nights, longer.	日短夜長。
13.	Sometimes we can see a thin layer of morning mist.	有時我們可以看到一層薄紗似的晨霧。
14.	Chrysanthemums are bright and beautiful.	菊花鮮艷美麗。
15.	Ladies are dressed in autumn style.	女士們穿上秋裝。

16. Children are singing in a merry atmosphere.   孩子們在歡樂的氣氛中歌唱。

17. We feel a sense of greenishness.   我們感到一片綠意。

18. People enjoy the bright moonlight.   人們欣賞明亮的月色。

19. It is like a million golden rays hanging from the sky.   它像是百萬道掛在天空中的金光。

20. It is changed into a coral sea.   它變成了一片珊瑚海。

21. The setting sun is fast receding.   夕陽正在迅速地消失。

22. Peace and tranquillity dominate everything.   和平與寧靜支配了一切。

23. Many things are worthy of our attention.   很多事物值得我們留意。

24. As leaves gradually wither away, people begin to feel gloomy and sad.   隨着樹葉逐漸枯萎，人們開始感到悲涼。

 Phrases

1. bare and bleak   荒涼寂寞

2. with hardly any life   幾乎沒有生命

3. beyond imagination   超乎想像的

4. natural beauty   天然的美麗

5. golden leaves   金黃色的樹葉

6. hazy sky   天色迷濛

7. tinges of Autumn   秋色

8. a scattering of   零零落落的

 Vocabulary

1.	orchards	果園	5.	countryside	郊野
2.	twigs	小樹枝	6.	insects	昆蟲
3.	dew	露水	7.	shade	樹蔭
4.	sunset	落日	8.	swan	天鵝

9.	chrysanthemum	菊花	21.	fascinating	迷人的
10.	harvest	收穫	22.	azure	天藍色的
11.	maple leaves	楓葉	23.	clear	澄澈的
12.	morning ray	晨光	24.	leisurely	悠閒的
13.	colourful	顏色鮮艷的	25.	stroll	散步
14.	charming	迷人的	26.	shine	發光
15.	lovely	可愛的	27.	appreciate	欣賞
16.	wonderful	神奇的	28.	wither	枯萎
17.	splendid	妙不可言的	29.	recede	後退
18.	serene	寂靜的	30.	fancy (v.)	想像
19.	scenic	天然景色的	31.	full moon	圓月
20.	fragrant	芳香的			

In a Bank

Sentences

1. Before a bank opens, many people are waiting at the door.

   銀行還沒開門，很多人已在門外排隊。

2. Some deposit the money in the bank. Some withdraw money from the bank.

   有人存款，有人提款。

3. Where do you bank?

   你的錢存在哪家銀行？

4. Some old ladies take the passbook to the bank to update.

   有些老婆婆拿着存摺到銀行「打簿」。

5. Some people go to the bank to pay the insurance fees.

   有些人到銀行繳交保險費。

6. Some open the safe deposit box to put the valuables there. | 有些人要開保險箱，存放貴重物品。

7. One lady remits money to her daughter studying abroad. | 有一位太太要匯款給她在外國讀書的女兒。

8. Some buy US dollars with Hong Kong dollars. | 有人用港幣買美鈔。

9. Some exchange Reminbi for Hong Kong dollars. | 有人以港幣兌換人民幣。

10. One old gentleman made a fixed deposit of Australian dollars for half a year. | 有一位老先生要做半年澳幣定期存款。

11. Many banks set up the stocks and shares department and install several computers for customers to enquire about the share prices. | 很多銀行設有股票部及安裝多部電腦，以便顧客查詢股價。

12. Moreover, in some banks, there are chairs for spot trading customers to rest. | 更有些銀行放置很多椅子，供進行即場買賣的顧客休息。

Phrases

1. a basket of currencies | 一籃子貨幣

2. to pay by installments | 分期付款

3. to mortgage a house to a bank | 把一幢房子押給銀行

4. deposit matures | 存款到期

5. to cash a cheque | 兌現一張支票

Vocabulary

1. loan | 貸款
2. listing | 上市
3. interim report | 中期報告
4. bankrupt | 破產
5. bank-note | 鈔票

6. market value | 市值
7. stamp duty | 印花稅
8. bad debt | 壞帳
9. bond | 債券
10. annual report | 年報

11.	analyst	分析員	23.	current account	來往戶口
12.	privatization	私有化	24.	rebate	回佣
13.	bubble economy	泡沫經濟	25.	banking hours	營業時間
14.	interest	利息	26.	minority share holder	小股東
15.	bank rate	銀行貼現率	27.	letter of credit	信用狀
16.	prime rate	優惠利率	28.	bill of lading	提貨單
17.	savings account	儲蓄戶口	29.	automatic teller machine	自動提款機
18.	bank balance	銀行存款餘額	30.	limited liabilities company	股份有限公司
19.	bank cheque	銀行支票			
20.	bank draft	匯票	31.	post dated cheque	期票
21.	bank book	存摺			
22.	gift coupon	禮券	32.	best lending rate	最優惠利率

At the Beach

 Sentences

1. Red flag is hoisted at the beach. It isn't suitable for swimming there.

   海灘懸掛紅旗，表示不宜游泳。

2. Red tide appears near the beach. It is dangerous to swim there.

   海灘附近出現紅潮，泳客在那裏游泳會有危險。

3. People short of moral litter at the beach.

   有些缺德的人把垃圾丟在沙灘上。

4. Children make castles on the sand.

   兒童在沙上造城堡。

5. Waves come rolling on the shore.　波浪滾到岸上來。

6. People like the brilliant sun, but are averse to the shimmering heat.　人們喜愛燦爛的陽光，但他們厭惡熠熠的熱力。

7. Many young people like living the present to the full.　很多年青人喜歡及時行樂。

8. Some young couples row a boat on the green water.　一些年青愛侶泛舟綠波上。

9. The waves are quiet.　風平浪靜。

10. Some people prefer basking in the sun.　有些人喜歡進行日光浴。

11. A nearby shop serves refreshments.　一家附近的商店供應點心。

12. Children romp round the beach.　兒童在海灘四週嬉戲。

13. Beaches are often swarmed with swimmers in summer.　在夏天，海灘經常擠滿弄潮兒。

14. Some people lay under the coloured tents.　有些人躺在彩色的帳幕下。

15. Although waves are sometimes violent, many people attempt to break through them and proceed forward.　雖然有時海浪洶湧，但是很多人仍然嘗試破浪前進。

16. A few dinghies can be seen floating on the surface of the sea.　我們可以看到幾艘橡皮艇在海面上浮着。

17. The sand glitters in the sun with a golden colour.　沙礫在太陽下閃出金黃色。

18. Three common ways of swimming are crawl stroke, breast stroke and butterfly stroke.　三種常見的泳式是自由式、蛙式和蝶式。

19. The sultry weather drives many people to the beach.　悶熱的天氣驅使很多人前往海灘。

20. Children are playing happily with the sand.　孩子們正在愉快地玩沙。

21. The sky and the sea merge into one.　天與海連成一片。

22. The breeze is blowing gently.　微風正在輕輕地吹着。

23. Some people tread on the sand with their bare feet.　有些人赤足在沙上走。

24. People descend the steps to reach the beach.　人們走下石階來到海灘上。

25. The most prominent object is an enormous stone statue.

最矚目的東西是一個巨大的石像。

26. Children are playing about in the shallow water near the beach.

兒童在沙灘附近的淺水處玩耍。

27. They chase one another.

他們互相追逐。

28. Paddling in the water can bring you a lot of fun.

涉水能帶給你很多樂趣。

29. Two girls are splashing each other.

兩個女孩正在互相潑水。

30. Three beginners are learning how to float on water.

三個初學者正在學習浮水。

31. People usually smear suntan lotion on the skin before taking a sun bath.

人們通常在進行日光浴前在皮膚上塗上太陽油。

32. Some people are sipping soft drinks and playing cards.

有些人正在喝汽水和玩紙牌。

33. Others like to relax in canvas chairs listening to the radio.

其他人喜歡躺在帆布椅上休息及聽收音機。

34. When night falls, swimmers rush to catch a bus home.

當夜幕低垂時，泳客匆匆乘搭巴士回家。

35. All forms of public transport are filled to capacity.

各種公共交通工具都載滿了人。

 Phrases

1. colourful tents — 色彩繽紛的帳幕

2. rows of tents — 一排排的帳幕

3. happy holiday-makers — 愉快的度假者

4. portable radios and CD player — 手提收音機及 CD 機

5. colourful umbrellas — 色彩繽紛的傘子

6. the most popular summer pastime — 最受歡迎的夏日康樂活動

7. boat rowing — 划艇

8. potential hazard — 潛在危險

Vocabulary

1.	tide	潮水	26.	travel bag	旅行袋
2.	raft	浮台	27.	slippers	拖鞋
3.	rubber dinghies	橡皮艇	28.	flipper	蛙鞋
4.	float	浮標	29.	thermos flask	熱水瓶
5.	speed boat	快艇	30.	sandwich	三文治（三明治）
6.	Repulse Bay	淺水灣	31.	ice-cream	雪糕（冰淇淋）
7.	sun parasols	大遮陽傘	32.	soft drinks	汽水
8.	beach umbrella	沙灘傘	33.	sea gulls	海鷗
9.	sand castles	沙堡	34.	lookout	瞭望台
10.	waves	波浪	35.	cut (n.)	割傷
11.	pebbles	小石子	36.	bruise (n.)	擊傷
12.	shells	貝殼	37.	cramp (n.)	抽筋
13.	horizon	水平線	38.	first-aid tent	救傷營幕
14.	litter	垃圾	39.	rubber ring	橡膠浮水圈
15.	spade	鏟	40.	sunburn (n.)	曬黑
16.	pail/bucket	桶	41.	water-skiing	滑水
17.	life-buoy	水泡	42.	overcrowded	擠滿了人
18.	beach ball	沙灘波	43.	calm	風平浪靜的
19.	beach chair	沙灘椅	44.	splash	濺起
20.	swimming suit	泳衣	45.	glitter	閃耀
21.	bikini	比堅尼式泳衣	46.	sun-bathe	進行日光浴
22.	life-guards	救生員	47.	dive	跳水
23.	suntan lotion	太陽油	48.	diving	潛水
24.	tan	黃褐色	49.	paddle	划水
25.	sun-glasses	太陽眼鏡	50.	drown	溺斃

51.	surfing	滑浪	61.	back stroke	背泳
52.	windsurfing	滑浪風帆	62.	floating bed	浮牀
53.	surfboard	滑浪板	63.	swimming trunks	泳褲
54.	water safety campaign	水上安全運動	64.	changing room	更衣室
55.	manage	管理	65.	swimming classes	習泳班
56.	sandy beach	沙灘	66.	gazetted beaches	憲報公布的泳灘
57.	sailing boats	帆船			
58.	free stroke	自由式	67.	shark prevention nets	防鯊網
59.	butterfly stroke	蝶泳			
60.	breast stroke	胸泳／蛙泳			

7

On a Bus

 ## Sentences

1. The temperature in some air-conditioned buses is too low and the passengers cannot stand it.

   有些空調巴士的溫度太低，使乘客抵受不住。

2. Some passengers do not like to take a seat too near the television for fear of radiation.

   一些乘客不喜歡坐得太貼近電視機，恐怕受到輻射影響。

3. Most passengers would like to take a seat near the window because they can have a view of the street.

   大部分乘客都會選坐車窗旁的座位，因為可以看到街景。

4. This bus will cross the harbour by the Western Harbour Tunnel but not the Hung Hom Cross Harbour Tunnel.

   這路巴士走西隧過海，不走紅隧。

5. You take the bus going in the opposite direction.

你乘坐反方向的巴士了。

6. The general capabilities and maintenance of the buses running on the roads now are quite good.

現在市面行走的巴士的性能和保養都很好。

7. In the compartment, it is quite clean too.

車廂內也很清潔。

8. The fare of the bus is lower than the fare of the minibus.

巴士的收費比小巴的便宜。

9. Sectional fare is available in the bus.

巴士設有分段收費。

10. The fare of the cross-tunnel bus is reduced after crossing the harbour.

隧道巴士過了海，就減收車費。

11. Passengers can roughly be classified into several types.

乘客可大約分為數類。

12. Some people carry heavy parcels on a bus.

有些人攜帶重的東西坐巴士。

13. Many Hong Kong people travel on a bus every day.

很多香港人每天都乘搭巴士。

14. Buses are usually extremely crowded during rush hours.

在繁忙時間，巴士通常十分擠迫。

15. At that time, late-comers can hardly get a seat.

在那時，遲上車的乘客難以找到座位。

16. Some passengers always give up their seats to old people or pregnant women.

有些乘客常常讓座給老人或孕婦。

17. Vulgar people often use abusive language while travelling on a bus.

粗鄙的人時常在乘搭巴士時說穢言惡語。

18. If buses run at a high speed, standing passengers may not be able to keep their balance.

巴士高速行駛，站立的乘客便不能保持平衡。

19. A push from behind is a common phenomenon on a crowded bus.

在一輛擠迫的巴士上，後面的乘客向前推是常見的現象。

20. Many passengers use the 'Octopus' to pay the fare.

很多乘客使用「八達通卡」繳付車費。

21. Passengers have to pay the exact fare.

乘客須繳足車費，不設找續。

22. Passengers insert the coins into the money box in an orderly manner.

乘客有秩序地把輔幣放入錢箱內。

23. On a busy route, there are usually many people getting on or getting off a bus.

在繁忙的路線上，通常有很多人上車或下車。

24. When a bus engine breaks down, it will remain stationary.

當巴士的引擎發生故障時，它便會停止不動。

25. At the time, things will be at a dead-lock.

那時候，事情便成為一個僵局。

26. They were violently pushed onto a bus.

他們被粗暴地推上車。

27. The crowded passengers felt uncomfortable.

擠迫的乘客感到不舒服。

28. We have to elbow our way off a crowded bus.

在一輛滿載乘客的巴士上，我們要盡力擠開別人才能下車。

29. The quarrel could be avoided.

爭吵是可以避免的。

30. It is an embarrassing experience to be stared at on a bus.

在巴士上被人注視使人感到侷促不安。

31. Passengers ring the driver to stop the bus.

乘客按鈴請司機停車。

32. The double decker is often packed with passengers.

雙層巴士經常擠滿乘客。

33. Passengers are squashed tightly together like tinned sardines.

乘客被擠得緊靠在一起，好像裝在罐頭內的沙甸魚。

34. Some people always like to travel on the upper deck of a bus.

有些人總喜歡坐在巴士的上層。

35. On rainy days, speeding buses easily cause accidents.

在下雨天，高速行駛的巴士易生意外。

36. Some passengers like reading newspapers on a bus.

有些乘客喜歡在巴士上閱讀報章。

37. When it rains heavily, buses are always caught in a traffic jam.

當下大雨時，巴士常被困於車龍中。

38. Many people will feel agitated if a bus does not move forward for one reason or another.

當巴士由於某種原因而停滯不前時，很多人會感到焦躁不安。

39. Some passengers kill the time by reading novels while others like to hum their favourite tone.

為了打發時間，有些乘客閱讀小說，有些喜歡哼他們所喜愛的調子。

40. In summer, a bus without air-conditioning becomes a living hell of fire.

在夏天，沒有空調設備的巴士成了一個活火爐。

41. Many people cannot stand the heat.

很多人不能忍受酷熱。

42. The long queue began to move slowly.

那條車龍開始慢慢移動。

43. The bus inched its way forward.

那輛巴士緩慢地前進。

44. In busy urban areas, a bus often moves at a snail's pace.

在繁忙的市區內，巴士常常以蝸牛般的速度行駛。

45. The stuffy air inside a bus nearly suffocates all the passengers.

巴士內混濁的空氣幾乎使所有乘客窒息。

46. Smelly clothes make the situation worse.

發出臭味的衣服使情況更壞。

47. It seems that passengers are caught in a helpless situation.

乘客如陷入一個無助的情況中。

48. At that very moment, they lost their temper.

就在那時，他們發脾氣了。

49. Some standing passengers sway with the turning of the bus.

有些站着的乘客隨着巴士轉彎而擺動。

50. Young couples can sometimes be seen clinging together in each other's arms, regardless of other passengers around them.

我們有時可以看到一雙雙年青情侶互相摟抱，旁若無人。

51. We are encouraged to offer our seats to disabled persons and seniors.

巴士公司鼓勵我們讓座給傷殘人士及長者。

52. They are sitting on the top deck of a double decker.

他們坐在一輛雙層巴士的上層。

53. Under sultry weather, passengers sweat profusely when they travel on a bus without air-conditioning.

在悶熱的天氣，乘客乘搭沒有空調的巴士會汗流浹背。

54. Some people behave in a vulgar manner on a bus.

有些人在巴士上行為粗鄙。

55. They are gazing out of the window.

他們正在望出窗外。

56. The poster reads: Be considerate of others.

那張海報寫着：為他人着想。

57. A courtesy campaign should be held.	巴士公司應該舉行一個禮貌運動。
58. Many passengers alight at the Admiralty Station.	很多乘客在金鐘站下車。
59. No smoking on the bus.	巴士內禁止吸煙。
60. No food and drink on the bus.	巴士內禁止飲食。

 Phrases

1.	screams and shouts	大聲叫喊
2.	in a frenzy of anger	狂怒
3.	to board a bus	登上巴士
4.	outings on holidays	在假日出外旅行
5.	on the upper deck	在上層
6.	on the lower deck	在下層
7.	passengers' blames and curses	乘客的譴責及咒罵
8.	to hold the handrail tight	緊握扶手
9.	to offer seats to the needy	讓位給有需要的人
10.	to skip the stop	飛站

 Vocabulary

1.	passengers	乘客	8.	package/parcel	包裹
2.	possessions	私人物品	9.	steps	階梯
3.	capacity	載客量	10.	pickpocket	小偷
4.	franchised buses	專利巴士	11.	purse/wallet	錢包
5.	bus-only lanes	巴士專用線	12.	regulations	規則
6.	bus fare	車費	13.	cross-harbour routes	過海路線
7.	air-conditioned bus	空調巴士	14.	chaos	混亂

15. commuters	經常乘搭某一路線的乘客	30. middle-aged people	中年人
16. stuffy	空氣不流通的	31. double decker	雙層巴士
17. squeeze	擠壓	32. concessionary fares	優惠票價
18. witness	目睹	33. shuttle bus	穿梭巴士
19. sway	搖擺	34. senior discount	長者優惠
20. swing	擺動	35. exact fare	不設找續
21. clutch	緊握	36. Eastern Harbour Tunnel	東區海底隧道（東隧）
22. struggle	掙扎	37. Hung Hom Cross Harbour Tunnel	紅磡海底隧道（紅隧）
23. rumble	發出隆隆聲	38. Western Harbour Tunnel	西區海底隧道（西隧）
24. collide/crash	相撞		
25. complain/grumble	抱怨		
26. smoke	吸煙		
27. chat	傾談		
28. criticize	批評		
29. Road Show	路訊通		

Bus Stop

 Sentences

1. Now the bus passengers in Hong Kong will queue up for boarding of their own accord. They seldom struggle their way to get on the bus.

   現在香港的巴士乘客都會自動自覺排隊上車，甚少爭先恐後。

2. All the important road marks that the bus goes past are listed on the signage at the bus stop.

   巴士站的路線牌都列明巴士經過的重要路標。

3. Most of the bus stops have a shelter.　　幾乎所有巴士站都有上蓋。

4. The shelter usually serves as an advertise-ment stand.　　巴士站的上蓋通常作賣廣告之用。

5. There is usually a litter box by the side of a bus stop.　　巴士站旁通常有一個廢紙箱。

6. Many office workers have to rush for the morning bus.　　很多寫字樓職員需要趕乘早班巴士。

7. They hurry to the bus stop, only to find that the bus has just left.　　他們趕往巴士站，但發現巴士剛開出。

8. To their dismay, the fully-packed double decker does not stop at the bus stop.　　滿載乘客的巴士沒有停站，候車的人感到失望。

9. The late-comers join the long queue.　　遲來者加入那條長長的候車人龍。

10. An increasing number of people take their place in the line.　　愈來愈多人加入候車隊伍。

11. Finally they get onto a bus.　　他們最後登上一輛巴士。

12. The bus is crowded with passengers.　　那輛巴士擠滿了乘客。

13. The passengers are nearly squashed.　　乘客幾乎給壓扁。

14. A lot of people get off the bus.　　很多人從巴士走出來。

15. It is a bitter experience waiting at a bus stop without a shelter on a rainy day.　　下雨天，在沒有上蓋的巴士站候車是一個痛苦的經驗。

16. They find it very difficult to get off the bus.　　他們發覺難以下巴士。

17. Many people are waiting to board a bus.　　很多人正在等候乘搭巴士。

18. A bus is approaching the bus stop.　　一輛巴士向巴士站駛過來。

19. They are ready to scramble with the crowd.　　他們準備好與眾人擠上車。

20. Whenever I am to board a bus, I often have a hard time scrambling with other passengers.　　我每次乘搭巴士，都要和其他乘客爭上車。

21. The bus services should be improved.　　巴士公司應要改善服務。

22. Buses are often packed to capacity before leaving the terminus.　　巴士離開總站前，常是載滿乘客的。

23. They do not queue up for a bus.　　他們沒有排隊等候巴士。

24. Minutes seem to fly.

時間好像飛走。

25. Passengers often push against each other in order to get on a bus.

乘客時常互相擠壓，以便登上巴士。

26. They wait impatiently at a bus stop.

他們不耐煩地在巴士站候車。

27. She goes hurriedly to catch a bus.

她匆忙地趕搭巴士。

28. Quarrels sometimes break out among the passengers.

乘客間有時會發生口角。

29. Many passengers pointed an accusing finger at the man who jumped the queue.

很多乘客指責那個不排隊的人。

30. To get on an overcrowded bus must be a trying experience.

登上過度擠迫的巴士真是一個令人厭煩的經驗。

31. A large crowd swarmed to the front gate of the bus.

大羣人一窩蜂地走向那輛巴士的前閘。

32. They jammed in a bus.

他們擠進一輛巴士內。

33. A large crowd of people gathered at the bus stop.

一大羣人在巴士站聚集。

34. A half-full bus sped its way past the bus stop.

一輛載着半滿乘客的巴士疾駛過巴士站。

35. Those people who had been waiting for a long time were very angry with the driver.

久候巴士的乘客對那個司機感到十分憤怒。

36. Buses came, dropped off a few passengers and picked up some more.

巴士來了，幾個乘客下了車，另一批乘客又上車。

37. The bus broke down suddenly.

那輛巴士突然發生故障，不能前進。

38. The bus pulled up at a bus stop.

那輛巴士在巴士站停下來。

 **Phrases**

1. inadequate service

服務不足

2. short of buses

缺乏巴士

3. peak-hour congestion

繁忙時間的擠迫情況

4. to ease traffic congestion

紓緩交通擠塞

Vocabulary

1.	route	路線
2.	station controller	站長
3.	queue-jumpers	不排隊的人
4.	frustration	挫折
5.	disturbance	騷亂
6.	pedestrians	行人
7.	minibus	小巴
8.	accident	意外
9.	road junction	十字路口
10.	traffic	交通
11.	passers-by	路人
12.	notice	告示
13.	vehicles	車輛
14.	factory workers	工廠工人

15.	office workers	在寫字樓工作的人
16.	clamorous	吵鬧的
17.	pant	氣喘
18.	alight	下車
19.	board	上車
20.	struggle	力爭
21.	block	阻塞
22.	persuade	勸告
23.	dissuade	勸阻
24.	bus route No. 68	第六十八號巴士路線
25.	peak hours	繁忙時間
26.	off-peak hours	非繁忙時間

9

Cafe

Sentences

1.	That cafe is famous for its magnificent interior decorations.	那家咖啡店以華麗的裝潢著稱。
2.	Light music is frequently played.	咖啡店經常播放輕音樂。
3.	It is a suitable place for social gatherings.	它是一個適宜社交的地方。

4. Some customers only order a drink.　　有些顧客只點一杯飲品。

5. The coffee smells delicious.　　咖啡聞起來十分美味。

6. Breakfast includes a cup of tea and a piece of buttered toast.　　早餐包括一杯茶和一件牛油多士。

7. She is on a diet.　　她正在節食。

8. All flavours of ice-cream are served.　　各式雪糕(冰淇淋)皆有供應。

9. Taking lunch in that cafe is a good experience.　　在那家咖啡店吃午餐是一個愉快的經驗。

10. I like to drink freshly squeezed orange juice.　　我喜歡喝鮮搾橙汁。

11. The cafe serves excellent roast beef.　　那家咖啡室供應非常好的燒牛肉。

12. Many people in Hong Kong have a buffet during holidays.　　很多香港人假日吃自助餐。

13. Customers have to buy a ticket at the cashier.　　顧客須在收銀處購票。

14. They follow the queue.　　他們跟着排隊。

15. They were full.　　他們當時吃得很飽。

16. Some people prefer the suggested "Today's Special".　　有些人比較喜歡餐廳所推薦的「今日好介紹」。

17. Thick soup seems too rich.　　濃湯看似很膩。

18. Sometimes he treats his friends to a meal.　　有時他請朋友吃飯。

19. We have made a reservation.　　我們已預訂了座位。

20. I asked the waitress to charge all the food to my account.　　我請那位女侍應生把所有食物算在我的帳上。

21. She cannot finish a complete dinner.　　她不能把一份全餐吃掉。

22. The cafe specializes in steak.　　那家咖啡室做的牛扒特別出色。

23. Ten percent service charge has been included.　　百分之十的服務費已計算在內。

24. The steak is overdone.　　那塊牛扒煎得過熟。

25. Many people do not like to share a table with others.　　很多人不喜歡「搭枱」。

26. All the tables are filled up in the cafe. 那家咖啡室已全部滿座。

27. He likes deep-fried chicken. 他喜歡吃炸雞。

28. Customers are well attended to. 顧客受到很好的招呼。

29. Customers take their meals in a cosy and relaxing atmosphere. 顧客在舒適和輕鬆的氣氛下進餐。

30. The cafe provides fabulous service. 那家咖啡室提供令人難以置信的優良服務。

31. The cafe features a spectacular variety of food. 那家咖啡室以食品種類繁多見稱。

32. The waiter packed up the remaining food with a box for her to take it back. 侍應用盒子替她把吃剩的食物裝好，讓她帶回去。

33. We accept cash and credit cards. We don't accept cheques. 本店只收現金及信用卡，不收支票。

34. We welcome customers to pay by 'Octopus' card. 本店歡迎顧客以「八達通卡」付帳。

Phrases

1. a five-course dinner 一個有五道菜的晚餐

2. a jug of coffee 一壺咖啡

3. an extra charge 另外算帳

4. at the cashier's desk 在收銀處

5. a couple of bottles of beer 兩瓶啤酒

6. wines of outstanding quality 品質超羣的餐酒

7. world-famous lamb 世界著名的羊肉

8. spaghetti with meat sauce 肉醬意粉

9. delicious food 美味的食品

10. economical set lunch 特價午餐

11. fresh and delightful 味道鮮美的

12. to foot the bill 結帳

Vocabulary

1.	snacks	小吃	
2.	buffet	自助餐	
3.	menu	菜牌	
4.	dish	菜餚	
5.	appetizer	開胃小吃	
6.	reservations	訂座	
7.	bill	帳單	
8.	service charge	服務費	
9.	tips	小費	
10.	credit card	信用卡	
11.	waiter	侍應生	
12.	tray	淺盤	
13.	napkin	餐巾	
14.	seat	座位	
15.	style	款式	
16.	hamburger	漢堡包	
17.	apple pie	蘋果批	
18.	chicken pie	雞批	
19.	doughnut	冬甩（炸麵圈）	
20.	sandwiches	三文治（三明治）	
21.	pancakes	班戟（煎餅）	
22.	pizza	意大利薄餅	
23.	fried eggs	煎蛋	
24.	scrambled eggs	炒蛋	
25.	softed-fried egg	荷包蛋	
26.	bacon	煙肉	
27.	roast chicken	烤雞	
28.	roast beef	燒牛肉	
29.	satay beef	牛肉沙爹	
30.	oyster	蠔	
31.	chicken wing	雞翼	
32.	garlic bread	蒜茸包	
33.	steak	牛扒	
34.	grilled pork chop	煎豬扒	
35.	curry chicken	咖哩雞	
36.	omelette	庵列（煎蛋捲）	
37.	sausage	腸仔	
38.	fried chicken leg	炸雞肶（炸雞腿）	
39.	French fried	炸薯條	
40.	fried onion rolls	炸洋葱圈	
41.	hot dog	熱狗	
42.	garoupa	石斑魚	
43.	tuna fish	金鎗魚（吞拿魚）	
44.	sardine	沙甸魚	
45.	smoked salmon	煙三文魚	
46.	macaroni	通心粉	
47.	onion soup	洋葱湯	

48.	Russian borsch	羅宋湯	74.	creamed corn	忌廉粟米
49.	ox-tail soup	牛尾湯	75.	lettuce	生菜
50.	Kaiser salad	凱撒沙律	76.	tomato	番茄
51.	desserts	甜品	77.	salad dressing	沙律醬
52.	pudding	布丁	78.	vinegar	醋
53.	lobster salad	龍蝦沙律	79.	pepper	胡椒粉
54.	mixed fruit salad	雜果沙律	80.	cube sugar	方糖
55.	assorted ice-cream	雜錦雪糕	81.	sumptuous	豐盛的
56.	banana split	香蕉船	82.	delicious	美味的
57.	fried ice-cream	炸雪糕	83.	rare	較生的
58.	ice-cream soda	雪糕梳打	84.	medium rare	半生熟的
59.	fruit jelly	雜果啫喱	85.	well-done	熟透的
60.	sundae	新地	86.	over done	過熟的
61.	strawberry	草莓	87.	full	肚子飽了
62.	drink/beverage	飲品	88.	revolving	旋轉的
63.	milk shake	奶昔	89.	order (v.)	點菜
64.	cream soda	忌廉疏打	90.	seafood chowder	周打海鮮湯
65.	fresh milk	鮮奶	91.	baked rice	焗飯
66.	soft drinks	汽水	92.	sole	龍脷（撻沙魚）
67.	Coca Cola	可口可樂	93.	brunch	早午餐
68.	San Miguel beer	生力啤	94.	afternoon tea	下午茶
69.	orange juice	鮮橙汁	95.	happy hour	歡樂時光（酒吧的減價時段）
70.	lemonade	檸檬水	96.	French dishes	法國菜
71.	fruit punch	雜果賓治	97.	Italian cusine	意大利菜
72.	almond milk	杏仁奶露	98.	Korean food	韓國菜
73.	red beans in ice	紅豆冰	99.	Japanese food	日本菜

100. Thai cusine	泰國菜	104. Hong Kong style restaurant	港式餐廳
101. Vietnamese food	越南菜		
102. Indian food	印度菜	105. Starbuck Cafe	星巴克咖啡
103. rotating sushi	迴轉壽司		

Choosing a Career

 Sentences

1. Many graduates are eager to get a job.　　很多畢業生渴望找到一份工作。

2. Proper guidance is indispensable.　　正確的輔導是不可或缺的。

3. The absence of careful career planning will lead to a waste of time and effort.　　沒有周詳的職業計劃會浪費時間與努力。

4. We should know the sources of career information.　　我們應該知道職業資料的來源。

5. Having the opportunities of in-service training and promotion is very important.　　有在職訓練及晉升機會是很重要的。

6. Some jobs require special training and higher academic qualifications.　　有些工作需要特別的訓練及較高的學歷。

7. Some employers require applicants to pass an aptitude test.　　有些僱主要求申請人通過一個能力測驗。

8. Keeping a close contact with the outside world is essential.　　與外邊世界保持密切的接觸是必要的。

9. Big firms and organizations usually provide better welfare for their employees.　　大公司及機構通常為員工提供較好的福利。

10. Newspaper advertisements play an important role in linking together employers and job-seekers.　　報章廣告在聯繫僱主及求職者方面擔任一個重要的角色。

11. Job-seekers must be well prepared before attending an interview.

求職者在面試前必須作好準備。

12. Copies of certificates and testimonials should be ready.

我們應準備好證書和推薦信的副本。

13. Some people attach a lot of importance to personal interest, job satisfaction and a sense of achievement.

有些人十分注重個人的興趣，工作的滿足感及成就感。

14. Others are more interested in the starting pay, maximum salary, terms of employment and conditions of work.

其他人則對起薪點、最高薪酬、僱用和工作條件更感興趣。

15. Choosing a career is an important decision in life.

選擇職業是人生中一個重要的決定。

16. Working experience is not required when applying for some positions.

對一些職位而言，申請人是不需要有工作經驗的。

17. All factors concerned should be seriously considered before choosing a career.

我們在擇業前須認真考慮一切有關的因素。

18. To take on an uninteresting job is torturing.

投身於自己沒有興趣的職業是痛苦的。

19. We should pay more attention to interpersonal relationships.

我們應該多留意人際關係。

20. Career exhibitions usually provide detailed career information.

職業展覽通常提供詳盡的職業資料。

21. Some people have a flair for languages.

有些人具有語言天賦。

22. Personal qualities also count.

個人的品質也是重要的。

23. Other fringe benefits should also be taken into account.

其他額外福利也應在我們考慮之列。

24. It is useful to take part in career talks and seminars.

參加職業講座及座談會是有用的。

25. The Labour Department provides useful careers information and practical guides for numerous job-seekers.

勞工處為無數的求職人士提供有用的職業資料及實際的指導。

26. It is extremely important to enter a suitable field of work.

從事合適的工作是極其重要的。

27. We all hope to realize our dreams.   我們都希望夢想成真。

28. We have to weigh and consider carefully all related factors.   我們必須小心衡量及考慮所有有關的因素。

29. It is advisable to start planning early for one's future career.   及早開始計劃將來的職業是合宜的。

30. It should be examined from every angle.   我們應從每個角度去考查。

31. Professional training is almost a must for better career development.   對較佳的職業發展而言，專業訓練幾乎是必需的。

32. Professional knowledge and professional ethics are equally important.   專業知識及專業操守同樣重要。

33. We must grasp more than one skill to earn a living in modern society.   我們須掌握多項技能，才能在現代社會謀生。

34. Higher academic qualifications are often linked to better employment opportunities.   較佳的就業機會常與較高的學歷有關。

35. Success is often determined by individual experience and working ability.   成功常決定於個人的經驗及工作能力。

36. Individual career development should be in line with social needs.   個人的事業發展應與社會的需求配合。

Phrases

1. parking for customers   代客泊車

2. on official business   出差

3. pressure from work   工作壓力

4. nature of the work   工作的性質

5. bent of mind   傾向

6. letter of recommendation   推薦信

7. a stepping stone   踏腳石

8. physical endurance   身體的忍耐能力

9. research and theory   研究及理論

10. being well received by   深受歡迎

11.	large retrenchments	大量裁員
12.	to make job referrals	轉介求職個案
13.	structural changes in the economy	經濟結構轉型
14.	being best suited to their interests and talents	配合他們的興趣和才能
15.	on an equal footing	平等對待
16.	to live up to	實踐
17.	to make it	成功
18.	to stand a good chance	有個好機會
19.	to make the most of opportunities	好好利用機會
20.	out of touch	與現實脫節
21.	a stop-gap measure	權宜之計
22.	to remiss in one's work	疏忽職責
23.	neglect of duties	曠工
24.	to think ahead	詳加思考

Vocabulary

1.	abilities	能力	11.	contentment	滿意
2.	interest	興趣	12.	sociability	好社交
3.	inclination	性向	13.	initiative	主動性
4.	character	性格	14.	adaptability	適應力
5.	aptitude	能向	15.	requirements	要求
6.	preference	喜愛	16.	qualifications	條件／資格
7.	strengths	長處	17.	experience	經驗
8.	weaknesses	弱點	18.	salary	薪酬
9.	aims	目的	19.	increment	薪金的增加
10.	ambition	大志	20.	bonus	獎金

21. promotion/ advancement	擢升	44. commercial school	商科學校
22. pension	退休金	45. labour market	勞工市場
23. mandatory provident fund	強積金	46. job-seekers	求職者
24. workers insurance	勞工保險	47. Labour Department	勞工處
25. prospects	前途	48. Youth Employment Advisory Service	青年就業輔導組
26. profession	專業		
27. engineering	工程	49. pamphlets	小冊子
28. commerce	商業	50. careers master	職業輔導主任
29. finance	金融業	51. careers information centre	職業資料中心
30. banking	銀行業		
31. service industries	服務業	52. suitable	適合的
32. tourism	旅遊業	53. challenging	具挑戰性的
33. hotel trade	酒店業	54. imaginative	富想像力的
34. public relations	公共關係	55. suit	適合
35. advertising	廣告業	56. affect (v.)	影響
36. manufacturing industries	製造業	57. enrich (v.)	充實
37. apprentice	學徒	58. Vocational Training Council	職業訓練局
38. craftsman	技工		
39. technician	技術員	59. Employees Retraining Board	僱員再培訓局
40. manager	經理		
41. executives	行政人員	60. Education and Careers Expo	教育及職業博覽會
42. professionals	專業人士	61. job vacancies	職位空缺
43. technical institute	工業學院	62. employment contract	僱用合約

63. credentials	介紹信	82. stipendiary class	受薪階級
64. commitment	承擔	83. express delivery services	速遞服務
65. sandwich courses	實習課程	84. computer information	電腦資訊
66. attachment scheme	實習計劃	85. vocational training	職業訓練
67. odd job	散工	86. working environment	工作環境
68. sideline	副業	87. employee benefits	員工福利
69. dismiss	解僱	88. promotion opportunities	晉升機會
70. unemployed	失業	89. practical work	實際的工作
71. under-employment	就業不足	90. secretarial work	秘書的工作
72. Youth Pre-employment Training Programme	展翅計劃	91. clerical work	文書的工作
73. sun-setting trade	夕陽行業	92. blue-collar workers	藍領工人
74. overtime subsidy	加班津貼（補水）	93. skilled workers	熟練工人
75. minimum wage	最低工資	94. physical fitness	體格
76. unemployment statistics	失業數據	95. import and export firms	出入口公司
77. employment statistics	就業數字	96. placement service	就業服務
78. overtime work	超時工作	97. Job Matching Programme	就業選配計劃
79. food and beverage trade	飲食業	98. skills retraining	技術訓練
80. realty agency	地產代理	99. skills upgrading	技術提升
81. white collar class	白領階級	100. prospective employer	未來僱主

Chinese Festivals and Customs

Sentences

1.	Every place is filled with a happy atmosphere.	到處都充滿愉快的氣氛。
2.	For safety's sake, fire-crackers have been forbidden to be let off.	政府基於安全的理由，禁止市民燃放爆竹。
3.	When the Lunar New Year comes, every home is cheerfully decorated.	農曆新年來臨，家家戶戶都裝飾得充滿愉快的氣氛。
4.	It is celebrated with the utmost spirit and happiness.	人們興高采烈地慶祝農曆新年。
5.	The Spring Festival is the most important traditional festival in China.	春節是我國最重要的傳統節日。
6.	It is always a great festival.	它總是一個盛大的節日。
7.	The Eve of the New Year is a day for family reunion.	大除夕是家人團聚的日子。
8.	Every family cooks special and delicious dishes.	家家戶戶都烹調特別的及美味的菜餚。
9.	Auspicious words are uttered by every one.	人人都説吉祥的語句。
10.	It is an occasion for rejoicing.	這是一個歡樂的時節。
11.	Gifts and visits are exchanged among friends and relatives.	親友間互相交換禮物及探訪。
12.	Most traditional women worship gods.	絕大多數傳統婦女都拜神。
13.	There are five major festivals in the Chinese calendar.	中國曆上有五個主要的節日。
14.	The observance of the various festivals enriches the lives of the Chinese people.	中國人的過節習俗使他們的生活多姿多彩。

15. It is conventional practice to observe the various festivals.

過節是一個俗例。

16. During Ching Ming and Chung Yeung festivals, the Chinese sweep graves to commemorate their ancestors.

在清明節及重陽節，中國人去掃墓以紀念他們的先人。

17. Many grave-sweepers kneel down in front of the grave and pray solemnly with a heavy heart.

很多掃墓者跪在墓前，帶着沉重的心情莊嚴地禱告。

18. The worship of ancestors is an important event.

拜祭祖先是一件重要的事。

19. People pay homage to the ancestor's tombs to show respect to their ancestors.

人們拜祭祖先墳墓以表示對先人的敬意。

20. The day is filled with a mournful atmosphere.

當日充滿了哀悼的氣氛。

21. In ancient times, many Chinese people went up mountains during the Chung Yeung Festival to escape the plagues.

在古時，很多中國人在重陽節那天登高，藉以躲避瘟疫。

22. The Chinese have a high regard for mutual love and respect.

中國人推崇互敬相愛。

23. The Dragon Boat Festival is of historical significance.

端午節具有歷史意義。

24. Dragon boat races take place during that festival.

在那個節日中，人們舉行龍舟競賽。

25. Rice dumplings are wrapped in bamboo leaves.

糭子以竹葉包裹。

26. The festival is in memory of a patriotic poet in ancient China.

這個節日是紀念中國古代一位愛國詩人。

27. Lantern carnivals are usually held during the Mid-Autumn Festival.

花燈晚會通常在中秋節期間舉行。

28. Many children play with colourful lanterns and burst out laughing.

很多兒童玩彩燈及發出大笑。

29. The major Chinese festivals have been made statutory holidays in Hong Kong.

在香港，政府把主要的中國節日列為法定公眾假期。

30. China is a highly civilized country and many old customs are worth preserving.

中國是一個有高度文化的國家，很多古老習俗是值得我們保留的。

Phrases

1.	special features	特色
2.	traditional festivals	傳統的節日
3.	a great festival	盛大的節日
4.	in memory of	紀念
5.	to queue up	排隊
6.	embarrassed behaviour	困惑的行為
7.	items of worship	祭品

 Vocabulary

1.	Lunar New Year	農曆新年	13.	candle	蠟燭
2.	Ching Ming Festival	清明節	14.	paper money	紙錢
3.	Dragon Boat Festival	端午節	15.	descendants	子孫
4.	Mid-Autumn Festival	中秋節	16.	rice dumplings	糭子
5.	Chung Yeung Festival	重陽節	17.	lantern carnival	花燈晚會
6.	Winter Solstice	冬至	18.	moon cakes	月餅
7.	presents/gifts	禮品	19.	lotus paste	蓮蓉
8.	ornaments	裝飾品	20.	egg yolks	蛋黃
9.	fire-crackers	爆竹	21.	festive lantern	花燈
10.	graveyard	墳場	22.	pomelo	柚子
11.	sacrifices	祭品	23.	persimmon	柿子
12.	joss sticks/ incense	線香	24.	star fruit	楊桃
			25.	taro	芋頭
			26.	Tin Hau Temple	天后廟

27.	Wong Tai Sin Temple	黃大仙祠	
28.	gods	神	
29.	Buddhist Po Lin Monastery	佛教寶蓮寺	
30.	feast	宴會	
31.	bridegroom	新郎	
32.	bride	新娘	
33.	sedan-chair	轎	
34.	traditional	傳統的	
35.	magnificent	壯麗的	
36.	excited	興奮的	
37.	mournful	悲哀的	
38.	bury	埋葬	
39.	commemorate	紀念	
40.	bow	鞠躬	
41.	observe	遵守	
42.	respect	尊敬	

43. celebrate	慶祝
44. decorate	佈置
45. drizzle	下微雨
46. International Dragon Boat Races	國際龍舟邀請賽
47. red packets/ lucky money	紅封包
48. wedding ceremonies	結婚儀式
49. lunar calendar	農曆
50. ancestral hall	祠堂
51. ancestral tablet	祖先靈牌
52. Goddess of Mercy	觀音
53. sticky rice	糯米
54. starting point	起點
55. finishing line	終點線
56. background music	背景音樂

Chinese New Year

 **Sentences**

1. With the coming of the New Year, everything appears in a new and happy state, and everyone puts on a cheerful look.　　新年到來，萬象更新，喜氣洋洋。

2. Every Chinese household is busy with preparations.

每個中國家庭都忙着準備。

3. The house is swept clean and everything is specially treated.

房子打掃乾淨，每件東西都經過特別處理。

4. The old and the young, men and women will all have a good time.

男女老幼將享受快樂的時光。

5. Kumquat is a symbol of good luck for the New Year.

金桔是一年好運的象徵。

6. The New Year Day is a day of merry-making and feasting.

新年是一個飲宴與作樂的日子。

7. Streets are filled with brightly-dressed children and grown-ups.

街道上滿是衣着看光鮮的孩子與成年人。

8. People put on cheerful looks.

人們流露着歡欣的神情。

9. Plants show new signs of life.

植物顯出新生的跡象。

10. Everyone hopes that he will make profit by the coming of the New Year.

人人都希望因新年的來臨而得到好處。

11. Lunar New Year is the most important traditional festival.

農曆新年是最重要的傳統節日。

12. It is also known as the Spring Festival.

新年又稱為春節。

13. A particular animal is associated with each Lunar New Year.

每個農曆新年都有一種特別的動物跟它配合。

14. They stand for good fortune.

牠們代表好運。

15. People greet their relatives and friends a happy New Year.

人們恭祝親友新年快樂。

16. Children wish their parents a happy, healthy and wealthy New Year.

孩子們恭祝父母有一個快樂、健康及富裕的新年。

17. People greet one another with such auspicious words as "Kung Hei Fat Choy".

人們以「恭喜發財」的吉祥語互相問候。

18. Parents give their children red packets stuffed with "lucky money".

父母給子女裝着「吉利錢」的紅封包。

19. People call on their relatives and friends, bringing them New Year's greetings.

人們探訪親友，並向他們拜年。

20. The New Year is a suitable time for looking back to the past and looking forward to the future.

新年是一個適宜緬懷過去、展望將來的日子。

21. We all hope that the New Year will bring us success.

我們都希望新的一年能帶給我們成功。

22. We should advance as the years accumulate.

我們應隨歲月的增加而進步。

23. Many people make plans for the New Year, hoping that they can turn over a new leaf.

很多人定下新年大計，希望能翻開新的一頁。

24. They are determined to fulfil their ambitions.

他們有實現志向的決心。

25. Everywhere overflows with a merry, festive atmosphere.

到處都洋溢着歡樂的節日氣氛。

26. When we go out, we have to thread our way through the crowd of jostling people.

我們上街的時候，需要穿過擠擁的人羣。

27. Sometimes we watch a Chinese martial arts performance.

有時我們可看到中國武術的表演。

28. When the traditional lion dances are performed, we can hear the sounds of gongs and drums.

當人們表演傳統的舞獅時，我們可聽到鑼鼓聲。

29. During the Spring Festival, there is usually a spectacular fireworks display in the harbour.

春節期間通常有一個在海港進行的壯麗煙花匯演。

30. Cinemas are crowded with people.

電影院內擠滿了人。

31. People welcome the New Year because they think it can bring them good luck.

人們歡迎新的一年，因為他們認為新年能帶來好運。

32. In the New Year, the Chinese try their best to prevent quarrels and unhappy situations.

在新年期間，中國人盡量避免爭吵和不愉快的事情。

33. Most homes are brightly decorated.

大多數的家庭都佈置得色彩明艷。

34. It is a traditional custom to paste up red-paper scrolls with lucky words written on them.

傳統的習俗是貼上寫着吉祥語的紅聯。

35. Many housewives are doing their last minute shopping.

很多主婦正在進行最後一刻的採購。

36. New Year's Eve is a day for family reunion.

除夕是家人團聚的日子。

37. When the New Year approaches, people rush to stock up on provisions for the New Year.

新年快到，人們紛紛趕辦年貨。

38. They usually discharge all their debts before the New Year.

他們通常在新年前償還所有的債務。

39. New Year is a festive season and people usually have a great deal of busy activities.

新年是一個大節日，人們通常有許多繁忙的活動。

40. It is also a time for visiting friends and relatives.

它也是一個探訪親友的時刻。

41. Many superstitious Chinese conduct rituals.

很多迷信的中國人拜神。

42. They perform kowtow to their ancestors at the same time.

他們同時向祖先叩頭。

43. Many families make sacrifices to the gods and their ancestors.

很多家庭都供奉神靈及祖先。

44. In village families, the most noticeable feature is the household altar.

在鄉村的家庭中，最引人注意的特色是屋內的神壇。

45. On the first day of the New Year, people usually have a vegetarian diet.

在新年元旦，人們一般吃齋菜。

46. Many adults play a game of mahjong at home.

很多成年人在家中打麻將。

47. Indeed, every person would like to prosper in wealth.

事實上，每個人都喜歡發財。

48. On the third day of the New Year, many people go on a pilgrimage to Che Kung Temple in Shatin to make offerings to the gods.

在農曆年初三，很多善信前往沙田車公廟向車公供奉祭品。

49. To the Chinese people, red means good luck and white is bad luck. In the New Year, children in particular, mostly put on red clothes. They do not put on white clothes.

中國人以紅色為吉利，白色為凶險。新年期間，尤其是孩童，大多穿紅色衣服，不會穿白色衣服。

50. In Hong Kong, setting off fire crackers is banned, but in China, people in villages still set off fire crackers.

香港禁止燃放爆竹，但在中國內地鄉間，人們仍然燃放。

51. Life returns to a normal routine after two or three weeks.

兩、三個星期後，生活又回復正常。

Phrases

1.	good luck and good fortune	大吉與好運
2.	auspicious sayings	吉詳語
3.	flowers bringing wealth and honour	花開富貴
4.	assorted sweets	各式糖果
5.	festive season	節日
6.	smoked and salted meat and poultry	臘肉臘味
7.	let bygones be bygones	讓過去成為過去
8.	a thorough clean-up	大掃除
9.	pay new year calls/visits	拜年

 Vocabulary

1.	Lunar New Year	農曆新年	14.	reunion dinner	團年飯
2.	Spring Festival	春節	15.	favourites	喜愛物
3.	Kung Hei Fat Choy	恭喜發財	16.	sweets/candies	糖果
4.	New Year Fair	年宵市場	17.	water melon seeds	瓜仁／瓜子
5.	flower fair	花展	18.	New Year's Eve	除夕
6.	peach blossoms	桃花	19.	laughter	笑聲
7.	narcissus flowers	水仙花	20.	red-packets	紅封包
8.	chrysanthemums	菊花	21.	present/gift	禮物
9.	peony blossoms	牡丹花	22.	toys	玩具
10.	flower stalls	花檔	23.	prosperity	興盛
11.	New Year cakes	年糕	24.	Che Kung Temple	車公廟
12.	turnips	蘿蔔	25.	worshippers	拜祭者
13.	mushrooms	香菇			

26. windmills	風車	47. prosperous	興盛的
27. fortune	幸運	48. celebrate	慶祝
28. fortune tellers	相士	49. decorate	裝飾
29. bamboo sticks	竹籤	50. symbolise	象徵
30. ornaments	裝飾品	51. gamble	賭博
31. blessing	祝福	52. dumplings	湯圓
32. scrolls	春聯	53. Gods of good fortune, prosperity and longevity	福祿壽
33. lotus seeds	蓮子		
34. kumquats	金桔		
35. willow sticks	柳枝	54. God of Wealth	財神
36. Door God	門神	55. God of the Hearth	灶君
37. drums	鼓		
38. gongs	鑼	56. Cantonese opera	粵劇
39. cymbals	鐃鈸		
40. puppet shows	木偶表演	57. spring charms	揮春
41. incense	線香，燒香	58. ancestral home	祖宗靈位
42. customs	習俗	59. confectionery box	全盒
43. tradition	傳統		
44. auspicious	吉祥的	60. potted plants	盆栽植物
45. spectacular	壯觀的	61. martial art	武術
46. joyous	歡樂的	62. evil spirits	鬼

Christmas

 ## **Sentences**

1. The whole city is covered with the merry festivity of Christmas.

   整個城市籠罩着聖誕節的歡樂氣氛。

2. Many people enjoy the specially arranged amusements.

   很多人享受特別安排的娛樂。

3. They all enjoy themselves heartily.

   他們個個都盡情地享受。

4. Hong Kong is a place of mixed cultures.

   香港是一個文化混合的地方。

5. Western civilization has greatly influenced the Chinese residents in Hong Kong.

   西方的文化深深地影響着香港的中國居民。

6. Young people usually receive many invitations to Christmas parties.

   年青人通常接到很多參加聖誕派對的邀請。

7. A lot of devoted Christians go to church.

   很多虔誠的基督徒上教堂去。

8. Numerous Christmas cards are sent abroad.

   無數的聖誕卡被寄往國外。

9. Locally, it is common to exchange Christmas cards and presents among friends.

   在本地，朋友間互贈聖誕卡及禮物是很普遍的。

10. Countless Christmas parties are held and Christmas carols sung.

    人們舉行數之不盡的聖誕舞會及唱聖誕歌。

11. Many people celebrate the birthday of Jesus Christ.

    很多人慶祝耶穌基督的誕生。

12. They put up attractive decorations in their home.

    他們在家中掛上吸引人的裝飾品。

13. Thanksgiving services are held in churches.

    教堂舉行感恩崇拜。

14. Everywhere is filled with an air of festivity.

    每個地方都充滿節日的氣氛。

15. Large department stores are crowded with customers.

    各大百貨公司擠滿了顧客。

16. They select presents for friends and relatives. 他們為親友選購禮品。

17. Streets are crowded with pedestrians and cars. 街上車水馬龍，行人熙來攘往。

18. A lovely little girl is staring at a toy Santa Claus in the display window. 一個可愛的小女孩正在凝視着窗櫥內的一個玩具聖誕老人。

19. She is wearing beautiful silk ribbons. 她戴上了美麗的絲帶。

20. People are busy decorating their sitting room. 人們正忙於佈置客廳。

21. They receive many greeting cards. 他們收到很多賀卡。

22. Many children are particularly interested in candies. 很多兒童對糖果特別感興趣。

23. A lot of Hong Kong residents make use of the holidays to take an overseas trip. 很多香港居民趁着假期往外地旅行。

24. We must not lose sight of the deep significance of Christmas. 我們不要忘記聖誕節的深層意義。

25. We should think of and show concern for others. 我們應想念及關心他人。

26. The majority of people are in a holiday mood. 大多數人都懷着放假的心情。

27. They go to church and attend the ceremony. 他們上教堂及參加儀式。

28. A number of festive events follow. 一連串的慶祝活動接踵而來。

29. Now, many people do not mail Christmas cards. Instead, they use electronic cards to replace them. It is convenient and fast. 現在很多人不郵寄聖誕卡，而以電子賀卡代替，方便快捷。

30. Some websites provide free on-line electronic card services. The varieties are numerous. 有些網站提供免費網上賀卡服務，種類繁多。

 Phrases

1. exchange of gifts 交換禮物

2. preparations for the celebrations 籌備慶祝活動

3. real security and prosperity 真正的安全與繁榮

4. lasting peace and justice 永久的和平與公正

5. brightly decorated 色彩繽紛地裝飾着

Vocabulary

1.	Christmas Eve	聖誕前夕	13.	fun	樂趣	
2.	Christmas cards	聖誕卡	14.	merry-making	歡樂	
3.	Christmas trees	聖誕樹	15.	preparations	籌備	
4.	Christmas carols	聖誕歌	16.	light bulbs	燈泡	
5.	Christmas party	聖誕舞會	17.	coloured paper	顏色紙	
6.	Christmas meal	聖誕大餐	18.	turkey	火雞	
7.	Jesus Christ	耶穌基督	19.	variety show	綜合表演	
8.	cathedral	大教堂	20.	gorgeous	華美的	
9.	priest	牧師	21.	merry	愉快的	
10.	prayer	祈禱	22.	celebrate	慶祝	
11.	Santa Claus	聖誕老人	23.	commemorate	紀念	
12.	holidays	假期	24.	rejoice	使喜悅	
			25.	fancy ball	化裝舞會	

City Life

Sentences

1. City dwellers enjoy a lot of comforts and conveniences. 城市居民享受眾多的舒適及方便。

2. There are up-to-date facilities. 這裏有現代化的設施。

3. Well-equipped hospitals and modern clinics look after our health. 設備良好的醫院及現代化的診所照顧我們的健康。

4. We cannot deny that city life is comparatively busy. 我們不能否認城市生活是較繁忙的。

5. Many streets are crowded.　　很多街道都擠滿了人。

6. There are loud shouts and clattering noises of vehicles.　　這裏有呼叫聲及車輛的嘈雜聲。

7. Flashing, dazzling and colourful neon-lights are the characteristics of a busy city.　　閃耀的、燦爛的及多姿多彩的霓虹燈是一個繁忙城市的特徵。

8. People lead a hectic life.　　人們過着刺激的生活。

9. Life presses them hard and they can hardly breathe.　　生活緊緊地壓迫着他們，使他們喘不過氣來。

10. The population increases rapidly.　　人口急速地增加。

11. Citizens have to make a greater effort in order to survive.　　市民為了生存，只得更加努力。

12. Competition is especially keen.　　競爭特別激烈。

13. It is undeniable that only the fittest can survive.　　無可否認，只有適者才能生存。

14. People work hard all day long.　　人們整天辛勤工作。

15. They often worry about thousands of things.　　他們常常憂慮很多事情。

16. They have to learn how to deal with others.　　他們必須學習如何應付別人。

17. Housing is often a problem and as a result people are forced to crowd together.　　居住空間常是一個難題，所以人們被迫擠在一起。

18. People can hardly stretch their limbs in their small flats.　　在細小的單位內，人們難以伸展其四肢。

19. Under such circumstances, many people cannot have a good rest.　　在這種情形下，很多人不能得到好好的休息。

20. Stress and strain in life are very common.　　生活上的壓迫及緊張是十分普遍的。

21. Time is changing fast.　　時代正在迅速地改變。

22. People are living in a struggling, competitive world.　　人們在一個掙扎、競爭的世界中生活。

23. They must constantly adapt themselves to new circumstances.　　他們必須不停地適應新環境。

24. Clanging sounds always jar our ears.

嘈雜的聲音總是在刺我們的耳朵。

25. The streets are jammed by public vehicles and private cars.

街道被公共車輛和私家車擠滿。

26. Everywhere is filled with all sorts of people and noises.

到處滿溢着各種各樣的人和聲音。

27. We have to endure the television noises coming from our neighbours late into the night.

我們須忍受來自鄰居的電視吵鬧聲，一直至深夜。

28. Some people are tired of the city life.

有些人厭倦了都市的生活。

29. It seems that annoyances of the city life are endless.

似乎城市生活的煩擾是無窮無盡的。

30. Jostling pedestrians and heavy traffic are a common scene in a big city.

擠擁的行人及繁忙的交通是大城市常見的景象。

31. Local people have got used to the hustle and bustle of city life.

本地居民已習慣了城市生活的擾攘。

32. Most people are only obsessed with making more money.

大多數人只顧賺取更多的金錢。

33. Life in a metropolitan city is busy.

大城市生活十分忙碌。

34. Some people live a busy life in ugly surroundings.

有些人在簡陋的環境中過着忙碌的生活。

35. Anyway, a garden city is always more desirable.

無論如何，一座花園城市是較為理想的。

Phrases

1. hustle and bustle of city life

城市生活的擾攘

2. the supply of water, electricity and gas

水電煤氣的供應

3. exhausting thoughts and considerations

費盡心神的思念和考慮

4. financial difficulties

財政困難

5. fatigue of work

工作疲勞

6.	health conditions	衞生情況
7.	thundering sound of music	雷鳴似的音樂
8.	yells and roarings	呼喊和咆哮
9.	all sorts of people	各種各樣的人
10.	survival of the fittest	適者生存
11.	throngs of pedestrians	大羣的行人
12.	mills and factories	工廠
13.	to line up	排隊
14.	to meet the challenge	迎接挑戰
15.	to go with the current of the times	迎合潮流
16.	to enhance the quality of life	提高生活素質
17.	to speculate on the rise and fall of the share market	買空賣空 (投資股票)
18.	the centre of cultural activities	文化活動中心
19.	computerized ticketing	電腦售票網
20.	cross section of society	社會各階層
21.	worthy causes	善事
22.	a caring society	有愛心的社會
23.	hectic city life	繁忙的都市生活
24.	worship of money	拜金主義
25.	a pragmatic society	功利社會
26.	hundreds of thousands	盈千累萬
27.	the urban scene	都市觀景
28.	to distribute handbills	派發傳單
29.	double-glazed panels	雙層玻璃幕牆
30.	enterprising spirit	進取精神

Vocabulary

1.	entertainment	娛樂	25.	shopping	購物
2.	concerts	音樂演奏會	26.	fashion	時裝
3.	theatres	劇場	27.	competition	競爭
4.	television sets	電視機	28.	banks	銀行
5.	hi-fi stereo equipment	音響設備	29.	transport	運輸
6.	universities	大學	30.	communications	通訊
7.	libraries	圖書館	31.	pollution	污染
8.	museums	博物館	32.	unhealthy	不健康的
9.	art galleries	藝術館	33.	modern	現代化的
10.	zoo	動物園	34.	sanitary	衛生的
11.	skyscrapers	摩天大廈	35.	luxurious	奢侈的
12.	citizens	市民	36.	magnificent	宏偉的
13.	chimneys	煙囪	37.	expensive	昂貴的
14.	pile-driving	打地基	38.	precious	寶貴的
15.	"rock and roll" music	搖擺音樂	39.	relax	休息
16.	street sweepers	清道夫	40.	Hong Kong City Hall	香港大會堂
17.	hawker	小販	41.	Hong Kong Coliseum	香港體育館 （紅館）
18.	city dwellers	城市居民	42.	exhibitions	展覽
19.	mahjong	麻將	43.	variety shows	綜合表演
20.	cinemas	電影院	44.	Cantonese opera	粵劇
21.	casinos	賭場	45.	highlights	精彩項目
22.	crimes	罪惡	46.	home makers	主婦
23.	attractions	吸引人的事物	47.	hustling	熱鬧的
24.	temptations	引誘	48.	civic-minded	有公德心的

49.	facinating	令人着迷的	54.	cultural and entertainment performances	文娛表演
50.	public services	公共服務			
51.	mental illness	精神病	55.	financial turmoil	金融危機
52.	visual art	視覺藝術			
53.	hot issues	熱門話題			

15

Clean Hong Kong Campaign

Sentences

1. Maintenance of public health is extremely important.

保持公共衛生是極為重要的。

2. Under no circumstances should we neglect cleanliness.

在任何情況下，我們都不應忽視清潔。

3. We should therefore avoid littering everywhere.

故此我們不要到處拋垃圾。

4. A disgusting mass of litter always gives off a sickening smell.

一大堆討厭的垃圾常常發出令人難受的氣味。

5. More campaigns should be launched to arouse public attention to this matter.

我們應多發起清潔運動以引起大眾對這件事的注意。

6. Dirty water must be properly treated.

污水必須經過適當的處理。

7. The Government has already imposed heavier punishment on litter-bugs.

政府已加重對垃圾蟲的處罰。

8. Unhygienic conditions cannot be tolerated.

不衛生的情況是不能容忍的。

9. A lot of collected rubbish is burnt in incinerators.

很多被收集的廢物在焚化爐中燒掉。

10. Many major streets are swept three times a day.

很多主要的街道一日清掃三次。

11. Beach-goers are urged to keep the beach clean.

政府力勸去海灘的人保持海灘清潔。

12. There are many litter black spots in Hong Kong and the rubbish there must be cleared away in no time.

香港有很多垃圾黑點，這些地方的廢物必須立即被清除。

13. The importance of environmental health has never been over-emphasized.

環境衛生的重要從來沒被人過份強調。

14. Publicity through the mass media is effective.

通過大眾傳播媒介宣傳是有效的。

15. The Government appeals to all the citizens to keep Hong Kong clean.

政府向所有市民呼籲要保持香港清潔。

16. As a citizen, we should set a good example and positively participate in the Clean Hong Kong Campaign.

作為一個市民，我們應建立一個良好的榜樣，並積極參與清潔香港運動。

17. It is always a civic duty to keep the city clean.

保持城市清潔一向是公民的責任。

18. Poster design competition is part of the publicity campaign.

海報設計比賽是宣傳運動的一部分。

19. The angry eyes of the girl in the poster are very effective in deterring people from being litter-bugs.

那張海報上的女孩怒目而視，對阻嚇垃圾蟲十分有效。

20. Actually, the public must be educated if Hong Kong is to become a clean city.

事實上，假如香港要成為一個清潔的城市，大眾必須接受教育。

21. Laws have been enacted to impose heavier penalties on the offenders.

政府已制定法律對違法者加以重罰。

22. The dumping of agricultural waste in the New Territories is still serious.

在新界，傾倒農業廢物的情形仍然嚴重。

23. Dirty places provide a breeding ground for germs.

骯髒的地方為病菌提供一個繁殖的場所。

24. It poses a serious threat to our health.

它對我們的健康構成嚴重的威脅。

25. We should always properly dispose of the waste.

我們應常常適當地處理廢物。

26. It seriously affects the outlook and international image of Hong Kong.

它嚴重地影響香港的觀瞻及國際形象。

27. The Government must rigorously enforce penalties on litter-bugs.

政府必須對垃圾蟲嚴格執行處罰。

28. The public's whole-hearted co-operation is very much needed.

公眾全心全意的合作是十分需要的。

29. Cockroaches, mosquitoes, flies and rats can spread diseases. We should remove all the flavourable environment for their growth and breeding.

蟑螂(曱甴)、蚊子、蒼蠅和老鼠都能傳播疾病。我們應消除有利於牠們生長和繁殖的環境。

30. Empty all the stagnant water to completely eradicate the growing of mosquitoes.

傾倒積水，杜絕蚊子滋生。

31. Clear out the rubbish to prevent the insects and ants from gathering together.

清除垃圾，防止蟲蟻聚集。

32. People without public morality dump the rubbish from their home into the litter box by the roadside. If the litter box is full, they just leave the rubbish by its side giving out a disgusting smell.

沒有公德心的人把家中的垃圾丟進街上的廢紙箱內。如果廢紙箱滿了，他們就把垃圾放在旁邊，發出惡臭。

 **Phrases**

1.	evil-minded people	存心不良的人
2.	breeding grounds	繁殖的地方
3.	a smell of decay	腐爛的氣味
4.	physical and mental ill-health	身心的不健康
5.	a difficult job	一項艱巨的工作
6.	good personal habits	良好的個人習慣
7.	streets and gullies	街道及溝渠
8.	noticeable improvement	顯著改善
9.	to educate the public	教育市民

10. to step up law enforcement action   加強執法行動

11. to prosecute litter-bugs   檢控垃圾蟲

12. to trigger off   引起

13. to pitch in   響應支持

14. well-organized   組織完善的

 # Vocabulary

1. cartons	紙盒	
2. orange peel	橙皮	
3. cigarette ends	煙頭（煙蒂）	
4. fines	罰款	
5. health education	衛生教育	
6. mass media	大眾傳播媒介	
7. measures	措施	
8. disease	疾病	
9. germs	病菌	
10. malaria	瘧疾	
11. sewer/gully	溝渠	
12. sewage	溝渠的污物	
13. removal	去除	
14. cleanliness	清潔	
15. sanitation	衛生	
16. co-operation	合作	
17. dirt	污物	
18. rubbish/waste/refuse/litter	廢物	

19. pamphlets   小冊子

20. litter bins   廢紙箱

21. drainage   污水

22. drain-pipe   水渠

23. beaches   海灘

24. picnic spots   旅行地點

25. ordinances   法例

26. rotten/putrefied   腐爛的

27. polluted   污染的

28. effective   有效的

29. filthy   污穢的

30. infectious   傳染的

31. selfish   自私的

32. inconsiderate   不為人設想的

33. unhygienic   不衛生的

34. toxic   有毒的

35. emphasize   強調

36. safeguard   保障

37. support   支持

38. enact   制定

39.	bathhouses	浴室	50.	cockroach trap	甲由屋

39. bathhouses　　浴室
40. public toilets　　公廁
41. night soil　　糞便
42. dog droppings　　狗糞
43. disposable　　用後即棄的
44. recycle　　循環再用
45. ovitrap　　誘蚊產卵器
46. dengue fever　　登革熱
47. Japanese encephalitis　　日本腦炎
48. mosquito coil　　蚊香
49. electronic mosquito repeller　　電子驅蚊器

50. cockroach trap　　甲由屋
51. empty bottles　　空瓶
52. rusty tins　　生銹的罐
53. public places　　公眾場所
54. public spirit　　公德心
55. refuse collection　　垃圾收集
56. community involvement programmes　　參與社區活動
57. pest control　　防治蟲鼠

16

Clothing

Sentences

1. Clothes are originally intended for protection against cold.　　衣服原本用以禦寒。

2. For the sake of decency, people wear clothes.　　為了符合禮節，人們穿上衣服。

3. In order to keep up with the times, many people wear stylish clothes.　　為了追上時代，很多人穿着時髦的衣服。

4. Some people like to wear clothing of famous brands so as to satisfy personal vanity and show off themselves.　　有些人喜穿名牌衣服，藉以滿足個人的虛榮及向人們誇耀一番。

5. People who always wear odd clothing like to draw others' attention.

時常穿上奇裝異服的人每每喜歡引人注目。

6. Young ladies are often faithful followers of the fashion.

年青的女士常常是時裝的忠實追隨者。

7. Styles of clothing are subject to change.

服裝的款式是會轉變的。

8. Some styles of clothing are fast dying out.

有些服裝的款式很快不再流行。

9. Fashion is a hot topic of conversation among girls.

時裝是女孩子們的一個熱門話題。

10. It especially appeals to young people.

它特別吸引年青人。

11. The colours of her dress and handbag are well-matched.

她所穿的裙子與手袋的顏色配襯得很好。

12. Fashion magazines often influence and promote new styles.

時裝雜誌時常影響及推廣新的款式。

13. Style changes take place quickly.

款式的改變是很迅速的。

14. New styles may become outmoded in a few years' time.

新的款式可能在幾年間便過時了。

15. Many young girls wear beautiful clothes to attract the attention of the opposite sex.

很多女孩子穿上漂亮的衣服以吸引異性的注意。

16. Extravagance on clothes should be avoided.

我們應避免在衣服上過份浪費。

17. What is most important is to dress neatly and in a becoming manner.

最重要的還是穿着整齊合適的衣服。

18. Different types of clothes are designed for different uses.

不同種類的衣服為不同的用途而設計。

19. The primary function of clothes is to keep our body warm.

衣服的首要功能是使我們的身體溫暖。

20. Wearing clothes makes us look more dignified and graceful.

穿着衣服使我們看起來更高貴優雅。

21. Her skirt looks nice.

她的裙子很好看。

22. Particular clothes often show that the wearer has authority or power.

特別的衣服往往顯露穿着者擁有的權力。

23. People are treated with respect probably because of the clothes they wear.

人們受到尊敬很可能是由於他們所穿的衣服的緣故。

24. Some clothes are an essential part of ceremonial occasions.

有些衣服是某些典禮場合所必要的。

25. You need to wear shirts and long trousers to enter this restaurant. T-shirts and shorts are not welcome.

你進入這家餐廳，要穿襯衣長褲，穿短衣短褲的人不受歡迎。

26. Clothes are also connected with religious beliefs.

衣着也與宗教信仰有關。

27. Until now, many people still prefer suits made to measure.

時至今日，很多人仍然較喜歡度身訂造套裝。

28. Many ladies would like to wear clothes entirely different from others.

很多女士喜歡穿着完全與眾不同的衣服。

 Phrases

1. neat and tidy — 整齊清潔

2. complete and stylish — 完美與時髦

3. beautiful fabrics — 漂亮的料子

4. iron free — 免熨

5. crease proof — 防縐

6. dry cleaning — 乾洗

7. washable in water — 可水洗

8. eye-catching — 奪目的

9. feather and down — 羽絨

 Vocabulary

1. vanity — 虛榮心
2. comfort — 舒適
3. trend — 趨勢

4. contrast — 強烈的對比
5. vogue — 時尚
6. wardrobe — 衣櫥

7.	fashion designers	時裝設計師	31.	ornaments/ trimming	裝飾品
8.	model	模特兒	32.	accessories	配飾（衣服的）
9.	uniform	制服	33.	velvet	絲絨
10.	gown	禮服／大學學士長袍	34.	lace	花邊
11.	national costume	民族服裝	35.	brooch/lapel pin	胸針
12.	jacket	短上衣	36.	cardigan	有鈕羊毛背心
13.	suit	套裝	37.	silk stockings	絲襪
14.	overcoat	外衣	38.	charming	迷人的
15.	evening dress	晚服	39.	grotesque/ eccentric	奇異的
16.	fur coat	皮草大衣	40.	simple	簡單的
17.	blouse	寬身外衣	41.	decent	適當的
18.	swimsuit	泳衣	42.	graceful	大方的
19.	sportswear	運動衣	43.	suitable	合適的
20.	unisex wear	男女合穿的衣服	44.	dignified	高貴的
21.	lovers' wear	情侶裝	45.	elaborate	精密的
22.	vest	背心	46.	stylish	時款的
23.	jeans	牛仔褲	47.	creative	有創作性的
24.	bra	胸圍	48.	harmonious	和諧的
25.	necktie	領帶	49.	striped	有條紋的
26.	bow tie	領花	50.	plaid	有格子的
27.	trousers/slacks	長褲	51.	current	流行的
28.	shorts	短褲	52.	attractive	吸引的
29.	skirt	短裙	53.	luxurious	奢侈的
30.	mini-skirt	迷你裙	54.	prevail (v.)	流行
			55.	match	配合

56.	whole-length	全身		
57.	mantle	斗篷		
58.	lingerie	女裝內衣		
59.	panty hose	襪褲		
60.	see-through	透視式		
61.	translucent	半透明的		
62.	designer clothes	名牌服飾		

17

Complaint

Sentences

1. You have never reserved a table for two for dinner.
   你從未預訂一張雙人枱吃晚餐。

2. We felt this matter to be entirely your responsibility.
   我們覺得你應對此事負全責。

3. We must comply to our customers' request.
   我們必須依從顧客的要求。

4. This complaint concerns the discrepancy in colour.
   這是有關顏色不一致的投訴。

5. Thank you for your complaint letter dated 23 July 2008.
   多謝你在2008年7月23日所寫的投訴信。

6. We are aware of the difficulties you encounter.
   我們知道你所遇到的困難。

7. I would like to take this opportunity to thank you for your help.
   我希望借此機會多謝你的幫忙。

8. The manager refused to give me a boarding pass.
   那個經理拒絕給我一張登機証。

9. I expect I can get back a partial refund.
   我預期可得回部分退款。

10. I will consider taking legal action against your company.
    我將考慮對 貴公司採取法律行動。

11. I have not yet received a satisfactory reply.
    我仍沒有收到滿意的答覆。

12. We received many complaints during the election.

我們在選舉期間收到很多投訴。

13. They used force to drive away the demonstrators.

他們用武力驅散示威群眾。

14. They never respond to the complaint.

他們從沒對投訴作出回應。

15. We complain about their misconduct over the telephone.

我們用電話投訴他們的不當行為。

16. You can use the complaint form to complain.

你可利用投訴表格投訴。

17. Those officers have been reprimanded, suspended or fired.

那些官員已被譴責、停職或開除。

18. We are now investigating your complaint seriously.

我們正認真地調查閣下的投訴。

19. These letters prove that we have handled your complaint.

這些信件証明我們已經處理閣下的投訴。

20. He is charged with forging.

他被指控偽造罪。

21. I continuously received threatening and annoying telephone calls.

我不停地接到恐嚇和令人煩惱的電話。

22. I wonder if you could investigate this complaint promptly.

我想知道你能否迅速地調查這宗投訴。

23. Please advise us as soon as possible.

請盡早通知我們。

24. We don't want this to happen again.

我們不想此事情再次發生。

25. You have no grounds to complain that they are lazy.

你沒有理由投訴他們是懶惰的。

26. You must make sure your home is secure.

你一定要確保家居安全。

27. Hong Kong is generally one of the safest cities in the world.

整體而言,香港是世界上最安全的城市之一。

28. The thief snatched my watch and mobile telephone.

那個賊人搶走我的手錶及手提電話。

29. The shopkeeper sold me the imitation brand name goods.

那個店員把冒牌貨品售賣給我。

30. It is best to write a letter to complain.

我們最好用書面投訴。

31. If you are unable to identify the assistant, you can write to the head of the department to complain.

如果你不能認出該助手，你可寫信向部門主管投訴。

32. Please use a couple of sentences to state your complaint.

請用幾句句子說出你的投訴。

33. You should make sure that your demands are reasonable.

你需要確定你的要求是合理的。

34. Please explain what action you think the company should take to solve your problem.

請解釋你認為公司應採取甚麼措施去解決你的問題。

35. If you are in urgent need of help, you can dial 999.

如你需要緊急援助，請打999。

36. We must educate the public to respect intellectual property right.

我們必須教育市民尊重知識產權。

37. We welcome the public to give us information on copyright or trade mark infringement activities.

我們歡迎市民提供有關侵犯版權或商標的活動的資料。

38. Other categories of counterfeit goods are sportswear, foodstuff and pharmaceutical products.

其他類別的冒牌貨品包括運動服裝、食品和藥物。

39. I wish to draw your attention to the fact that this building has had no water supply for 3 days.

我想引起你注意，本大廈已經三日沒有食水供應了。

40. I regret to inform you that your shipment of food is not up to the standard.

我很抱歉通知你，你所付運的食品未合水準。

41. I lost my baggage at the airport.

我在機場遺失了行李。

42. The hawker shouted loudly continuously.

那個小販不停地大聲呼叫。

43. All taxis in Hong Kong are equipped with an electronic fare meter.

所有香港的士都裝上電子收費表。

44. The policeman abused his power.

那個警察濫用權力。

45. The bus driver refuses to surrender his driving licence.

那個巴士司機拒絕交出他的駕駛執照。

46. My neighbour sang and danced till small hours.

我的鄰居又唱歌又跳舞，直至下半夜。

Phrases

1.	a formal complaint	正式投訴
2.	a waste of time	浪費時間
3.	legal action	法律行動
4.	stress from the outset	一開始已有壓力
5.	fake jade bracelets	假玉鐲
6.	fake electronic parts	假電子零件
7.	age discrimination	年齡歧視
8.	report corruption	舉報貪污
9.	drug trafficking	販毒
10.	sexual abuse	性虐待
11.	counterfeit goods	冒牌貨品
12.	counterfeit leather goods	冒牌皮革貨品
13.	allergic to medicine	對藥物敏感
14.	disturbing noise	噪音
15.	seriously injured	嚴重受傷
16.	forced to leave	被迫離開
17.	with reference to	有關
18.	a partial refund	部分退款
19.	poor quality goods	劣質貨品
20.	telephone deception	電話行騙
21.	credit card fraud	信用卡騙案
22.	sex discrimination	性別歧視
23.	child abuse	虐待兒童
24.	sexual harassment	性騷擾
25.	infringement of copyright	侵犯版權

26. fake brand-named garments	冒牌成衣
27. in the smoking area	在吸煙區內
28. victim of an injustice	受到不公平對待的受害者
29. false imprisonment	非法禁錮
30. to refuse to apologize	拒絕道歉
31. absent without a reason	無故缺席
32. bad manners	沒禮貌

 Vocabulary

1. impatient	不耐煩的		15. tempt	引誘
2. negligent	疏忽的		16. gang of spiritual blessing	祈福黨
3. rough	粗暴的			
4. violent	兇惡的		17. pyramid schemes	層壓式計劃
5. tough	強硬的			
6. cunning	狡猾的		18. gang of borrowing money	借錢黨
7. unfair	不公平			
8. dishonest	不誠實		19. triad society	黑社會
9. unreasonable	不合理的		20. addiction treatment centre	戒毒所
10. unscoupulous	不講道德的			
11. unqualified	不合資格的		21. overcharged	叫價過高
12. deceive	欺騙		22. air pollution	空氣污染
13. pretend	假裝			
14. bribe	賄賂			

Sentences

1.	All the audience applauded thunderously.	所有聽眾都熱烈喝采。
2.	They clapped their hands.	他們拍手。
3.	It was a pleasant evening.	這是一個愉快的晚上。
4.	Many people enjoy listening to the music.	很多人喜歡聽音樂。
5.	Music is a universal language.	音樂是世界語言。
6.	Performers give joy to listeners.	演奏者給聽眾帶來快樂。
7.	The pianist touched the audience's hearts through their ears.	那個鋼琴家通過聽眾的耳朵感動他們的心。
8.	Their feelings will be changed according to the music they hear.	他們的感覺會隨着他們所聽到的音樂而變化。
9.	They hold a concert regularly.	他們定期舉行音樂演奏會。
10.	The concert features the performance of three internationally renowned pianists.	那個音樂演奏會的特色是有三位國際知名的鋼琴家演奏。
11.	Tickets for the concert are now available at the Box Office in the Hong Kong City Hall Low Block.	音樂演奏會的門票現已在香港大會堂低座售票處發售。
12.	Beautiful singing filled the air.	悦耳的歌聲充滿空氣之中。
13.	Two notes were played simultaneously.	表演者同時演奏兩個音符。
14.	Many girls relish the music.	很多女孩子愛好音樂。
15.	A long queue can be seen at the box office.	我們可以看到售票處前出現人龍。
16.	People struggle to buy a ticket.	人們爭購入場門票。

17. The sound and light effects were excellent. 　　　音響和燈光的效果極佳。

18. A concert is usually a grand occasion. 　　　音樂演奏會通常是一件盛事。

19. That performance stirred the hearts of the audience. 　　　那個演奏項目扣人心弦。

20. The concert won high acclaim from the public. 　　　那個演奏會贏得公眾的喝采。

21. The performers played to a full house. 　　　演奏者在全場滿座的觀眾面前表演。

22. Rousing cheers could be heard from the audience. 　　　我們可聽到觀眾的高聲喝采。

23. The choir had good co-operation. 　　　那個合唱團有良好的合作性。

24. Many people have a good sense of music. 　　　很多人都有良好的音樂感。

25. Their performance was quite good. 　　　他們有不俗的表演。

26. The audience concentrated on the music at an open-air concert. 　　　觀眾在一個露天音樂會中入神地傾聽音樂。

27. The audience sensed a rapport with the performers. 　　　觀眾與表演者產生共鳴。

28. It is no easy task conducting an orchestra. 　　　指揮一個樂團不是一件容易的事。

29. A lot of people enjoy very much the great Ninth Symphony of Beethoven. 　　　很多人十分欣賞偉大的貝多芬第九交響樂。

30. The performers are often full of deep emotion. 　　　表演者往往充滿深摯的感情。

31. She dedicates her life to a music career. 　　　她畢生致力於音樂事業。

32. The audience encored the singer. 　　　觀眾要求那個歌星再唱一次。

33. He performed skilfully on the guitar. 　　　他熟練地彈奏結他。

Phrases

1. a lively piece of music 　　　一首生動的音樂

2. enchanting songs 　　　迷人的歌曲

3. internationally renowned performers   國際知名的表演者

4. an orchestra of international standing   達到國際水準的樂團

5. renowned vocal musicians   著名的聲樂家

6. graceful composition   優美的作品

7. admission tickets for a concert   音樂演奏會的入場門券

8. full house   全場滿座

 # Vocabulary

1.	piano	鋼琴	20.	composer	作曲家
2.	pipe organ	風琴	21.	composition	作品
3.	accordion	手風琴	22.	overtures/ prelude	前奏曲／序樂
4.	violin	小提琴	23.	sonata	奏鳴曲
5.	harmonica	口琴	24.	serenade	小夜曲
6.	clarinet	豎笛	25.	symphony	交響曲
7.	flute	笛子	26.	soloist	獨奏／唱者
8.	cello	低音提琴	27.	duo	二部曲
9.	erhu	二胡	28.	trio	三重奏
10.	pipa	琵琶	29.	quartet	四重奏
11.	yangqin	揚琴	30.	philharmonic orchestra	管弦樂團
12.	pipe	簫	31.	symphony orchestra	交響樂團
13.	gong	鑼	32.	conductor	樂團指揮
14.	drum	鼓	33.	recital hall	演奏廳
15.	guitar	結他	34.	concert hall	音樂廳
16.	harp	豎琴	35.	Beethoven	貝多芬
17.	curtain	幕	36.	Bach	巴哈
18.	programme	節目			
19.	musician	音樂演奏家			

37. Tchaikovsky	柴可夫斯基	63. appreciation	欣賞
38. Chopin	蕭邦	64. chamber music	室樂
39. Mozart	莫札特	65. critics	評論員
40. Schubert	舒伯特	66. highlight	精彩片段
41. audience	觀眾	67. events	項目
42. recital	音樂獨奏	68. rehearsal	排練
43. A Major	A 大調	69. choir	合唱團
44. G Minor	G 小調	70. solo piano	鋼琴獨奏
45. resonance	回聲／共鳴	71. percussion	敲擊樂器
46. rhythm	節奏	72. performing	演奏的
47. timbre	音色	73. humorous	有幽默感的
48. melody	旋律	74. distinguished	著名的
49. pianist	鋼琴演奏家	75. talented	有才華的
50. Opus (Op.)	音樂作品	76. commence	開始
51. pop concert	流行音樂會	77. applaud	喝采
52. fans	樂迷	78. tune	使音調和諧
53. suprano	最高音歌手	79. accompany	伴奏
54. tenor	男高音	80. musical instruments	樂器
55. alto	中音歌手		
56. bass	男低音	81. musical scores	樂譜
57. masterpiece	傑作	82. violin player	小提琴演奏者
58. gesture	手勢	83. piano concerto	鋼琴演奏曲
59. organizer	主辦機構	84. string instruments	弦樂器
60. debut/premiere	首次登台表演		
61. brass band	銅管樂隊	85. artistic songs	藝術歌曲
62. creation	創作	86. small group performance	小組演奏

Corruption

Sentences

1. Corruption is a deep-rooted social evil.

    貪污是根深蒂固的社會大害。

2. It has far-reaching consequences.

    它的影響十分深遠。

3. It is illegal to offer and accept bribes.

    行賄與受賄都是非法的。

4. To root out corruption is no easy task.

    根絕貪污不是一件容易的事。

5. Public support and assistance are instrumental in preventing corruption.

    公眾的支持及協助有助於防止貪污的發生。

6. We must emphasize the harmful repercussions of corruption.

    我們必須強調貪污所帶來的惡果。

7. Syndicated corruption was once very serious.

    集團式貪污曾一度十分嚴重。

8. The old ways of doing business should be changed.

    我們應該改變舊式經營方法。

9. It is human greed to receive bribes.

    受賄是人類貪婪的表現。

10. We should not do favours for people with a view to getting some other benefit in return.

    我們不應予人恩惠，藉此得到其他的利益回報。

11. Heavier punishment and penalty must be imposed on offenders.

    我們對犯貪污罪的人必須加強處罰。

12. We must make an all-out effort to clean up corruption and pursue a clean administration.

    我們必須全力肅清貪污，建立一個廉潔的政府。

13. At the same time, the idea of a fuller life should be promoted.

    同時我們應提倡一個較完全的生活概念。

14. Materialistic gain should not be the sole purpose of life.

    物質上的收穫不應是人生的唯一目的。

15. Social education and character training are important in preventing citizens from corruption.

社會教育及人格訓練對防止市民貪污很重要。

16. The staff of ICAC investigate suspected corruption offences.

廉政公署職員調查可疑的貪污罪行。

17. ICAC often comes into direct contact with individual citizens and organizations.

廉政公署常與個別市民及團體直接接觸。

18. Corruption spoils the fruit of our hard labour.

貪污腐蝕我們辛勤工作的成果。

19. We should educate the public on the evil of corruption.

我們應教育大眾有關貪污的害處。

20. It is also very important to promote honesty and a sense of civic responsibility in schools.

在學校提倡誠實及公民責任感也是十分重要的。

21. The "satisfied customer" type of corruption is still posing a problem to the authorities.

「顧客滿意式」貪污對當局仍然是一個難題。

22. ICAC tackles the problem of corruption through detection, prevention and education.

廉政公署通過偵查、防止及教育去解決貪污問題。

23. Public confidence in ICAC has greatly increased.

公眾對廉政公署的信心已大為增加。

24. The Government takes disciplinary action against its corrupted officers.

政府對貪污的官員採取紀律處分。

25. Suspected corruption offenders will be taken to a law court for hearing.

犯貪污罪的疑犯被帶上法庭審訊。

26. It will become the breeding ground for corrouption.

它將成為貪污的培殖場所。

27. ICAC hopes to change the community's attitude towards corruption.

廉政公署希望改變社會人士對貪污的態度。

28. Television drama series on corruption have been produced.

電視台製作有關貪污的劇集。

29. Through changes in working procedures, existence of corruption opportunities could be eliminated.

通過工作程序的改變，貪污機會的存在是可以消除的。

30. Anti-bribery laws have been enacted by the Government.

政府已定立反賄賂的法例。

Phrases

1.	public response	公眾的反應
2.	investigation of bribery	調查貪污
3.	defiance of law	蔑視法律
4.	a serious and long-standing social problem	一個長期存在的、嚴重的社會問題
5.	corruption complaints	有關貪污的投訴
6.	conflict of interest	利益衝突
7.	the evils of corruption	貪污的禍害
8.	to fight corruption	肅貪倡廉
9.	to enlist public support	獲得市民支持
10.	to promote higher ethical standards of citizens	致力提高市民的道德水平
11.	to promote youth ethics	推廣青年道德
12.	corruption prevention	防止貪污
13.	to keep Hong Kong fair and just	維持香港公平正義
14.	stable and prosperous	安定繁榮
15.	being cautioned	受警誡

 Vocabulary

1.	Independent Commission Against Corruption	廉政專員公署	6.	mass media	大眾傳播媒介
			7.	anti-corruption	反貪污
			8.	ordinance	法例
2.	"tea money"	「茶錢」	9.	offence	犯罪
3.	injustice	不公道	10.	means	手段
4.	report centre	舉報中心	11.	seminars	座談會
5.	telephone hotline	熱線電話	12.	publicity	宣傳

13.	involvement	參與	30. support	支持
14.	perception	認識	31. investigate	調查
15.	uneasy	不安的	32. prosecute	起訴
16.	unconscious	不知不覺的	33. bribe	賄賂
17.	unjust	不正義的	34. consult	諮詢
18.	unjustifiable	不正當的	35. foster	助長
19.	organized	有組織的	36. procedures	程序
20.	suspected	被懷疑的	37. policies	政策
21.	accountable	有責任的	38. responsibilities	責任
22.	effective	有效的	39. advocate	提倡
23.	curb	抑制	40. review	檢討
24.	arrest	拘捕	41. public bodies	公共機構
25.	confiscate	充公	42. private sector	私人部門
26.	misuse	濫用	43. personal contact	個別的接觸
27.	purge	肅清	44. moral education training	德育培訓
28.	eliminate	消除	45. business ethics	商業道德
29.	spread	散播		

Country Life

 Sentences

1. Villagers usually go to bed early and rise early. 　村民通常是早睡早起的。

2. They go to the field for the day's work. 　他們到田裏做當天的工作。

3. It is comfortable to take a rest in the shade of a tree.

在樹蔭下休息是很舒服的。

4. People live a simple, healthy and useful life.

人們過着簡單的、健康的和有用的生活。

5. Beautiful views can be seen everywhere.

美麗的景色隨處可見。

6. The gentle morning breeze often has a soothing effect on people.

溫柔的晨風常常給人平靜的感覺。

7. Farmers are busy digging the soil and pulling out the weeds.

農夫們正忙於翻土及拔除莠草。

8. Two girls are gazing at the white geese in the pond.

兩個女孩子凝視着池中的白鵝。

9. Thanks to the congenial environment, our minds become peaceful and calm.

感謝適意的環境,它使我們內心寧靜安然。

10. Everywhere is filled with a peaceful atmosphere.

四周都充滿寧靜的氣氛。

11. The picturesque landscape is very charming.

圖畫般的風景十分迷人。

12. We can enjoy the sweet scent of flowers and the lucidity of the stream water.

我們可欣賞芬芳的花朵及清澈的溪水。

13. The twigs swing gently in the breeze.

小樹枝在微風中輕微搖動。

14. Leading a country life makes us closer to nature.

鄉村的生活使我們接近大自然。

15. We can sit on a patch of grass and enjoy the mystery of nature.

我們坐在一塊小草地上,欣賞大自然的奧妙。

16. There are plenty of open areas.

這裏有很多空曠的地方。

17. Morning exercises are good for the health.

做早操可使身體健康。

18. If we like, we may collect specimens of plants.

如果我們喜歡的話,我們可以採集植物的標本。

19. The view of the natural landscape refreshes us.

天然的風景畫使我們心曠神怡。

20. People live a regular life.

人們過着有規律的生活。

21. The villagers live mainly on farming.

村民主要以務農為生。

22. City life pales in comparison.

比較之下,都市生活頓覺失色。

Phrases

1. at dawn   黎明
2. after sunset   日落後
3. chatting with friends   與朋友談天
4. in the shade of trees   在樹蔭下
5. more meaningful   更有意義
6. tranquil villages   寧靜的村莊
7. to lose touch with   與……脫節

Vocabulary

1.	farmyard	農場	16.	stream	小溪
2.	fields	田野	17.	orchard	果園
3.	meadow	草地	18.	woodland	林地
4.	boughs	樹枝	19.	hills	小丘
5.	daybreak	破曉	20.	valley	山谷
6.	temples	廟宇	21.	irrigation	灌溉
7.	harvest	收割	22.	villagers	村民
8.	reap	收穫	23.	entertainment	娛樂
9.	tranquillity	平靜	24.	inaccessible	不能通達的
10.	fragrance	香氣	25.	graze	吃草
11.	dew drops	露水	26.	plough	犁田
12.	fertilizers	肥料	27.	water (v.)	澆水
13.	path	小徑	28.	weed	野草
14.	pond	池塘	29.	walled villages	圍村
15.	geese	鵝	30.	genealogy	族譜

Countryside

 Sentences

1. Parts of the countryside are not easily accessible. 一些郊野地方交通不便。

2. The countryside on urban fringes has become popular picnic spots. 市區邊緣的郊野已成為受歡迎的旅遊地點。

3. The countryside abounds in open space. 郊野有很多空曠的地方。

4. The countryside is a good place for physical exercise. 郊野是進行體能運動的好地方。

5. There are beautiful wooded valleys. 那裏有風景美麗的林谷。

6. Rambling across the hills should be very enjoyable. 越山漫遊應該是十分寫意的。

7. More country parks have been built to cater for an increasing demand for outdoor recreation. 為了應付市民對戶外康樂的需求的增長,政府已興建了很多郊野公園。

8. Almost all the picnic sites are in the countryside. 幾乎所有旅遊點都在郊野。

9. Children's play equipment is extremely popular. 兒童的遊玩設備深受歡迎。

10. Many young people like to walk on rural footpaths. 很多年青人喜歡在鄉村小徑上步行。

11. In order to protect the countryside, afforestation programmes have been carried out. 為了保護郊野,政府已經展開植林計劃。

12. During holidays, picnic and barbecue places in the countryside are crowded with people. 每逢假日,郊外的旅行及燒烤地點都擠滿了人。

13. The countryside is scenically very attractive. 郊野的景色十分迷人。

14. Many people spend the weekend in the countryside to temporarily escape the pressures of city life. 很多人在郊野渡週末，藉以暫時逃避城市生活的壓力。

15. We should be careful with fire and not litter while enjoying ourselves in the countryside. 我們在享受郊野的樂趣時，應小心防火及不要亂拋垃圾。

16. To enjoy the natural beauty of the countryside is a happy thing in life. 享受郊外的自然美是人生一大快事。

17. We should always observe the regulations aimed at conserving the countryside. 我們應常常遵守保護郊野的規則。

18. We can have a view from above the hill. 我們可在山上向下俯瞰風景。

19. The views far and near all come within our eyesight. 遠近風光，一覽無遺。

20. It is delightful to see a hundred flowers in full bloom. 觀賞百花齊放的美景是十分愉快的事。

21. Green hills and beautiful rivers are features of the countryside. 山青水秀是郊野的特色。

Phrases

1. green plants 綠色的植物

2. refreshing air 清新的空氣

3. trickling stream 小溪潺潺

4. noted places and historic sites 名勝古蹟

5. protection of vegetation 保護植物

6. wild animal protection 保護野生動物

Vocabulary

1. landscape 風景

2. slope 山坡

3. path 小徑

4. peak 山頂

5.	picnic-goers	郊遊人士	22.	magnolias	木蘭
6.	shelters	避雨處	23.	camellias	茶花
7.	wildlife	野生動物	24.	bellflower	吊鐘花
8.	guidebooks	指南	25.	scarecrow	稻草人
9.	city-dwellers	城市住戶	26.	remote areas	偏遠地區
10.	facilities	設施	27.	scenic areas	風景區
11.	benches	長櫈	28.	recreational amenities	康樂設施
12.	fireplace	火爐	29.	tourist resorts	旅遊勝地
13.	barbecues	野火燒烤	30.	ecological resources	生態資源
14.	campsite	露營地點	31.	conservation education	保護教育
15.	hikers	遠足人士			
16.	litter bins	廢紙箱	32.	nature education centre	自然教育中心
17.	flourish	長得茂盛			
18.	relax	休憩			
19.	beech	山毛櫸	33.	nature trails	自然教育徑
20.	azaleas	杜鵑	34.	marine reserves	海岸保護區
21.	orchids	蘭花			

In a Court

 ## Sentences

1. The accused sits in the dock.　被告坐在犯人欄內。

2. Members of the public sit in the public gallery.　公眾人士坐在公眾席上。

3. The lawyers sit in front of the judge's bench.

律師坐在法官席前。

4. Court clerk knocks on judge's door.

法庭書記敲一敲法官的門。

5. Judge comes into court and bows.

法官進入法庭並鞠躬。

6. Everyone in the court bows to the judge.

法庭內所有人向法官鞠躬。

7. The court clerk reads out the charge and the brief facts of the case.

法庭書記讀出控罪及案情摘要。

8. The court clerk asks the defendant whether he/she pleads guilty or not guilty and agrees with the brief facts of the case.

法庭書記詢問被告認罪與否，以及是否同意案情摘要的內容。

9. The defendant pleads guilty / not guilty.

被告認罪／不認罪。

10. The defendant agrees / disagrees with the brief facts of the case.

被告同意／不同意案情摘要的內容。

11. The case is adjourned until a date specified by the judge.

案件延至法官指定的日期審理。

12. The jury is empanelled if the defendant pleaded not guilty.

如被告不認罪，陪審團便會組成。

13. The prosecution makes the opening submission.

控方發表開案陳詞。

14. The defence makes the opening submission.

辯方發表開案陳詞。

15. The prosecution calls prosecution witness.

控方傳召控方證人。

16. The prosecution witness takes the oath / affirmation.

控方證人宣誓。

17. The prosecution examines the prosecution witness in chief.

控方主要證人接受控方盤問。

18. The defence cross examines the prosecution witness.

控方證人接受辯方盤問。

19. The prosecution re-examines the prosecution witness.

控方證人接受控方覆問。

20. The defence calls defence witness.

辯方傳召辯方證人。

21. The defence witness takes the oath / affirmation.

辯方證人宣誓。

22. The defence examines the defence witness in chief.　　辯方主要證人接受辯方盤問。

23. The prosecution cross examines the defence witness.　　辯方證人接受控方盤問。

24. The defence re-examines the defence witness.　　辯方證人接受辯方覆問。

25. The defence makes the closing submission.　　辯方發表結案陳詞。

26. The prosecution makes the closing submission.　　控方發表結案陳詞。

27. The judge sums up and directs the jury to consider the verdict.　　法官作出總結並指示陪審團考慮裁決。

28. The jury is retired to deliberate their verdict.　　陪審團退庭商議裁決。

29. The jury returns a unanimous / majority verdict.　　陪審團作出一致／多數裁決。

30. The defendant is released in court if he/she is acquitted.　　如被告被裁定無罪，他／她會被當庭釋放。

31. The defence mitigates if the defendant pleaded guilty / is convicted.　　如被告認罪／被定罪，辯方會求情。

32. The judge delivers judgment and fixes the sentence.　　法官宣告判決及判處刑罰。

Phrases

1. no plea taken　　毋須答辯
2. to detain in custody　　還押監管
3. to release in court　　當庭釋放
4. insufficient evidence　　證據不足
5. contempt of court　　藐視法庭罪
6. binding over　　監守行為
7. commencement of hearing　　開庭
8. life imprisonment　　終身監禁
9. to release from imprisonment　　出獄

10. commercial fraud — 商業欺詐

11. to retire to deliberate the verdict — 退庭商議裁決

12. to enter into a recognizance — 簽保

13. to surrender travel documents — 交出旅遊證件

14. delivery of judgment — 宣判

15. obscene articles — 不雅刊物

16. indecent assault — 猥褻罪

17. possession of dangerous drug — 藏毒罪

18. trafficking in dangerous drug — 販毒罪

19. plead guilty — 認罪

20. plead not guilty — 不認罪

21. alibi evidence — 不在場證據

22. legal aid — 法律援助

23. false imprisonment — 非法禁錮

24. judicial review — 司法覆核

25. evidence through live television link — 視像作供 (透過電視直播聯繫提供的證據)

26. inflicting grievous bodily harm — 嚴重傷害他人身體

27. closing submissions — 結案陳詞

Vocabulary

1.	judge	法官	7.	witness	證人
2.	prosecutor	主控官	8.	evidence	證物
3.	bailiff	執達吏	9.	mention	提堂
4.	usher	庭警	10.	sentencing	判刑
5.	plaintiff	被告	11.	barrister	大律師
6.	defendant	原告	12.	solicitor	(事務) 律師

13. paralegal	師爺	37. mitigation	求情
14. perjury	作假證供罪	38. trial	審訊
15. conviction	定罪	39. case law	案例
16. imprisonment	監禁	40. ordinance	條例
17. robbery	搶劫罪	41. defamation	誹謗
18. wounding	傷人罪	42. estates	遺產
19. jail	監獄	43. injunction	禁制令
20. imprisoned	坐監（坐牢）	44. summons	法庭傳票
21. adjournment	休庭	45. settlement	和解
22. handcuff	手銬	46. surety	擔保人
23. juror	陪審員	47. warrant	搜查令
24. jury	陪審團	48. charge	控罪
25. abetting	教唆犯罪	49. fine	罰款
26. Civil Court	民事法庭	50. retrial	重審
27. Criminal Court	刑事法庭	51. acquittal	無罪釋放
28. appeal	上訴	52. victim	受害人
29. High Court	高等法院	53. murder	謀殺
30. District Court	區域法院	54. manslaughter	誤殺
31. Magistrates' Courts	裁判法院	55. oath / affirmation	宣誓
32. Lands Tribunal	土地審裁處	56. determinate sentence	有期徒刑
33. Family Court	家事法庭	57. community service order	社會服務令
34. Coroner's Court	死因裁判法庭	58. Correctional Services	懲教署
35. Labour Tribunal	勞資審裁處	59. sentencing term	刑期
36. Juvenile Courts	少年法庭	60. Justices of the Peace	太平紳士

61.	Court of Final Appeal	終審法院	
62.	Small Claims Tribunal	小額錢債審裁處	
63.	Obscene Articles Tribunal	淫褻物品審裁處	
64.	criminal record	案底	

A Crowded Street

 Sentences

1.	Pavements are overcrowded with pedestrians.	行人道上擠滿了行人。
2.	Constant streams of cars keep on coming.	車輛川流不息地駛來。
3.	Drivers impatiently press the horn.	駕駛者不耐煩地響號。
4.	Hawkers yell at the top of their voice to attract customers.	小販們高聲叫喊以招徠顧客。
5.	The traffic is extremely busy.	交通極其繁忙。
6.	It is situated in the hub of the city.	它位於市中心。
7.	The street is terribly congested.	那條街道十分擠塞。
8.	It is a busy street with shops on both sides.	這是一條兩邊有商店的繁忙街道。
9.	Pedestrians are walking in the midst of a crowd.	行人在人堆中行走。
10.	Nearly all the public vehicles are full of passengers.	幾乎所有公共車輛都載滿了乘客。
11.	Some people are chatting freely and happily.	有些人正在無拘無束地和愉快地傾談。
12.	Shops selling electrical appliances are filled with many customers.	電器店擠滿很多顧客。

13. Hong Kòng people have got used to the phenomenon of large crowds.

香港人已習慣到處是人羣的情景。

14. Pedestrians surge forward continuously.

行人不停地像波浪般向前移動。

15. The people behind often push and jostle those in front, hoping to get on more quickly.

後面的人時常向前面的人推擠，希望快點前進。

16. Many people fill the pavement.

很多人充塞於行人道上。

17. The audience pours out of all the cinema exits.

觀眾由電影院的每個出口湧出來。

18. Pedestrians overflow into the street.

街道上擠滿行人。

19. Some shops are offering a grand sale.

有些商店正進行大減價。

20. Many people stop to watch the beautifully decorated display window of the large department store.

很多人停下來觀看那個佈置得美輪美奐的大百貨公司的櫥窗。

21. The goods of some hawkers block the way.

有些小販擺賣的商品阻塞通道。

22. People thread their way through the crowd.

人們在羣眾中穿梭。

23. Everywhere is packed with people.

到處都擠滿了人。

24. Pedestrians have to elbow their way through the crowd.

行人需要以肘推開羣眾前行。

25. People move in different directions.

人們從不同的方向走去。

26. Different kinds of people are mingling in the street.

不同種類的人混雜在那條街道上。

27. Many citizens go out on public holidays.

很多市民在公眾假期外出。

28. Special events often attract large crowds.

特別的節目時常吸引一大羣人。

29. Many beautifully dressed girls come into view.

很多衣着漂亮的女孩子出現。

30. Those in a hurry can easily tread on the feet of others.

趕路的人很容易踏在他人的腳上。

31. A lot of cars can be seen lining both sides of the street.

我們可以見到很多汽車在街道兩旁排成直線。

 **Phrases**

1.	to dash past	越過
2.	a stream of pedestrians	像流水般的行人
3.	to squeeze through	推擠而過
4.	at festival times	在節日
5.	window-shopping	逛商店櫥窗
6.	No Parking	不准停泊車輛

 Vocabulary

1.	vehicles	車輛	18.	pavement/ sidewalk	行人路
2.	zebra-crossing	斑馬線	19.	newspaper stall	報攤
3.	shoppers	購物者	20.	banks	銀行
4.	hawkers	小販	21.	supermarkets	超級市場
5.	pedestrians	行人	22.	hi-fi stereo	音響器材
6.	noises	噪音	23.	signboards	招牌
7.	pickpockets	小偷	24.	traffic policeman	交通警員
8.	loud-speakers	擴音器	25.	safety island	安全島
9.	mini-bus	小型公共巴士	26.	parking meters	停車收費錶
10.	motor-cycles	摩托車（電單車）	27.	cinema	電影院
11.	pram	嬰兒車	28.	audience	觀眾
12.	bus-stop	巴士站	29.	overcrowded	過度擁擠的
13.	telephone booth	電話亭	30.	alongside	沿着
14.	post box	郵筒	31.	parade	巡遊
15.	restaurant	酒樓	32.	rush hours	繁忙時間
16.	private cars	私家車	33.	central business district	商業中心區
17.	double decker	雙層巴士			

Description of Persons

  ### **Sentences**

1.	She has a pleasant and outgoing character.	她性格爽朗。
2.	She has a flair for music.	她有音樂才華。
3.	He appreciates Chinese painting very much.	他十分欣賞國畫。
4.	He likes challenges.	他喜歡有挑戰性的事物。
5.	She is the only girl in the family.	她是家中的獨女。
6.	He never gets tired.	他孜孜不倦，樂此不疲。
7.	He is fond of demanding work.	他喜愛要求高的工作。
8.	He is a judo enthusiast.	他是一個柔道愛好者。
9.	She is a keen swimmer.	她是一個游泳健將。
10.	She is gentle and soft spoken.	她溫文婉雅。
11.	He has an abundance of energy.	他幹勁十足。
12.	He devotes much time and attention to English studies.	他花很多時間和精力在英文的研習上。
13.	He is willing to give voluntary service.	他願意做義務工作。
14.	He is a most responsible person.	他是最負責任的人。
15.	He is casual and relaxed.	他是一個無拘無束的人。
16.	She is a devoted lover of music.	她是一個音樂愛好者。
17.	She is a lady of many interests.	她是一個興趣廣泛的女士。
18.	She often wears a friendly smile on her face.	她臉上常掛着友善的笑容。
19.	He handles all his work with meticulous care.	他做每一件事都一絲不苟。

20. He always sticks to his purpose. 他總是堅持目標。

21. She is a beautiful girl. 她是一個美女。

22. She is nimble and amiable. 她玲瓏可愛。

23. Her beautiful hair is always well groomed. 她的秀髮總是經過好好地梳理。

24. Her beauty is incomparable. 她的美麗是無可比擬的。

25. Her posture is graceful. 她的姿勢優雅。

26. She has bronze skin. 她有古銅色的皮膚。

27. She is specially gifted. 她得天獨厚。

28. She usually keeps abreast with the fashion. 她時常跟上潮流。

29. He will feel terribly embarrassed when he is being jeered at by his peers. 當他被同儕恥笑的時候，他覺得非常難堪。

30. He has a hideous face. 他有一張醜陋的臉。

31. He sometimes uses malicious abuses. 他有時使用惡毒的語言罵人。

32. He is rather quiet and unsociable. 他頗為沉默寡言，不善交際。

33. His temper flares up easily. 他很容易發脾氣。

34. She was a greedy girl and easily put on a kilogram. 從前她是一個貪吃的女孩子，重量很容易增加一千克。

35. Now she is a fat middle-aged woman and is eager to lose weight. 現在她是一個肥胖的中年女人，她正熱衷於減肥。

36. He is a morally upright person. 他為人正直。

37. His conscience kept on blaming him. 他的良心一直在責備他。

38. He used to burst into temper. 他經常大發脾氣。

39. His behaviour is so strange that he sometimes scares other people to death. 他的行為古怪，有時把其他人嚇得要死。

40. She has not yet reached mature years. 她尚未成年。

41. She is fond of wearing skin-tight pants. 她喜歡穿着緊身的褲子。

42. Cosmetics spoil her natural beauty. 化妝品破壞了她的天然美。

43. She acts older than her age. 她的行為比實際的年齡成熟。

44. She has an immature mind. 她的心智尚未成熟。

45. He has experienced some hardship. 他曾經歷艱苦歲月。

46. From the lines on his face, we can see that he has worked and struggled hard. 我們從他臉上的皺紋，可知他曾辛苦工作及奮鬥。

47. He is the first born in the family. 他是家中的長子。

48. He is always devoted to his studies. 他時常很用功讀書。

49. He constantly stammers. 他經常口吃。

50. He always wears jeans at whatever time and on whatever occasion. 不論在何時何地，他總是穿着牛仔褲。

51. She enjoys herself to her heart's content. 她盡情享受。

52. She is in the prime of her life. 她正在生命的高峰。

53. She is fashion-conscious and always follows new trends. 她崇尚時裝，常常跟隨潮流。

54. She has soft, smooth hair, a high, straight nose and beautiful dark eyes. 她有柔軟光滑的頭髮，高而直的鼻子及美麗的黑眼睛。

55. She wears make-up — putting on lipstick, eye shade, powder base and rouge. 她用化妝品打扮 —— 塗口紅、眼蓋膏、粉底與胭脂。

56. Many boys are attracted to her. 很多男孩子都被她吸引。

57. He is full of youthful spirits and enthusiasm. 他充滿年青人的朝氣和熱誠。

58. He comes first in his form nearly every term. 他幾乎每個學期都是全級第一名。

59. He is well grown. 他好好地成長。

60. Sometimes he wears a pair of sun-glasses. 有時他戴上一副太陽眼鏡。

61. She has a high-pitched voice. 她有高調的嗓子。

62. She likes to spread the secrets of others. 她喜歡洩露他人的秘密。

63. No wonder she is not welcomed by her friends. 難怪她不受朋友歡迎。

64. She is easily scared. 她很容易受驚。

65. She has listless eyes, pale lips and a skinny body. 她有無神的眼睛，蒼白的嘴唇和一個皮包骨的身軀。

66. She often screams at the top of her voice.

她常常高聲叫喊。

67. He dresses shabbily and his hair is in knots.

他衣衫襤褸，頭髮糾纏成一團。

68. He is often highly strung.

他的情緒經常十分緊張。

69. He is very generous to his friends.

他對朋友非常慷慨。

70. He always takes an interest in girls.

他總是對女孩子發生興趣。

71. She is a delicate girl.

她是一個嬌滴滴的女孩子。

72. Her hands dangle with silver bracelets.

她手上搖蕩着銀鐲。

73. She is always on diet in order to trim her figure.

為了使身裁窈窕，她常常節食。

74. She buckles her belt to the innermost hole.

她把腰帶扣至最後的孔上。

75. He often puts on a bright floral shirt and pointed shoes.

他時常穿着一件鮮明的花襯衣及一雙尖頭鞋。

76. He likes to sing his idol's hits.

他喜歡唱他的偶像的流行曲。

77. He used to indulge in fights.

他經常沉迷於打鬥。

78. His parents felt let down.

他的父母感到失望。

79. He would easily engage in a heated argument over trivial matters.

他很容易為了一些小事而與人發生激烈的爭論。

80. His voice is low and hoarse.

他的聲音低沉沙啞。

81. She excels in every subject.

她每一科的表現都很優異。

82. She is a big sister to the students of lower forms.

她是低年級學生的大姊姊。

83. She is very polite to her elders.

她對長輩十分有禮貌。

84. She has got a big kind heart.

她有一個寬宏的心。

85. Although she is the only child, she is not spoilt.

雖然她是個獨生女，但她並沒有給寵壞。

86. He always sticks to the morality of propriety, righteousness, integrity and modesty.

他常常謹守禮、義、廉、恥。

87. He usually tries his best to attain perfection.

他時常力求做事盡善盡美。

88. He is elegant and courteous.　　　　　　他優雅有禮。

89. He has an unswerving determination to achieve his aim.　　　　　　他有不撓的決心去達成目標。

90. He is indeed a nice youngster.　　　　　他實在是一個優秀的少年。

91. She is a remarkable young lady.　　　　她是一個超凡的少女。

92. She is far from weak.　　　　　　　　她決不是一個弱者。

93. She may seem weak physically, yet behind her soft face is a strong will.　　她的身體看來柔弱，但在柔和的臉孔後面隱藏一個堅強的意志。

94. She cannot bear injustice.　　　　　　她不能忍受不公平的事情。

95. He speaks with an accent.　　　　　　他説話帶鄉音。

96. He does not like to argue with others.　　他不喜歡和別人爭論。

97. He is full of sympathy.　　　　　　　他充滿同情心。

98. Sometimes he is a laughing stock among his friends.　　　　　　　　　有時他是朋友的笑柄。

99. She is a sweet-looking girl.　　　　　她是一個可人兒。

100. She is fond of fantasy.　　　　　　　她喜愛幻想。

101. Perhaps she is a spoilt daughter of indulgent parents.　　　　　　　或許她是被父母溺愛的驕養女兒。

102. She is hard to please.　　　　　　　她很難侍候。

103. He always dresses modestly.　　　　　他常常穿着樸素的衣服。

104. Occasionally, he has witty expressions.　　有時他表情詼諧。

105. He is a man of principle.　　　　　　他是一個有原則的人。

106. He is outstanding in both conduct and academic performance.　　　　他品學兼優。

107. She is susceptible to flattery.　　　　她易於受諛。

108. She always indulges in material enjoyment.　　　　　　　　　她常常縱情於物質上的享受。

109. Her behaviour is sometimes very eccentric.　　她的行為有時十分怪異。

110. She is easily offended.　　　　　　　她易被激怒。

111. He overflows with vivacity. 他朝氣勃勃。

112. He has persistent vitality. 他有持久的活力。

113. He speaks in a free and easy manner. 他的談吐灑落。

114. He is firm in purpose. 他的意志堅定。

115. He has a good temper. 他的性情溫柔敦厚。

116. She is well-proportioned and her complexion is fair. 她有美好的身段及白皙的肌膚。

117. Her outward appearance is very attractive. 她的外表十分迷人。

118. She has a pair of clear dark eyes. 她有一雙明亮的黑眼睛。

119. Her voice is soft and sweet. 她的嗓子柔和甜美。

120. She is very pretty to look at. 她看起來十分美麗。

121. She makes a deep impression on people. 她給予人們深刻的印象。

 Phrases

1. a cheerful spirit 愉快的精神

2. of middle stature 身裁中等

3. free carriage 瀟灑的風度

4. fluent speech 流利的詞鋒

5. simple in dress 衣着簡樸

6. severe features 冷酷的容貌

7. facial expression 面部表情

8. shabby clothes 襤褸的衣服

9. haggard face 憔悴的面容

10. without expression 毫無表情

11. to think little of others 輕視他人

12. a sour face 不高興的臉

13. childish smile 稚氣的微笑

14. rosy cheeks	紅潤的臉頰
15. captivating smile	嫣然一笑
16. extremely sensitive	極端敏感的
17. a lovely smile	可愛的笑容
18. practical jokes	笑謔
19. to joke about others	戲弄別人
20. a bald head	禿頭
21. loud-coloured shirts	顏色耀目的襯衫
22. fashionably dressed	裝扮入時的
23. dresses and accessories	服裝與配件
24. well formed	輪廓優美
25. a good-for-nothing person	無用的人
26. cunning and deceitful	奸狡詭詐的
27. fond of company	喜歡交朋友
28. a man of handsome features	英俊的男子
29. handsome looks	儀表出眾
30. physically attractive	天生麗質
31. pleasing to the eye	順眼
32. a plump stature	身裁豐滿
33. polite and elegant	溫文爾雅
34. modest and demure	端莊嫺靜
35. a graceful figure	身裁窈窕
36. beaming with delight	滿面笑容
37. to wear a warm smile	笑容親切
38. with a friendly smile	笑容可掬
39. a cheerful disposition	天性開朗
40. an easy-going attitude	隨和

41. frank and outspoken   為人爽直

42. to throw a fit   發脾氣

43. a quick temper   性急

44. has moral courage   有堅持正義的勇氣

45. to uphold justice   維護正義

46. passive by nature   個性內向

47. has a heart for   有同情心

48. to make a show of   炫耀

49. fond of kidding   喜歡開玩笑

50. in good shape   處於良好狀態

51. being well versed in   精通於

52. to take great pains to   費盡苦心

53. to strive to improve himself   自強不息

54. good deed   喜事

55. being highly motivated   充滿幹勁的

56. aspire to become   有志成為

57. a man of ideas   足智多謀者

58. take heart   鼓起勇氣

59. first-rate calibre   第一流人才

60. uncommon taste   品味不凡

61. gentle and amiable   和藹可親

62. caring and considerate   關懷體貼

63. worldly wise   世故

64. animated expression   表情十足

65. to give full play to   發揮

66. a face-lift operation   整容

67. to take after   貌似

68.	to pose as	扮作
69.	a prominent woman executive	女強人
70.	the apple of their eye	他們的心肝寶貝
71.	a whiz kid	神童
72.	a dignified and commanding look	威嚴
73.	did not lose heart	未失信心
74.	have her hair permed	燙髮
75.	to become obsessed with	着迷
76.	tastes and flavour	品味和情趣
77.	to pass the time	打發時間
78.	to talk nonsense	胡扯
79.	to spread gossip	搬弄是非
80.	at odds with	爭執
81.	to weep and sob	哭哭啼啼
82.	to flare up	大吵大鬧
83.	a disagreeable fellow	令人討厭的人
84.	fed up with	極其厭倦
85.	to drag on	拖延
86.	being infatuated with	迷戀

 Vocabulary

1.	carriage/ demeanour	舉止風度	6.	character	性格
			7.	appearance	儀表
2.	eyebrows	眉毛	8.	bearing/ manners	儀態／禮貌
3.	complexion	膚色			
4.	expression	表情	9.	hair-style	髮型
5.	personality	個性	10.	nickname	綽號

11. chatterbox	話匣子	37. handsome	英俊的
12. cosmetics/ make-up	化妝品	38. good-looking	好看的
13. vanity	虛榮心	39. ladylike	像上流女子的
14. mood	心境	40. feminine	有女性氣質的
15. forehead	前額	41. expressionless	沒有表情的
16. chin	下顎	42. unreliable	不可靠的
17. beard	鬚	43. active	活躍的
18. mole	痣	44. sympathetic	富同情心的
19. scar	疤痕	45. majestic	高貴的
20. curls	鬈髮	46. moderate	溫和的
21. extrovert	外向者	47. graceful	優雅大方的
22. introvert	內向者	48. sharp-witted	聰穎機敏的
23. perseverance	毅力	49. cute	嬌小可愛的
24. petite/slim	窈窕的	50. studious	好學的
25. charming	嬌媚迷人的	51. diligent/ industrious	勤奮的
26. lovely/likable	可愛的	52. self-possessed	泰然自若的
27. pure	純潔的	53. friendly	友善的
28. mature	成熟的	54. enthusiastic	熱誠的
29. care-free	無憂無慮的	55. modest/humble	謙遜的
30. stylish	時髦的	56. confident	有信心的
31. haggard	憔悴的	57. intelligent	聰明的
32. chubby	肥而圓的	58. impressive	動人的
33. bony/skinny	骨瘦如柴的	59. sincere	誠懇的
34. well-built	體格良好的	60. good-tempered	好脾氣的
35. muscular	肌肉發達的	61. low-spirited	憂鬱的
36. robust/stout	強壯的	62. uneasy	侷促不安的

63. impetuous	急躁的	89. emotional	易激動的
64. irritable	易怒的	90. energetic	精力充沛的
65. selfish	自私的	91. passive	被動的
66. parsimonious	吝嗇的	92. demure	嫻靜的
67. courageous	勇敢的	93. determined	堅決的
68. humorous	幽默的	94. experienced	經驗豐富的
69. sweet	可愛的	95. hysterical	神經質的
70. kind-hearted	仁慈的	96. comb	梳（頭髮）
71. optimistic	樂觀的	97. fancy	幻想
72. pessimistic	悲觀的	98. stammer	口吃
73. disagreeable	可厭的	99. bully	欺負
74. disheartened	沮喪的	100. whistle	吹口哨
75. untidy	不整潔的	101. gossip	談論別人長短
76. argumentative	愛辯論的	102. tease	嘲弄
77. good-natured	好性情的	103. adore	崇拜
78. loyal	忠心的	104. match	相配
79. trustworthy	可信賴的	105. insight	見識
80. altruistic	利他人的	106. dimple	酒窩
81. outspoken	爽直的	107. socialite	社會名流
82. inquisitive	好發問的	108. celebrity	名人
83. ambitious	有志氣的	109. stash	小鬍子
84. thrifty	節儉的	110. laughing stock	笑柄
85. slovenly	散漫的	111. marvellous	了不起
86. forgetful/ absent-minded	善忘的	112. pony-tailed	梳馬尾的
		113. uncompromising	堅持
87. hideous	可憎的	114. broad-minded	心胸廣闊的
88. stubborn	頑固的	115. open-minded	坦率的

116. narrow-minded	小器的	132. well-behaved	有禮的
117. money-minded	唯利是圖的	133. immaculate	完美無瑕的
118. fastidious	吹毛求疵的	134. warm-hearted	富同情心的
119. self-assertive	自我肯定	135. prudent	審慎的
120. gallant	風流倜儻的	136. presentable	大方得體的
121. thoughtful	細心體貼的	137. genial	和藹可親的
122. sentimental	多愁善感的	138. hypocritical	虛偽的
123. fair-skinned	膚色白皙的	139. lousy	討厭的
124. skittish	膽小的	140. deep-seated	根深蒂固的
125. frantical	緊張萬分的	141. quick-tempered	性急的
126. fussy	大驚小怪的	142. nonsensical	荒謬的
127. giggling	咯咯而笑	143. bronzed	古銅色的
128. eloquent	有口才的	144. limp	跛行
129. steadfast	堅定不移的	145. social intercourse	社交活動
130. unswerving	不屈不撓的		
131. self-made	白手興家的	146. high-heeled shoes	高跟鞋

25

Description of Views

Sentences

1. The whole sky is a shadowless blue.　整個天空是一片明淨的蔚藍色。

2. Flowers give forth pleasant odour.　花兒發出令人愉快的芬芳。

3. It is enjoyable to sit and rest in the shaded retreat.　坐在沒有陽光的地方休息是愉快的。

4. The sun slowly appears, mapping out the lines of the surrounding environment.

太陽慢慢鑽出來，顯現出四周環境的輪廓。

5. A slight rustling of wind can be heard.

我們可聽到微風沙沙作響。

6. It is situated in a secluded and remote place.

它位於一個幽遠的地方。

7. The trees are in luxuriant growth.

林木葱鬱。

8. The water is clear blue.

河水澄清蔚藍。

9. Before us is an indescribable picture.

在我們面前的是一個難以描述的景象。

10. We can take in all the picturesque surroundings.

我們可飽覽湖光山色。

11. We are delighted to see the flowers in full bloom.

我們欣然看見花朵盛開。

12. The serene and crystal clear water is very lovely.

澄清的水，十分可愛。

13. The range of our vision gradually widens.

我們的視野逐漸擴闊。

14. Everything appears to be as beautiful as in a dream.

一切都顯出夢境般的美麗。

15. Spring has set in and the surroundings take on a completely new appearance.

春天來了，四周煥然一新。

16. At night, we can see the sparkling stars of the Milky Way.

在晚上，我們可以看到銀河中閃爍的星星。

17. They are staring at the clear and rippling water.

他們凝視着那清澈的漣漪。

18. Many people are rowing boats on the tranquil water.

很多人在風平浪靜的水面上划艇。

19. They fully enjoy themselves in the sunny landscape.

他們充分享受那風和日麗下的景色。

20. The flowers are fresh and vivacious.

花兒鮮艷而有生氣。

21. Girls are especially fond of the glossy and crystalline drops of water.

女孩子們尤其喜愛那晶瑩的水珠。

22. It seems that the bright full moon augurs well for us.

那圓圓的明月好像是為我們帶來吉兆。

23. We are engrossed in the poetical and picturesque environment.

我們陶醉於那詩情畫意的環境中。

24. The earth with its mantle of refreshing green is especially attractive.

大地一片青葱，特別吸引。

25. The scene is very lovely.

景色宜人。

26. Nature is wonderful.

大自然是美妙的。

27. The trees are rustling in the soft breeze.

樹木在溫柔的風吹拂下沙沙作響。

28. White clouds float leisurely across the sky.

白雲悠閒地飄過天空。

29. The heat has gradually dispersed.

熱氣漸漸散去。

30. Green hills lie in the back.

後面有青翠的小山。

31. Darkness veils the whole town.

黑暗籠罩着整個小鎮。

32. Silence falls upon every home.

寂靜降臨每個家中。

33. The sun is setting in the west.

夕陽西下。

34. There is an air of unfathomable magnificence.

這裏有一種無以名狀的宏麗氣派。

35. A wealth of grass covers the rich earth like a green carpet.

豐盛的草蓋滿了肥沃的土地，好像一張綠色的地氈。

36. The setting sun is fast disappearing beyond the horizon.

落日很快在水平線上消失。

37. There are several seagulls whirling over the waves.

幾隻海鷗在波浪上盤旋。

38. The sun is scorching.

太陽猛烈地照耀着。

39. There is hardly any life.

那裏毫無生氣。

40. They dread the sight of desolate and melancholy villages.

他們害怕看到蕭索的荒村。

41. Everywhere is dull and lonely.

四周一片孤寂。

42. There were no moon and stars; only some moving lights of the fishing boats dotted the vast dark sea.

那裏沒有月亮和星星，只有漁舟上一些移動的燈光點綴黑暗的大海。

43. It was a windy night.　　　　那是一個有風的晚上。

44. Everything sank into silence.　　萬籟俱寂。

45. The moon peeped through a hole of the cloud.　月兒從雲洞向外窺視。

46. Stars appeared in the sky like countless diamonds sparkling on a vast sheet of black velvet.　星兒在天空中出現，有如無數鑽石在一大片黑色天鵝絨上面閃閃發光。

47. The stars seemed to wink their eyes at you like your friends.　那些星兒恍如你的朋友一般，對你眨眼。

48. Dawn is wonderful.　黎明美極了。

49. The cocks crow.　公雞啼了。

50. The cool air is refreshing.　涼爽的空氣使人精神為之一振。

51. The sun gives forth dazzling rays.　太陽發出使人目眩的陽光。

52. The brightly-coloured flower square makes us feel refreshed and happy.　那繽紛的花圃使我們感到舒適和快樂。

53. The birds chirp and twitter.　鳥兒喇啾鳴囀。

54. A few seagulls circled over the water in search of food.　幾隻海鷗在水面上盤旋覓食。

55. It was an impressive sight.　這是一個使人印象深刻的景象。

56. What a beautiful scene!　多麼美麗的風景呀！

57. A stream of water runs down to the lake, creating a waterfall curtain.　溪水流下湖中，形成一個瀑布帷幕。

58. The surface of the lake glistens like a great mirror with the reflection of all the surrounding hills.　湖面猶如一面大鏡子，反映着四周的小山。

59. We waded in the water.　我們涉水而行。

60. The sun rises at dawn.　黎明日出。

61. We could not help admiring the wonder of nature.　我們禁不住驚歎大自然的神奇。

62. They were deeply attracted by the inviting scenes.

他們被那美景深深吸引。

63. The view is intensively attractive.

風景十分引人。

64. We were all wholly fascinated by the view.

我們每一個人都給風景迷住。

65. There were short undulations made by the passing oars.

船槳點過處，泛起一輪輪輕淺的波紋。

66. We could even see the reflection of soft, lazy clouds floating across the sky.

我們甚至看見輕軟而緩慢的雲在空中浮過的倒影。

67. The dream-like indistinct scenes seemed to have enchanted us.

如夢一般的景色把我們迷住了。

68. We constantly stared at the lovely scenery.

我們凝視着美景。

69. As the sun rises higher, the clear sea seems to become a mirror, reflecting the beauty of nature.

當太陽升至較高處的時候，澄清的大海彷如一面鏡子，反映大自然的瑰麗。

70. The tides splash at some near shore rocks, giving off soft musical tunes, harmonizing with the quiet universe.

潮水在近岸的大石處濺起，發出柔和的樂韻，與寧靜的大自然和諧地交融着。

71. The quiet day creeps slowly, and eventually evening comes.

寧靜的白天慢慢地溜走，最後黃昏到來。

72. The shadows of the trees are slanting on the beach, knitting a beautiful pattern along the golden sand.

海灘樹影橫斜，在金黃色的砂礫上交織成美麗的圖案。

73. The town below comes into view.

在下面的城鎮，盡人眼簾。

74. They could not help feeling sad and depressed.

他們不禁有悲涼之感。

75. We stood, mystified.

我們迷惘地站立着。

76. The weather turned gloomy.

天氣變得陰晦。

77. The weather was sultry and warm.

天氣悶熱，使人煩躁。

78. The weather was exceedingly gloomy and oppressive.

天色非常陰沉，使人十分氣悶。

 **Phrases**

1.	high noon	正午
2.	broad daylight	白晝
3.	sweet aroma	甜甜的香氣
4.	night and darkness	夜幕與暝色
5.	fragrant flowers	馥郁的鮮花
6.	beauties of nature	大自然的美麗
7.	the murmur of the stream	潺潺的流水
8.	the fragrance of spring	春天的芬芳
9.	luxuriant foliage	茂盛的綠樹
10.	mirror-like rivers	明鏡似的河水
11.	a chill wind	冷風
12.	without the least sign of life	沒有一絲生氣
13.	by the riverside	沿河
14.	golden yellow leaves	金黃的葉子
15.	serene and charming	寧靜而迷人
16.	now and then	不時地
17.	a wonderful place	一個可愛的地方
18.	cloudless blue sky	沒有雲的藍天
19.	under the sweltering heat of the sun	在炙人的太陽下
20.	gentle slope	微斜的山坡
21.	fragrant swell of wild flowers	野花的芳香
22.	sturdy undergrowth	茁壯的矮林
23.	picturesque view	圖畫似的風景
24.	fallen leaves	落葉
25.	the cool breeze of autumn	秋天的涼風
26.	freshening cool wind	使人感到清新的涼風

27. layers of clouds   雲層

28. soft, fascinating moonlight   溫柔而迷人的月光

29. blossoms in full bloom   盛開的花

30. crimson clouds   深紅色的雲塊

31. the howling of the cold wind   寒風的號叫

32. a secluded place   一個幽僻的地方

33. a pair of smiling eyes   一雙微笑的眼睛

34. a lofty mountain   一座高聳入雲的高山

35. under the silvery moonlight   在銀色的月夜中

36. the overhanging clouds   懸垂的雲

37. one of the wonders of nature   大自然奇觀之一

38. intricate arches of interlacing leaves   交枝接葉造成的拱門

39. the soft masses of waving grass   起伏如波的柔弱草叢

40. the drowsy, balmy air   令人陶醉的芬芳氣息

41. sun-rays in slanting gleams   斜照着的太陽光線

42. as far as our eyes could see   我們目力所及

43. with dots of distant sails   點綴着幾葉遠帆

44. to add colour to   增添色彩

45. bare hills   禿山

46. evening glow   夕陽

47. fleecy clouds   軟白的雲

48. peace and tranquillity   平靜

Vocabulary

1.	breeze	微風		4.	creek	小溪
2.	ripples	漣漪		5.	bank	河岸
3.	azure	蔚藍色		6.	azaleas	杜鵑花

7.	petals	花瓣	22.	sultry	悶熱的
8.	pond	池塘	23.	windless	沒有風的
9.	passage	通路	24.	crescent-shaped	新月形的
10.	water plants	水生植物	25.	exquisite	優美的
11.	orchard	果園	26.	lovely	可愛的
12.	pavilion	涼亭	27.	fascinating	迷人的
13.	landscape	風景	28.	splendid	妙不可言的
14.	reflection	反射	29.	wonderful	奇妙的
15.	pagoda	塔	30.	crystal-like	通明透亮的
16.	impression	感受	31.	bare	空虛的
17.	miracle	奇蹟	32.	bleak	荒涼的
18.	rainbow	彩虹	33.	lonely	寂寥的
19.	dew	露水	34.	resemble	彷似
20.	sunset	日落	35.	encircle	環繞
21.	shade	樹蔭			

26

The Disabled

Sentences

1. Training facilities are far from adequate.

   訓練設施十分不足。

2. Some organizations hold fund-raising campaigns to help the disabled.

   有些機構舉行籌款運動以幫助傷殘人士。

3. Disability allowance is granted to those who need it.

   傷殘津貼是給予有需要的人士。

4. Rehabilitation services are being rapidly expanded.

康復服務正在迅速擴展中。

5. We should help the disabled people to develop their various capabilities to the greatest possible extent.

我們應幫助傷殘人士，使他們的能力得以充分發揮。

6. We have the responsibility of helping them integrate into the community.

我們有責任幫助他們成為社會的一分子。

7. Voluntary agencies play an important role in helping the disabled.

志願團體在幫助傷殘人士方面扮演着一個重要的角色。

8. Social, recreational and counselling services for the disabled are still inadequate.

為傷殘人士提供的社會、康樂及輔導服務仍然不足。

9. Special transport facilities have been provided for the disabled.

有關方面已為傷殘人士提供特別的交通設施。

10. Severely disabled people must be taken good care of.

嚴重的傷殘人士必須受到良好的照顧。

11. The Government plans to provide more residential facilities for the disabled.

政府計劃為傷殘人士提供更多的居住設施。

12. The provision of pre-vocational training is very important.

提供職前訓練是十分重要的。

13. We have to teach them some basic selfcare knowledge.

我們必須教導他們一些基本的自理常識。

14. Simple work skills training is very useful.

簡單的工作技能訓練是很有用的。

15. We should cultivate in them good working habits and operational skills.

我們應使他們養成良好的工作習慣及操作技巧。

16. In this way, the disabled can live a comparatively independent life.

這樣，傷殘人士就能過較獨立的生活。

17. In treating the disabled, love, concern and patience are necessary.

對待傷殘人士，愛心、關懷及忍耐是必需的。

18. They have a right to enjoy various social and recreational activities.

他們有權享受各種社交及康樂的活動。

19. The Government also provides them with some informal educational activities.

政府也為他們提供一些非正式的教育活動。

20. They are taught skills for earning a living.　　有關方面教導他們謀生的技能。

21. Many welfare agencies provide free lunches for them.　　很多福利機構為他們供應免費午膳。

22. More community nursing services are urgently needed.　　我們急需要更多的社區護理服務。

 Phrases

1. mental retardation　　　　　　　　精神上的遲緩

2. special recreation and sports　　　特別的康樂與運動

3. extension of abilities　　　　　　　展能

4. social skills　　　　　　　　　　　社交技巧

5. basic concept　　　　　　　　　　基本概念

6. personal hygiene　　　　　　　　　個人的衛生

7. the physically disabled　　　　　　傷殘人士

8. the mentally handicapped　　　　　弱智人士

9. voluntary agencies　　　　　　　　志願機構

10. special education　　　　　　　　　特殊教育

11. the blind　　　　　　　　　　　　盲人

12. the deaf　　　　　　　　　　　　聾人

13. co-ordinated efforts　　　　　　　共同努力

14. adjustment problems　　　　　　　有適應困難

15. special education needs　　　　　　有特殊教育需要

16. to provide information　　　　　　提供資料

17. to enhance employment prospects　加強就業前景

18. to integrate into the community　　融入社會

Vocabulary

1.	rehab bus	復康巴士	23.	mild	輕度的
2.	nursing	護理	24.	contributing	有貢獻的
3.	deficiency	不足	25.	incorporate	合併
4.	subvention	補助	26.	physically handicapped	弱能
5.	psychologists	心理學家	27.	sight-impaired	弱視
6.	facilities	設施	28.	hearing-impaired	弱聽
7.	recreation	康樂	29.	artificial limb	義肢
8.	concern	關懷	30.	physiotherapists	物理治療師
9.	treatment	治療	31.	speech therapists	言語治療師
10.	wheelchair	輪椅	32.	Labour Department	勞工處
11.	unbalance	不平衡	33.	skills centre	技能訓練中心
12.	pressure	壓力	34.	ramp	斜坡道
13.	able-bodied	身體健全的人	35.	empathy	同感
14.	Community Chest	公益金	36.	vocational training	職業訓練
15.	Social Welfare Department	社會福利署	37.	sheltered workshops	庇護工場
16.	training centres	訓練中心	38.	remedial services	矯正的服務
17.	day-care centres	日間護理中心	39.	muscle training	肌能訓練
18.	Hong Kong Society for Rehabilitation	香港復康會	40.	intelligence quotient (IQ)	智商
19.	rehabilitation centres	復康中心	41.	medical social workers	醫務社會工作者
20.	community centres	社區中心	42.	screening and assessment services	甄別及評估服務
21.	potential	潛能			
22.	severe	嚴重的			

Drug Addiction

Sentences

1. A person can easily become addicted to heroin.

   一個人很容易變成吸食海洛英的癮君子。

2. He should be cut off from the drug.

   他應與毒品隔絕。

3. Drug addicts are often compelled to commit crimes.

   吸毒者很多時被迫犯罪。

4. Ill effects can easily be seen.

   不良的效果顯而易見。

5. Medical treatment is a must.

   接受醫藥治療是必需的。

6. A drug addict can hardly lead a normal life.

   吸毒者難以過正常的生活。

7. In recent years, electronic acupuncture has been used as a cure for drug addiction.

   近年來，人們用針灸電療醫治毒癮。

8. An increasing number of drug addicts are open to voluntary treatment.

   愈來愈多吸毒者傾向自願戒毒。

9. Yet, many others are unable to resist temptation.

   有很多人仍然不能抗拒引誘。

10. Drug addicts are deprived of a happy life.

    吸毒者不能享受快樂的人生。

11. A hectic life often results in stress and strains.

    繁忙的生活常導致壓力與緊張。

12. Some young people take the drug for fun.

    有些年青人吸毒是為了好玩。

13. Others take it in order to escape from the realities of life.

    有些人為了逃避現實而吸毒。

14. They easily indulge in drugs.

    他們很容易迷沉於毒品。

15. They will soon become physically and psychologically depenedent on drugs.

    他們很快會在身體上及精神上依賴毒品。

16. Once addicted, they will find it very difficult to abstain from taking drugs.

他們一經吸食，將難以戒除毒癮。

17. They will lose their appetite for food.

他們將失去食慾。

18. They only crave for drugs.

他們只切望得到毒品。

19. Outbreaks of tempers are very common among drug addicts.

吸毒者發脾氣是很常見的。

20. Drug addiction brings immeasurable harm to society and the consequences are far-reaching.

吸毒為社會帶來極大的禍害，其影響是深遠的。

21. We should do our best to uproot the vice of drug addiction.

我們應盡可能根除吸毒的禍害。

22. We must educate the young people to avoid the insidious attraction.

我們必須教育青年人去避免那隱伏的引誘。

23. "The first mouthful of drugs will make you feel sorry for the rest of your life."

「第一口白粉將使你終身悔恨。」

24. Drug addicts easily associate themselves with bad people.

吸毒者很容易與壞人結交。

25. Drug-pushers lure people into taking drugs.

毒品的推銷者引誘人吸毒。

26. Many of them are triad members.

他們之中有很多是三合會會員。

27. Many people wrongly believe that taking drugs can increase their sexual ability.

很多人誤信吸毒可增強性能力。

28. Drug addicts have no self-confidence and self-respect.

吸毒者沒有自信心及自尊心。

29. Drug addiction often causes a breakdown in family relationships.

吸毒往往造成家庭關係的破裂。

30. It wastes the valuable economic resources of society.

它浪費了社會上寶貴的經濟資源。

31. It undermines the stability of society as crime is often related to drug addiction.

它破壞了社會的安定，因為犯罪常與吸毒有關。

32. All in all, drug addiction ruins one's future, brings about broken families and does inestimable harm to society.

總而言之，吸毒摧毀一個人的前途，帶來破碎的家庭及對社會造成無可估計的禍害。

33. The Government has encouraged the public to take part in anti-drug campaigns.

政府已鼓勵公眾參與反吸毒運動。

34. Drug trafficking and peddling are still serious.

私運毒品和販毒仍然嚴重。

35. The Customs and Excise Service has always tried its best to detect and seize all kinds of narcotic drugs.

香港海關一向盡力偵查及搜捕各種毒品。

36. We should help the ex-addicts to stand on their own feet in society so that they can lead a normal life.

我們應幫助前吸毒者在社會上自立謀生，使他們能過正常生活。

37. They must be prevented from relapsing into drug addiction.

我們必須防止他們毒癮復發。

38. At the same time, financial help and counselling services are very much needed.

與此同時，金錢上的幫助及輔導服務是十分需要的。

39. Young people must be discouraged from experimenting with drugs.

我們必須勸阻青年人嘗試吸毒。

40. Prevention is better than cure.

預防勝於治療。

41. Citizens should fully co-operate with the authorities in the fight against drug addiction.

在反吸毒方面，市民應與當局通力合作。

 Phrases

1. nervous tension

神經緊張

2. physical discomfort

身體不適

3. an aching stomach

胃痛

4. compulsory treatment

強迫性治療

5. for fun or excitement

為了好玩及刺激

6. frustration of life

生活中所受的挫折

7. huge expenditure

龐大的支出

8. voluntary treatment

自願性治療

9. acupuncture and electro-stimulation

針灸電療法

10. illicit drug trafficking

非法運毒

11. to eradicate drug abuse   根絕毒禍

12. to increase fines for offences   增加違例罰款

13. to help at-risk youth   協助邊緣青年

14. to develop a healthy life style   採取健康的生活方式

15. positive attitudes   正確的態度

16. to say no to drugs   拒絕濫用藥物

17. to resist temptation   抗拒引誘

18. narcotics control   禁毒

19. a roving exhibition   巡迴展覽

20. halfway house service   中途宿舍服務

Vocabulary

1.	drug addict	吸毒者	15.	ecstasy	fing 頭丸 (搖頭丸)
2.	dosage	分量	16.	marihuana	大麻
3.	heroin	海洛英	17.	impulse	衝動
4.	cramps	抽筋	18.	diet	食物
5.	vomiting	嘔吐	19.	narcotics	麻醉劑
6.	diarrhoea	肚瀉	20.	Golden Triangle area	金三角地區
7.	treatment	治療	21.	drug addiction treatment centre	戒毒中心
8.	methadone	美沙酮			
9.	overdose	過量的藥物	22.	fatigue	疲勞
10.	symptom	病徵	23.	information	情報
11.	opium	鴉片	24.	opium poppy	罌粟
12.	LSD	迷幻藥	25.	ex-addicts	前吸毒者
13.	halcion	藍精靈			
14.	flunitrazepam	十字架			

26. after-care service	善後服務	47. tranquillisers	鎮靜劑
27. curious	好奇的	48. stimulants	興奮劑
28. ignorant	無知的	49. syringes	針筒
29. restless	不安靜的	50. peers	同儕
30. nervous	神經緊張的	51. ringleaders	販毒頭目
31. disgusting	厭惡的	52. lucrative	賺錢的
32. fatal	致命的	53. confiscate	充公
33. irrational	不合理的	54. seize	檢獲
34. eradicate	根絕	55. arrest	拘捕
35. support	支持	56. combat	搏鬥
36. wreck/ruin	摧毀	57. social and psychiatric therapy	社會及心理治療
37. alleviate	減輕	58. rehabilitation programme	康復計劃
38. misbelieve	誤信	59. methadone detoxification programme	美沙酮戒毒計劃
39. deteriorate	衰退		
40. repent	後悔	60. anti-drugs publicity campaigns	反吸毒宣傳運動
41. compel	迫使		
42. isolate	隔離	61. Drug Education Resource Centre	藥物教育資源中心
43. smuggle	走私		
44. co-ordinate	協調		
45. cough medicine	咳藥水		
46. cocaine	可卡因	62. rave party	迷幻派對

Elderly People

Sentences

1. According to Government estimation, elderly people will constitute one fourth of Hong Kong's population in 30 years.

   據政府估計，三十年後老人佔香港人口的四分一。

2. With the advancement of science and medicine, more and more elderly people are able to live longer.

   隨着科學及醫藥的進步，愈來愈多老年人能有較長的壽命。

3. We are now enjoying the fruits of the old people's hard labour.

   我們現正享受老年人昔日辛勤工作的成果。

4. We must appreciate the status and dignity that the elders deserve.

   我們必須重視長者應有的地位與尊嚴。

5. However, elderly people are often forgotten.

   然而老年人常被遺忘。

6. We should respect the elderly.

   我們應尊重老年人。

7. The Government should cultivate among the public the proper attitude towards the elderly.

   政府應培養公眾對老年人的正確態度。

8. Some low-income elderly people lack the friends and relatives to take care of.

   一些收入低微的老人缺乏親友的照顧。

9. Many elderly people have psychological or social problems.

   很多老年人在精神或社交上有困難。

10. Some elderly people cannot maintain proper care of themselves or their homes.

    有些老人難以照顧自己或家庭。

11. There is a serious shortage of services and facilities catering for the particular needs of the elderly people.

    配合老年人特別需要的服務及設施非常缺乏。

12. More hostel-type accommodation and related institutional facilities must be provided by the Government.

    政府必須提供更多宿舍形式的居住單位及有關的住院設施。

13. We should have a spirit of respect and a willingness to care for the elderly.

我們應有敬老的精神及願意照顧他們的心。

14. Elderly people can also contribute to society and their potential may further be developed.

老年人亦可對社會作出貢獻，而他們的潛能也可進一步得以發揮。

15. It is our responsibility to promote the well-being of the elderly.

促進老年人的幸福是我們的責任。

16. Elderly people are entitled to more social and recreational facilities.

老年人有權享有更多的社會和康樂的設施。

17. Through visits to Hostels for the Aged, we show our concern for the neglected.

我們到老人宿舍探訪，表示關心被社會忽略的一羣。

18. A large number of old people require personal or nursing care.

很多老人需要個人的照顧或護理服務。

19. House help includes services such as bathroom, laundry, canteen, etc.

家務助理包括提供浴室、洗衣、飯堂等服務。

20. In Hong Kong, there are many voluntary workers who use their leisure time to take care of the elderly and help organize recreational activities for them.

在香港，有很多義工利用餘暇照顧老人，以及為他們安排康樂活動。

21. Both the Social Welfare Department and voluntary welfare agencies play an important part in looking after the interests of elderly people.

社會福利署及各志願福利機構都在照顧老人的利益上擔當一個重要的角色。

22. The Government promotes the spirit of mutual help and care among the elderly.

政府提倡老人互助互愛的精神。

23. We should help old people to live a meaningful life.

我們應幫助老人過一個有意義的人生。

24. The value of the aged should not be under-estimated.

老年人的價值不應被低估。

Phrases

1. voluntary welfare agencies

志願福利機構

2. joint gathering for the elderly

耆英同樂

3.	socially isolated	與社會隔離
4.	social service groups	社會服務團體
5.	care and attention homes	護理安老院
6.	social centre for the elderly	老人康樂中心
7.	social gathering	社交聚會
8.	physical activities	運動
9.	social groups	聯誼小組
10.	social service activities	社會服務性活動
11.	personal care	個人護理
12.	care by the community	社區照顧
13.	residential care	院舍照顧
14.	pool bus service for the aged	老人專車服務
15.	financial and housing assistance	經濟及房屋援助
16.	provided for those in need	為有需要的人提供
17.	to grow haggard	日漸憔悴
18.	the same old story	老生常談
19.	life's highway	漫漫人生路

Vocabulary

1.	retirement	退休	9.	meal delivery	送飯
2.	experience	經驗	10.	household cleaning	家居清潔
3.	attitude	態度	11.	laundry service	洗衣服務
4.	contented	滿足	12.	escort service	護送
5.	visits	探訪	13.	house help service	家務助理
6.	variety show	綜合表演	14.	counselling service	輔導服務
7.	fun fair	攤位遊戲			
8.	interest group	興趣組			

15.	facilities	設施	28. senior discount	高齡優惠
16.	self-confidenc	自信心	29. longevity	長壽
17.	companions	同伴	30. wrinkle	皺紋
18.	concern	關懷	31. The Hong Kong Society for the Aged	香港耆康老人福利會
19.	Tai Chi	太極拳		
20.	calligraphy	書法	32. voluntary workers	義工
21.	Chinese painting	國畫	33. Festival of the Aged	老人節
22.	handicraft	手工		
23.	slides	幻燈片	34. homes for the aged	老人院
24.	dignified	可敬的	35. old age allowance	高齡津貼
25.	restore	恢復		
26.	elderly hostels	老人宿舍	36. outreach teams	外展服務隊
27.	day care centres	日間護理中心	37. senior citizen cards	長者卡

29 Entertainment and Recreation

Sentences

1. Cinema going is a very common kind of entertainment in Hong Kong.

    在香港，看電影是一種很普通的娛樂。

2. Many popular films often enjoy excellent box records.

    很多受觀眾歡迎的電影往往有極佳的票房紀錄。

3. Most locally produced films cater for different tastes of the audience.

    大部分本地製作的電影迎合觀眾的不同口味。

4. During holidays, many restaurants are fully packed.

每逢假日，很多酒樓皆擠滿了人。

5. Going to restaurants has become a way of life.

上酒樓已成為人們的一種生活方式。

6. Many citizens indulge in off-course betting.

很多市民沉迷於賭外圍馬。

7. It is very popular in Hong Kong.

它在香港很受歡迎。

8. An important football match is often broadcast live on the television screen.

電視台經常現場直播一場重要的足球賽事。

9. Many young people like listening to the pop music programme broadcast by radio stations.

很多年青人喜歡收聽電台廣播的流行音樂節目。

10. In Hong Kong, playing mahjong is a very popular indoor entertainment.

在香港，打麻將是一種很受歡迎的室內娛樂活動。

11. Watching television has become a part of life for many Hong Kong citizens.

對很多香港市民來說，看電視已成為了他們生活的一部分。

12. The activities of TV artists are often topics of Hong Kong citizens' daily conversation.

電視藝員的動態往往是香港市民日常的話題。

13. Many Hong Kong ladies like window-shopping.

很多香港女士喜歡逛公司櫥窗。

14. To them, the splendid goods on display in leading department stores are very attractive.

對她們來說，各大百貨公司所陳列的華麗商品是很具吸引力的。

15. Men usually like watching horse-racing.

男士通常喜歡觀看賽馬。

16. Others prefer quiet forms of recreation.

另一些人則較喜愛靜態的娛樂活動。

17. They take great delight in reading newspapers and magazines.

他們對閱讀報章雜誌有濃厚的興趣。

18. Reading newspapers is indeed an inexpensive entertainment.

閱讀報章實在是一種便宜的娛樂。

19. It is important to take sufficient recreation.

有充足的娛樂是很重要的。

20. "All work and no play makes Jack a dull boy."

「只有工作而沒有娛樂會使人愚鈍。」

21. Recreation brings some changes to our daily routine.

娛樂為我們刻板式的生活帶來一些變化。

22. It can also dispel our fatigue.

它同時能消除我們的疲勞。

23. On the whole, it brings us a fuller life.

總的來說，它帶給我們一個更完滿的生活。

 **Phrases**

1.	a variety of	各種不同的
2.	an excellent form of	最好的方式
3.	a full life	完滿的生活
4.	in the open air	在空曠地方
5.	to keep in good health	保持良好的健康
6.	cultural presentation	文化表演
7.	performing arts	表演藝術
8.	music appreciation	音樂欣賞
9.	to enrich the quality of life	提高生活素質
10.	pander to	迎合
11.	to steal the show	搶鏡頭
12.	to take a bow	謝幕
13.	to express their talent and creativity	發揮他們的才華和創造力
14.	never a dull moment	絕無冷場
15.	to play bridge	玩橋牌
16.	to sing karaoke	唱卡啦 OK
17.	soccer betting	足球博彩

 Vocabulary

1.	cinema	電影院	4.	feast	飲宴
2.	film	電影	5.	horse-racing	賽馬
3.	audience	觀眾	6.	race-track	馬場

7.	Happy Valley	跑馬地	31. folk dance	土風舞
8.	Hong Kong Jockey Club	香港賽馬會	32. Latin dance	拉丁舞
9.	off-course betting	賭外圍馬	33. aerobics	健體舞
			34. club	俱樂部
10.	Hong Kong Stadium	香港大球場	35. music	音樂
			36. popular	流行的
11.	fans	球迷	37. amusing	富娛樂性的
12.	neon light	霓虹光管	38. fascinating	精彩的
13.	ecology tour	生態旅行	39. crowded	擠滿了人的
14.	window-shopping	逛公司櫥窗	40. video	錄影
15.	mahjong	麻將	41. compact disc (CD)	光碟
16.	ball games	球類遊戲	42. video CD (VCD)	影碟
17.	bowling	保齡球	43. digital video disc (DVD)	數碼影碟
18.	billiard	桌球		
19.	golf	哥爾夫球	44. laser disc (LD)	鐳射影碟
20.	television	電視	45. car-racing	賽車
21.	poker	撲克	46. auction	拍賣
22.	weiqi	圍棋	47. hiking	遠足
23.	Chinese chess	中國象棋	48. gala	盛會
24.	camping	露營	49. Hong Kong Philharmonic Orchestra	香港管弦樂團
25.	fishing	垂釣		
26.	skating	溜冰	50. Hong Kong Cultural Centre	香港文化中心
27.	skating rink	溜冰場		
28.	surf-riding	滑浪	51. Hong Kong Museum of Art	香港藝術館
29.	surf-board	滑浪板		
30.	social dance	社交舞	52. Museum of Tea Ware	茶具文物館

30 Examinations

 Sentences

1. Examinations are a necessary evil.
考試是必要之惡。

2. It is used to judge the progress of students.
它被用來判斷學生的進度。

3. Examinations are often regarded as the key to success.
考試常被視為成功的關鍵。

4. Regarding examinations, many students are overwhelmed with anxiety.
很多學生對考試過度緊張。

5. They burn the midnight oil preparing for an approaching examination.
他們為了應付即將來臨的考試，通宵達旦地溫習。

6. Some students cram facts into their heads.
有些學生把資料塞進腦子裏。

7. In the examination hall, many candidates bite their pens in despair.
在試場內，很多考生失望地咬着筆桿。

8. Their nervous tension is at its highest.
他們的神經緊張達到最高峯。

9. They have no appetite for food and often lose a lot of sleep.
他們沒有食慾及時常失眠。

10. When the announcement of examination results comes, those who fail are often ashamed of themselves.
當公佈考試結果時，失敗者常對自己的表現感到羞恥。

11. Some weak-minded students may even commit suicide.
一些心靈脆弱的學生甚至會自殺。

12. Needless to say, examinations are a common headache to students.
不用說，考試是學生普遍感到頭痛的事。

13. Examinations are a popular form of testing students' ability to apply their knowledge.
考試是一種普遍的形式，藉以考核學生應用他們學識的能力。

14. Very often, examinations dominate one's future.

很多時候，考試支配了一個人的前途。

15. Most students have to sit for at least one important public examination.

大部分的學生都要參加至少一個重要的公開考試。

16. Critics point out that examinations bring a lot of harm to students.

批評者指出考試為學生帶來很多害處。

17. However, examinations may also do good to us.

然而，考試也可能為我們帶來好處。

18. Examinations may prevent us from indulging in other things.

考試可防止我們沉迷其他事上。

19. It drives students to learn more and study more thoroughly.

它促使學生們學得更多和更徹底。

20. It trains students to organize ideas and develop a quick mind.

它訓練學生組織意念及培養敏捷的思考。

21. Examinations force us to be careful and work out a way.

考試強迫我們要細心及找出解決的方法。

22. Many Hong Kong students have got used to the highly competitive examination system.

很多香港學生已習慣了那高度競爭的考試制度。

23. Some students may lose their confidence as a result of examination failure.

有些學生可能因考試失敗而失去自信心。

24. We should make good use of examinations to serve our positive purposes.

我們應善用考試，使它為我們正確的目的服務。

25. Students are often absorbed in studies and ponder over the books in order to get through an examination.

為了考試及格，學生常全神貫注埋首於書本上。

26. The heart begins to beat faster.

心開始急速地跳。

27. Their heads begin to ache as examinations draw nearer and nearer.

當考試愈來愈迫近的時候，他們開始感到頭痛。

28. When examinations are over, students heave a huge sigh of relief.

當考試結束時，學生發出一聲象徵解除痛苦的嘆息。

29. To the majority of students, attending an examination is a terrifying experience.

對大部分學生來說，考試是一個可怕的經驗。

30. In the examination hall, each face bears an expression of anxiety, nervousness or puzzle.

在考試大堂內，每張面孔都流露焦慮、緊張或困惑的表情。

31. Candidates have to try their best to squeeze out some inspiration.

考生必須盡力把一些靈感擠出來。

32. Their hands are sore with writing.

他們的手寫到痠痛。

33. Students wait for the results with great anxiety.

學生們十分焦慮地等待考試結果的公佈。

34. Many students resit the public examinations.

很多學生重考公開試。

35. Examinations are still subject to much criticism.

考試仍然受到很多批評。

36. Excessive pressures are often exerted on children by over-anxious parents.

高度緊張的父母往往對其兒女施加過度的壓力。

37. In this case, children might easily suffer from a nervous breakdown.

在這種情形下，兒童會很容易神經衰弱。

38. We should provide counselling service for those distressed students who fail in examinations.

我們應對受苦的失敗考生提供輔導服務。

39. Owing to the local examination system, moral education is often neglected.

由於本地的考試制度，道德教育常被忽視。

40. Little time is left for leisure.

餘暇很少。

41. Examinations are often used for the selection of students for admission to institutions of higher learning.

很多時候，考試被用以選拔學生進入高等院校。

42. The shortage of university places has something to do with the keen competition in entrance examinations.

入學試競爭激烈與大學學位的短缺有關。

43. Very often, too much emphasis is being put on examinations.

考試常被過份強調。

44. Examinations are a stimulus to work.

考試是一種對工作的刺激。

45. It also brings a sense of frustration and failure to many students.

它也為不少學生帶來一種挫敗感。

46. It cannot test moral qualities.

它不能測驗德性。

47. To get through an examination is a trying task. 考試及格不是一件易事。

48. Only a few students pass an examination with flying colours. 只有少數學生能考試及格並得到優異的成績。

49. Students taking an examination should leave nothing to luck. 參加考試的學生不應寄望於幸運。

50. Many critics argue that examinations serve no educational purposes. 很多批評者認為考試不能達到教育的目的。

51. Most students are too pre-occupied with examinations. 大部分學生太過專注於考試。

52. Examinations deprive students of normal extra-curricular activities. 考試剝奪學生正常的課外活動。

53. They bring undesirable pressures to students. 它們給學生帶來不必要的壓力。

54. There is a lack of balanced education among students. 學生們缺乏平衡的教育。

55. They merely manage to pass examinations. 他們只設法在考試中獲得及格。

Phrases

1. devotion to study 熱愛學習

2. extreme exhaustion 極度疲累

3. a physical collapse 身體不支而病倒

4. a full and useful life 完滿而有用的人生

5. as long as 只要

6. as good as others 像別人一樣好

7. inferior to others 比別人低劣

8. all in all 總括來說

9. intensive study 精深的研究

10. to come out a better student 成為一個好學生

11. an awfully tough time 十分困難的時間

12.	the heavy load of intense study	沉重密集的學習	
13.	highly strung	情緒十分緊張的	
14.	extra thick lenses	特別厚的眼鏡片	
15.	skeleton knowledge	皮毛的知識	
16.	peculiar circumstances in Hong Kong	香港的特殊環境	
17.	appealing to parents and teachers	對父母及教師所發出的呼籲	
18.	mental illness	精神病	
19.	element of luck	幸運的因素	
20.	cheating in examinations	考試作弊	
21.	in a muddle	處於一個混亂的狀態中	
22.	to keep one's nerve	保持鎮定	
23.	to make an eleventh hour effort	盡最後一刻努力	
24.	to take no chances	絕不靠運氣	
25.	to come off with flying colours	成績美滿	
26.	good time management	善用時間	
27.	elite selection	拔尖	
28.	King of the tutors	補習天王	
29.	school-based teaching	校本教學	
30.	internal assessment	校內評估	
31.	5 As and 1 C	五優一良	

Vocabulary

1.	merits	優點		5.	grade	等級
2.	demerits/ drawbacks	缺點		6.	certificate	證書
				7.	diploma	文憑
3.	elite	尖子		8.	degree	大學畢業學位
4.	scores/marks	分數				

9.	associate degree	副學士	
10.	bachelorship	學士資格	
11.	master's degree	碩士學位	
12.	doctor's degree	博士學位	
13.	future	前途	
14.	efficiency	效率	
15.	advantage	好處	
16.	disadvantage	壞處	
17.	tension	緊張	
18.	obstacles	困難險阻	
19.	criterion	標準	
20.	loophole	漏洞	
21.	critics	批評者	
22.	ordeal	使人難堪的經驗	
23.	officer-in-charge	主管	
24.	nervous	神經緊張的	
25.	anxious	焦慮的	
26.	haggard	憔悴的	
27.	pale	臉色蒼白的	
28.	harmful	有害的	
29.	numerous	無數的	
30.	fussy	慌張的	
31.	disappointed	失望的	
32.	crucial	重要的	

33.	reliable	可靠的
34.	indispensable	必要的
35.	memorize	記憶
36.	detest	憎恨
37.	exaggerate	誇大
38.	distribute	派發
39.	worry	憂慮
40.	cheat	欺騙
41.	cram	塞進
42.	overlook	忽視
43.	abolish	廢除
44.	replace	取代
45.	compete	競爭
46.	proficiency tests in Putonghua	普通話能力測試
47.	Test of English as a Foreign Language (TOEFL)	英語作為外國語言考試 (托福)
48.	tutorial school	補習學校
49.	Early Admission Scheme	優先錄取計劃
50.	subsidized school	津貼學校
51.	DSS (Direct Subsidary Scheme) School	直資學校

Exhibition

 Sentences

1. The exhibition covers an area of ten thousand square metres.

展覽場地廣達一萬平方米。

2. It is open to the public.

這是公開的展覽。

3. Admission is free.

免費入場。

4. The theme of the exhibition is the application of solar energy.

展覽的主題是太陽能的應用。

5. The exhibition was personally opened by the Chief Secretary for Administration.

展覽會由政務司司長主持開幕。

6. He also performed the ribbon-cutting ceremony.

他同時主持剪綵儀式。

7. The exhibition was a great success.

這次展覽會十分成功。

8. Many latest products were displayed.

展覽會展出很多新產品。

9. The exhibits have great educational value.

展品有很大的教育意義。

10. The works of art on display attracted a large audience.

展出的藝術品吸引了一大羣參觀者。

11. They give pleasure to the viewers.

它們為參觀者帶來快樂。

12. The exhibitors present their products artistically.

參展商以藝術的形式展出他們的產品。

13. The exhibition will last for ten days.

展覽為期十天。

14. It leaves the viewers with a deep and lasting impression.

它給參觀者留下一個深刻和難忘的印象。

15. The exhibition hall was nicely decorated.

展覽廳佈置得美輪美奐。

16. It successfully attracted a lot of visitors.　它成功地吸引了眾多的參觀者。

17. The audience enjoyed the visit very much.　參觀者對這次參觀感到十分愉快。

18. The exhibition is worth visiting.　這次展覽值得參觀。

19. Taking photographs was not permitted.　大會不准許人們拍照。

20. The exhibition was jointly organized by Education Burean and Hong Kong and Shanghai Banking Corporation.　這次展覽由教育局及香港上海匯豐銀行聯合主辦。

21. Visitors were very interested in the exhibits.　參觀者對展品感到濃厚的興趣。

22. The exhibition was both entertaining and educational.　這次展覽既富娛樂性，也具教育意義。

23. The staff in charge explained the exhibits to the visitors.　負責的職員向參觀者講解展品的特質。

24. The Hong Kong Book Fair attracted thousands and thousands of book lovers to visit.　香港書展吸引無數愛書人前往參觀。

25. The publishers in the exhibition come from different parts of the world.　參展出版社來自世界各地。

26. Most of the books exhibited can be bought on the spot.　人們可以即場購買絕大部分展出的書籍。

27. Hundreds and hundreds of youths line up early to wait for admission to the comic book exhibition.　在漫畫書籍展覽會門前，有數以百計的青少年一早排隊，等候入場。

28. In addition to books and posters, there are also toy weapons for sale in the comic books exhibition.　漫畫書展中，除了書籍和海報，更出售玩具武器。

29. The large scale flowers exhibition is held annually.　大型花卉展覽每年舉辦一次。

30. The peculiar flowers and grass are exhibited. The visitors have the feeling that everything is new.　場內展出來自各地的奇花異草，令參觀者耳目一新。

31. The work of the winners in the flower arrangement competition is exhibited.

場內展出插花比賽的優勝作品。

32. Many large-scale exhibitions are held at AsiaWorld-Expo.

很多大型展覽會在亞洲國際博覽館舉行。

33. Hong Kong Art Museum and other museums display many a time the collections of pottery porcelain, jadeware and copperware from many dynasties of the past.

香港藝術館及其他博物館在年中多次展出館藏歷代陶瓷、玉器和銅器。

34. They also borrow displays from museums in the Mainland and other countries for the citizens to visit.

他們更從國內或國外博物館借來展品，供市民參觀。

35. Most exhibitions are open for the public to visit and no admission fees are charged.

大部分展覽供大眾參觀，而且不收入場費。

36. For some exhibitions, admission is restricted to people in their trade only.

部分展覽只許業內人士進場。

Phrases

1.	the chief objective	主要的目的
2.	rich and colourful exhibits	豐富及多姿多采的展品
3.	beautiful design	精美的設計
4.	unique decoration	獨特的裝飾
5.	festive atmosphere	節日的氣氛
6.	audio-visual aids	視聽器材

Vocabulary

1.	theme	主題	6.	visitors	參觀者
2.	organizer	主辦者	7.	art gallery	美術館
3.	sponsor	贊助人	8.	spectators	觀眾
4.	project	計劃	9.	exhibition gallery	展覽廳
5.	exhibits	展品			

10.	features	特色	24. eye-catching	吸引人的
11.	entrance	入口	25. fascinating	迷人的
12.	publicity	宣傳	26. organize	組織
13.	careers exhibition	職業展覽	27. promote	促進
			28. encourage	鼓勵
14.	venue	展覽地點	29. arrange	安排
15.	queries	詢問	30. support	支持
16.	stalls	攤位	31. display	展出
17.	highlights	最精彩的部分	32. briefing	簡介
18.	exhibitors	參展單位	33. informative	資料豐富
19.	interchange	交流	34. opening ceremony	開幕典禮
20.	record	紀錄		
21.	handicrafts	手工藝品	35. Hong Kong Convention and Exhibition Centre	香港會議展覽中心
22.	numerous	無數的		
23.	prominent	顯著的		

Fear

Sentences

1. Fear is a common human experience.　恐懼是人類普遍的經驗。

2. It is a sound, natural instinct.　這是一個健全的、自然的天性。

3. Fear is often complex and unpredictable.　恐懼常是複雜及不能預測的。

4. It is part and parcel of physical reaction.　這是生理反應的一部分。

5. Fear will not do us immediate bodily harm.

恐懼不會即時傷害我們的身體。

6. There are a number of sources of fear.

恐懼的來源有多種。

7. We may have pangs of sudden fear in a state of emergency.

在危急的情形下，我們會有突發的恐懼。

8. Some people fear the wrath of gods.

有些人恐懼神的憤怒。

9. Others fear physical pain, mental distress and social disgrace.

其他人則恐懼身體和精神上的痛苦，以及在社會上遭受的恥辱。

10. Man has a strong motive for overcoming instinctive fear.

人類有一個強大的動機去克服本能上的恐懼。

11. We have to assess dangers correctly and overcome the fear.

我們需要正確地估計危險及克服恐懼。

12. We must be aware of risks without fearing them.

我們要知道危險的存在，不要對它產生恐懼。

13. We should have true courage without a sense of fear.

我們應有真正的勇氣而沒有恐懼的感覺。

14. Fear cannot be wholly welcomed, nor can it be rejected.

我們不能完全欣然接受恐懼，也不能拒絕它。

15. Fear is part of the natural development of things and is often related to the future.

恐懼是事物自然發展的一部分，它往往與將來有關。

16. Some people recoil from danger while others take action to deal with it.

有些人遇危險而退縮，其他人則採取行動去對付它。

17. It is important to gain a full understanding of the problem.

對問題有充分的了解是很重要的。

18. A sense of fear may sometimes inhibit potential law-breakers.

恐懼的感覺有時會抑制可能破壞法紀的人。

19. Many people have a fear of impending danger.

很多人恐怕即將來臨的危險。

20. Most people fear death.

大部分人都怕死。

21. The British fear God and honour the Queen.

英國人敬畏上帝，尊敬女王。

 **Phrases**

1.	to avoid danger	避免危險
2.	to take action	採取行動
3.	dreaded events	可怕的事情
4.	to shrink back	畏縮
5.	fear of failure	對失敗的恐懼
6.	fear of trying	對嘗試的恐懼
7.	fear of superiors	對上司的恐懼
8.	fear of breaking with convention	對違反習俗的恐懼
9.	defence against fear	對恐懼的防衛
10.	fear of ill health	對身體不健康的恐懼
11.	aim of self-preservation	自保的目的
12.	to break the heart	傷心
13.	to tremble with fear	戰戰兢兢
14.	to take heart	鼓起勇氣

 Vocabulary

1.	emotion	情感	10.	panic	恐慌
2.	cowardice	膽怯	11.	shock	吃一驚
3.	consequences	後果	12.	terrified	感到恐懼的
4.	courage	勇氣	13.	phobia	恐懼症
5.	impulse	衝動	14.	confidence	信心
6.	nervous	精神緊張的	15.	hair-raising	令人毛髮直豎的
7.	fearlessness	無懼	16.	rational	有理智的
8.	temperament	性情	17.	instinctive	本能的
9.	challenge	挑戰			

18. desperate	失望的	35. start	嚇一跳
19. excessive	過度的	36. ruin	摧毀
20. well-founded	有理由的	37. remedy	補救
21. shudder	顫慄	38. shiver	顫抖
22. cautious	謹慎的	39. scare	驚嚇
23. anxious	焦慮的	40. paralyse	麻痹
24. shy	害羞的	41. horror	恐怖
25. hopeless	失望的	42. stage-fright	怯場
26. helpless	無助的	43. terror-stricken	膽戰心驚的
27. timid	膽小的	44. terrorism	恐怖主義
28. imaginary	想像的	45. terrorist	恐怖份子
29. stimulate	刺激	46. alarm	恐懼
30. evoke	喚起	47. alarmist	大驚小怪的人
31. stifle	窒息	48. frightful	可怕的
32. overcome	克服	49. conscience-stricken	受良心責備的
33. suffer	受痛苦		
34. recover	恢復	50. chicken-hearted	缺乏勇氣的

33

Ferry

Sentences

1. During holidays, there are many fully occupied ferries.

   每逢假日，很多渡輪都載滿乘客。

2. Some ferries are available for hire.

   有些渡輪可供出租。

3. Passengers stepped on board the ferry.　乘客登上那艘渡輪。

4. Nowadays, the air-conditioned deluxe class is more popular.　在今天，設有空調的豪華艙較受歡迎。

5. We went across the harbour on a Star ferry.　我們乘坐天星小輪渡海。

6. There were strong winds and waves.　風浪很大。

7. It was still an enjoyable trip.　但仍然是一個愉快的旅程。

8. Many people caught a ferry back to Hong Kong.　很多人乘搭小輪返回香港。

9. They glanced over the scenery on the island.　他們欣賞島上的景色。

10. There are some signboards advertising various goods and services in the ferry.　在小輪內有一些廣告牌為各種產品和服務賣廣告。

11. Some passengers choose a seat by the window.　有些乘客選擇一個靠窗的座位。

12. They appreciate the beautiful view of the sea.　他們欣賞美麗的海景。

13. The sea wind was blowing gently.　海風正輕輕地吹着。

14. A group of seagulls could be seen flying over the sea.　我們可以見到一羣海鷗在海上飛翔。

15. Many passengers were reading newspapers.　很多乘客正在閱讀報章。

16. Some people were playing cards.　有些人正在玩紙牌。

17. They were indifferent to others.　他們對其他人漠不關心。

18. The sea was calm.　大海風平浪靜。

19. A walk on the deck was agreeable.　在甲板上散步是愉快的。

20. The wind was in our favour.　那時正是順風。

21. The ferry was just out of the bay.　小輪剛駛出了海灣。

22. The sea was rather rough.　大海有點風浪。

23. The ferry cut its way through the waves.　小輪破浪前進。

24. It heaved uncomfortably.　它搖擺不定。

25. It came to a standstill.　船停了。

26. It ran aground.　船擱淺了。

27. The anchor was dropped.   船已經落了錨。

28. Some passengers were grasping the handrail.   有些乘客正抓緊扶手。

29. The ferry finally reached the shore.   小輪終於到了岸。

30. Passengers were in a hurry, making for the gangway.   乘客們正匆忙上船。

31. Many other people were catching the ferry.   很多其他人正趕乘那班渡輪。

32. Some passengers leant out of the window.   有些乘客斜倚窗外。

Phrases

1. on weekdays   在週日

2. entrance to the ferry pier   小輪碼頭入口

3. a gloomy sky   陰晦的天空

4. by instinct   直覺地

5. much to my surprise   使我感到十分驚奇

6. to go on board   上船

7. agreeable passage   愉快的航程

8. at a high speed   高速

9. public demand   公眾的需求

10. attractive posters   有吸引力的海報

11. the inner harbour   港內

12. free travel   免費乘搭

13. concessionary fares   優惠票價

Vocabulary

1. deck   甲板   3. Public Pier   公眾碼頭

2. double-deck ferry   雙層渡海小輪   4. turnstile   旋轉柵門

5.	Star Ferry	天星小輪	27.	sail	航行
6.	fares	船費	28.	scream	叫喊
7.	route	航線	29.	depart	開行
8.	gangway	跳板	30.	steer	把舵
9.	porthole	船的側窗	31.	arrive	抵達
10.	bow	船頭	32.	vessels	渡輪
11.	stern	船尾	33.	Kaitos	街渡
12.	engine room	機房	34.	Discovery Bay	愉景灣
13.	mask	桅桿	35.	Lamma Island	南丫島
14.	funnel	煙囪	36.	Cheung Chau	長洲
15.	journey	旅程	37.	Peng Chau	坪洲
16.	seats	座位	38.	Mui Wo	梅窩
17.	conversation	談話	39.	Lantau Island	大嶼山
18.	helm	舵	40.	Po Tai Island	蒲台島
19.	anchor	錨	41.	Yung Shue Wan	榕樹灣
20.	high-tide	高潮	42.	Hung Shing Ye Beach	洪聖爺灣
21.	low-tide	低潮	43.	outlying districts	離島地區
22.	lifeboat	救生船	44.	ordinary class	普通艙
23.	lifebuoy	救生圈	45.	the deluxe class	豪華艙
24.	telescope	望遠鏡			
25.	casualties	傷亡			
26.	seasick	暈船			

Films, Broadcasting and Newspapers

Sentences

1. Cinema-going is still a very popular form of entertainment in Hong Kong.

   在香港，看電影仍然是十分受歡迎的娛樂形式。

2. Very often, people go to see a film to escape the monotony of daily life.

   很多時候，人們去看一套電影以擺脫單調的日常生活。

3. Amusing situations in a film always provoke laughter within the audience.

   電影中有趣的情景總是引起觀眾大笑。

4. Many Hong Kong people like to see a highly entertaining comedy.

   很多香港人喜歡看一部極富娛樂性的喜劇。

5. A light, amusing kung-fu film can often create a high box-office record.

   一部輕鬆滑稽的功夫片常能創下很高的票房紀錄。

6. The film industry provides employment for many people.

   電影工業為很多人提供就業機會。

7. Some people can develop their talent for acting in films.

   有些人能在電影中發揮他們的演戲才能。

8. Outstanding performance of the film stars is often acclaimed by the audience.

   電影明星的優異演出常受到觀眾的喝采。

9. Famous historical personalities and their deeds come to life on the screen.

   歷史名人的事蹟在銀幕上活現。

10. Spectators are very much impressed by this vivid presentation.

    觀眾對這生動的展示方式留下深刻的印象。

11. Some films have an educational value.

    一些電影具有教育價值。

12. These films, however, are very rare.

    然而，這些電影是十分稀少的。

13. Many films are produced locally while others are imported from other countries.

很多電影是本地製作的，有些則由外國進口。

14. Socially conscious film makers often take several years to produce a film.

有社會良知的電影製作者往往用數年的時間來拍攝一部電影。

15. This may include the time spent on outdoor shooting.

這可能包括拍攝外景所花的時間。

16. In some films, the manipulation of atmosphere is especially skilful.

有些電影的氣氛營造得特別巧妙。

17. Cinema attendance is often affected by the location of the cinema.

電影院的入場觀眾人數很多時受電影院的位置所影響。

18. In Hong Kong, a large number of films are not worth seeing.

在香港，很多電影是不值一看的。

19. They even do harm to the impressionable minds of young people.

它們甚至對青年人那易受影響的心靈有害。

20. Many films disseminate unhealthy ideas about sex and violence.

很多電影傳播色情、暴力等不健康的意識。

21. Without doubt, these films will have a far-reaching impact on the audience.

這些電影無疑會對觀眾產生深遠的影響。

22. Radio stations provide the local audience with news and entertainment.

電台為本港聽眾提供新聞及娛樂。

23. They provide round-the-clock news.

它提供二十四小時新聞報導。

24. The 24-hour broadcasting is welcomed by local people.

二十四小時廣播服務受到本地人士的歡迎。

25. Radio stations can play an important role in bridging the gap between the people and the government.

電台能扮演一個能讓人民與政府溝通的重要角色。

26. They also promote better mutual understanding between the two parties.

它們能促進彼此的了解。

27. Radio stations try to maintain balanced programmes.

電台嘗試保持節目的平衡。

28. All the programmes come on the air through different channels.

所有節目通過不同的波段廣播。

29. Information and public affairs programmes are very important.

新聞及公眾事務節目是十分重要的。

30. Youth programmes have not been neglected.

青年人的節目沒有被忽視。

31. In fact, many people find it enjoyable to listen to the radio during their leisure time.

事實上，很多人覺得在空餘聽收音機是一件愉快的事。

32. Radio stations serve society in many ways.

電台通過很多種方式為社會提供服務。

33. For instance, they provide valuable transport information for drivers.

例如它們為駕駛人士提供有用的交通消息。

34. They also provide emergency information during typhoons.

它們也在颱風時提供緊急消息。

35. Sometimes they teach the audience to appreciate classical music and other performing arts.

有時它們引導聽眾欣賞古典音樂及其他表演藝術。

36. Listening to the radio is indeed a good pastime.

聽收音機實在是一種很好的消遣。

37. Newspapers keep us well informed of the important daily happenings of the whole world.

報紙向我們詳細報導每日世界上發生的重要事情。

38. From reading newspapers we get not only knowledge but also pleasure.

我們閱讀報紙時不但獲得知識，也得到樂趣。

39. The spread of education has brought about a very large reading public.

教育的普及帶來眾多的讀者。

40. Many people find reading newspapers a daily necessity.

很多人發覺讀報是日常生活所必需的。

41. Reading newspapers has become a popular habit.

讀報已成為普遍習慣。

42. The local newspapers have a large daily circulation.

在本港，報紙每日銷量龐大。

43. The varied contents suit different tastes.

報紙內容多姿多采，適合人們不同的口味。

44. Newspapers provide the readers with up-to-date news and information.

報紙為讀者提供最新的新聞及資訊。

45. They report on both international and local events in detail.

它們詳盡報導國際及本港的新聞。

46. They also offer valuable services to the community.

它們也提供寶貴的社會服務。

47. The press can often profoundly influence public opinion.

報紙經常對公眾的意見有深遠的影響。

48. It even moulds public opinion.

它甚至塑造公眾的意見。

49. Readers are influenced to a great extent by the editor's discussion of current problems.

讀者在很大程度上受編輯對目前問題的討論所影響。

50. The press is a powerful force in shaping government policies.

報紙是塑造政府政策的一股強大的力量。

51. Indeed, it wields a great power.

它實在掌握很大的權力。

52. The press brings to light social injustice.

報紙揭示社會上不公平的事。

53. It upholds social justice and denounces social evils.

它維護社會正義，並公開指責社會的病害。

54. It is the mouthpiece of the people.

它是人民的喉舌。

55. It publishes the grievances of the public.

它刊登大眾的申訴。

56. It fights for the cause of people and promotes social harmony.

它為人民爭取福利並促進社會和諧。

57. The press reports the issues of common concern.

報紙報導大眾關心的事。

58. Through reading newspapers, people become conscious of the evils in society.

人們通過讀報意識到社會上的壞事。

59. The press often advocates social reforms.

報紙常常倡導社會改革。

60. It also keeps a vigilant eye on the activities of the government.

它也注視政府的活動。

61. It channels people's grievances to the authorities concerned.

它把人民的申訴傳達給政府有關的部門。

62. It reflects the public's views on a controversial issue.

它反映公眾對一個具爭論性的問題的意見。

63. When people read newspapers, they become more familiar with the background of an issue.

人們通過讀報加深對事件背景的了解。

64. Many newspapers encourage their readers to take an enlightened and progressive view of life.

很多報紙鼓勵讀者有一個開明及進步的人生觀。

65. The press often entertains readers by publishing vivid pictures and cartoons or amusing news and articles.

報紙常以生動的圖片與漫畫，或有趣的新聞和文章娛樂讀者。

66. The Letters to the Editor column provides an effective channel to air people's complaints or grievances.

報紙的讀者來信版為人們提供一個表達不滿或申訴的有效途徑。

67. High ranking government officers may hold a press conference to explain or clarify government policies.

政府高級官員會舉行記者招待會解釋或澄清政策。

68. The journalistic language style is simple and easy to understand.

報紙文體簡單易明。

69. We should get into the habit of reading newspapers every day.

我們應養成每天讀報的習慣。

70. Reading newspapers helps to improve our reading speed and writing.

讀報幫助我們增加閱讀速度及加強寫作能力。

71. Many secondary students read English newspapers mainly for the purpose of language learning.

很多中學生閱讀英文報紙主要是為了學習語文。

72. When we read newspapers, we must learn to judge what is right and what is wrong.

當我們讀報時，我們必須學習如何判別是與非。

73. Freedom of the press is extremely important.

新聞自由是極之重要的。

74. The press is not allowed to defame the good name of others.

報紙是不被准許誹謗他人的名譽。

75. Some unscrupulous publishers abuse the freedom of the press.

有些不良的出版人濫用新聞自由。

76. They pander to the pursuit of the lowest tastes by publishing obscene pictures and pornographic literature.

他們刊登猥褻圖片及色情文章，引人追求最低級的趣味。

77. Indeed, there are many newspapers in Hong Kong which corrupt public morals with indecent contents.　香港實在有很多報紙以淫穢的內容敗壞公眾道德。

78. The publishing of these newspapers should be prohibited.　我們應禁止這類報紙的出版。

79. The editor is legally responsible for the contents of a newspaper.　編輯對於報紙所刊登的內容有法律責任。

80. Advertisement is the main source of revenue for a newspaper.　廣告是報紙收入的主要來源。

 **Phrases**

1. thematic materials　題材

2. with particular emphasis on　特別注重

3. notable events　值得注意的大事

4. to keep in touch with　保持接觸

5. favourable comments　好的評論

6. tips on horse racing　賽馬貼士

7. first hand information　第一手資料

8. absence of censorship　沒有檢查制度

9. to enhance the public's access to information　加強市民的知情權

10. published on the Internet　透過互聯網出版

11. press freedom　新聞自由

12. to inform, entertain and educate　提供資訊、娛樂及教育

13. a popular leisure activity　一種受歡迎的消遣活動

14. to provide a balanced and objective programme　提供均衡和客觀的節目

15. news and current affairs　新聞及時事

16. special announcement　特別報告

17.	a three-tier film classification system		電影三級制
18.	harmful to		對……不良
19.	in line with community standards		根據社會尺度
20.	through competition		透過競爭
21.	to promote choice and diversity		提供多元化的選擇
22.	public standards of taste and decency		社會的口味和雅俗的標準
23.	to broadcast Chinese and Western "golden oldies"		播放中外經典金曲
24.	the biggest box-office hits		最賣座電影
25.	tune in to		收聽
26.	financial data		財經資訊
27.	mass culture		大眾文化

Vocabulary

1.	movie stars	明星		14.	melodrama	情節劇
2.	sex	性		15.	plot	情節
3.	violence	暴力		16.	art film	文藝片
4.	kung-fu films	功夫片		17.	film-makers	製片人
5.	movie fans	影迷		18.	theme	主題
6.	soap opera	肥皂劇		19.	announcer	播音員
7.	actor	演員		20.	disc jockey (DJ)	唱片騎師
8.	director	導演		21.	producer	監製
9.	style	風格		22.	audience	聽眾
10.	musicals	歌舞片		23.	functions	功能
11.	film script	劇本		24.	editor	編輯
12.	cast	主要演員		25.	editorial	社論
13.	comedy	喜劇				

26.	press conference	記者招待會	52. dub	配音
27.	reputation	名譽	53. broadcast	廣播
28.	bias	偏見	54. analyse	分析
29.	propaganda	宣傳	55. advocate	提倡
30.	doctrine	教條	56. praise	讚許
31.	news agency	新聞通訊社	57. disapprove	不贊同
32.	journalist/ reporter	新聞記者	58. eradicate	消除
33.	feature articles	特稿	59. cinema-going	看電影
34.	novels	小說	60. action films	動作片
35.	advertisement	廣告	61. block busters	賣座電影
36.	court news	法庭新聞	62. mini-cinemas	迷你電影院
37.	principles	原則	63. blue movies	小電影
38.	articles	文章	64. Cantonese pop music	粵語流行音樂
39.	cartoons	漫畫	65. Putonghua programme	普通話節目
40.	columnist	專欄作家	66. BBC World Service	英國廣播世界節目
41.	headline	標題	67. news summaries	新聞提要
42.	libel	誹謗	68. talk show	清談節目
43.	ridiculous	荒謬的	69. traffic reports	交通消息
44.	comical	諧趣的	70. weather reports	天氣報告
45.	refreshing	心曠神怡的	71. stop-press	最新消息
46.	romantic	浪漫的	72. tit-bits	花絮新聞
47.	sympathetic	同情的	73. gossip magazine	「八卦」周刊
48.	critical	批判的	74. sensational	煽情的
49.	vicious	邪惡的		
50.	ban	禁止		
51.	control	管制		

75.	Cantonese films	粵語片	
76.	Mandarin films	國語片	
77.	Western films	西片	
78.	Chinese subtitles	中文字幕	
79.	martial art films	武俠片	
80.	mysterious detective films	偵探懸疑片	
81.	indecent movies	不道德的電影	
82.	international news	國際新聞	
83.	local news	本地新聞	
84.	classified advertisement	分類小廣告	
85.	special columns	專欄	

86.	Mainly for Women	婦女版
87.	Sports Page	體育版
88.	Entertainment Page	娛樂版
89.	political and economic news	政治及經濟新聞
90.	phone-in programme	電話節目
91.	contemporary music	現代音樂
92.	informative programme	資訊節目
93.	song dedication programme	點唱節目
94.	Television and Entertainment Licensing Authority	影視及娛樂事務管理處

35

Fire

Sentences

1. It was a dreadful scene.　　　　　　　　　　那是一個可怕的景象。

2. A large crowd of people rushed out hurriedly.　一大羣人匆匆地走出來。

3. Huge flames of fire rose high in the sky.　　　巨大的火焰直衝雲霄。

4. The whole area was covered with black and thick smoke.　整個地區被濃厚的黑煙所籠罩着。

5. The fire spread rapidly all around.　火勢迅速向四方蔓延。

6. Firemen poured floods of water on the top of the fire.　消防員把大量的水射向火焰之上。

7. They finally brought the fire under control.　他們終於控制火勢。

8. The building was almost entirely destroyed.　整座建築物幾乎全被燒毀。

9. It was a third alarm fire.　這是一場三級大火。

10. Luckily, no one was killed in the fire.　幸而無人在這場大火中喪生。

11. Three residents were slightly injured.　三位住客受輕傷。

12. The injured were all rushed to hospital for treatment.　所有傷者都被迅速送往醫院接受治療。

13. About four hundred people were made homeless.　大約有四百位居民無家可歸。

14. It was a furious four-hour conflagration.　這是一場焚燒四小時的烈火。

15. Many houses were gutted by the fire.　很多房屋遭大火吞噬。

16. The fire covered an area of eighty thousand square metres.　災場面積廣達八萬平方米。

17. Through the efforts of the Fire Brigade, the fire was finally put out.　通過消防隊的奮力施救，大火終被救熄。

18. A man made a dramatic escape at almost the last minute.　一個男子在幾乎最後一分鐘內戲劇性地逃出生天。

19. He was narrowly averted.　他倖免於難。

20. It was the biggest and the most destructive blaze in recent years.　這是近年來火勢最大、損毀最重的祝融浩劫。

21. The rear part of the building collapsed.　那座建築物的後部塌了下來。

22. Many adjoining buildings were affected.　很多鄰近的建築物也受到波及。

23. The fire quickly spread to other floors of the building.　火勢迅速蔓延至大廈各層。

24. Within a few minutes, the entire building was ablaze.

在數分鐘內，整座大廈陷入火海中。

25. The cause of the fire is still unknown.

起火原因仍然未明。

26. Investigations are proceeding.

調查工作正在進行中。

27. Firemen used twenty jets at the height of the blaze.

消防員在火勢最猛烈時動用了二十條消防喉救火。

28. Most victims were recent arrivals from China.

大部分受害者是最近由中國大陸來港的移民。

29. The fire broke out at 2.44 a.m.

火警在上午二時四十四分發生。

30. It was raised to third alarm forty minutes later.

四十分鐘後大火升至三級。

31. There were explosions of LP gas cylinders.

液體石油氣罐發生爆炸。

32. Seventy firemen fought the blaze hard.

七十個消防員奮力救火。

33. Two children were missing.

兩個小童失了蹤。

34. An old woman might be trapped in the inferno.

一位老婦可能被困於火海中。

35. The fire victims were registered at the Kwun Tong Community Centre.

火災災民在觀塘社區中心登記資料。

36. The fire caused a blackout.

大火造成停電。

37. Electrical faults were probably to blame.

漏電可能是導致火災的原因。

38. Firemen made an eleventh-hour bid to save the building.

消防員作出最後一刻鐘的努力去搶救那座建築物。

39. It was a windy night.

那是一個有風的晚上。

40. Everywhere was buried by smoke.

周圍充滿濃煙。

41. Residents were running here and there.

居民四處奔跑。

42. Women and children were screaming and crying.

婦孺尖叫哭喊。

43. They were too frightened to do anything to save their property.

他們受驚過度，以致不曾搶救他們的財產。

44. The fire swept across the whole area.

大火橫掃整區。

45. Many people burst into tears.	很多人哭起來。
46. The whole affected area remained a heap of ashes, dead and motionless.	整個受影響的地區只剩下一堆殘灰,靜止而沒有生氣。
47. It was a scene of terror.	這是一個恐怖的景象。
48. Many people felt deeply sorry for the innocent victims.	很多人為無辜的受害者感到難過。
49. They were taken up with grief.	他們陷於哀傷中。
50. A woman nearly fainted.	一個婦人幾乎暈倒。
51. They gazed at the horrible mess.	他們凝視着那可怕的雜亂堆。
52. Three boys were caught in the fire and one of them was burnt to death.	三個男童被火困住,其中一人被火燒死。
53. I was deeply moved.	我深受感動。
54. Firemen managed to stop the fire from spreading.	消防員成功地阻止了火勢的蔓延。
55. The rescue team rushed to the scene.	救援隊迅速趕往現場。
56. To their relief, the fire was extinguished.	大火被救熄了,他們都如釋重負。
57. The authorities provided victims with blankets, cooking utensils and temporary shelters.	當局為災民提供毛氈、煮食用具及臨時居所。
58. Hot meals were also served.	政府同時供應熱烘烘的膳食。
59. Some affected houses were declared dangerous by the Government.	政府宣佈受影響的樓宇為危樓。
60. Many buildings were badly damaged.	很多建築物受到嚴重的損壞。
61. Some charred bodies could not be identified.	一些燒焦的屍體無法辨認。
62. Firemen were still searching for the trapped workers.	消防員仍在搜索被困的工人。

Phrases

1. multi-storey residential buildings	多層住宅樓宇

2.	a floor	一層樓
3.	inflammable things	易燃物體
4.	personal belongings	個人物品
5.	a mass of dense smoke	一團濃煙
6.	the shrilling sirens	一陣尖叫聲
7.	a big red ball of fire	一個大紅火球
8.	crumbling down	倒塌
9.	as black as coal	像炭般漆黑
10.	well-equipped firemen	裝備良好的消防員
11.	in vain	徒勞
12.	explosion of gas oven	石油氣爐爆炸
13.	the main switch	總掣
14.	compensate for the loss	補償損失
15.	a long turntable ladder	一條可轉動的雲梯
16.	two breathing apparatus fire-fighting teams	兩隊戴上呼吸器具的救火隊
17.	the three-hour fire-fighting operation	三小時的救火工作
18.	modern fire appliances and equipment	新型消防器具及裝備
19.	fires of No. 3 alarm	三級火警
20.	major causes of fires	起火的主要原因
21.	careless disposal of smoking materials	不小心棄置吸煙用品
22.	rescue services	救護服務
23.	fire prevention measures	防火措施
24.	fire hazards	火警危險
25.	devastating fires	大火
26.	fighting fire	滅火
27.	publicity campaign	宣傳運動
28.	to enhance public awareness of fire safety	提高市民的消防安全意識

29. to obstruct the means of escape in buildings　　在大廈內阻塞走火通道

30. a vegetation fire at Pat Sin Leng　　在八仙嶺發生的山火

 # Vocabulary

1.	fire engines	消防車	24.	installations	裝置
2.	alarm bells	警鐘	25.	debris	廢物堆
3.	fire victims	火災受害者	26.	destructive	具破壞性的
4.	exits	出路	27.	terrible/dreadful	可怕的
5.	firemen	消防員	28.	poor	可憐的
6.	scene/spot	肇事現場	29.	frightened	驚慌的
7.	stretcher	擔架	30.	fire-proof	防火的
8.	ladders	雲梯	31.	fierce	兇猛的
9.	water hose/jets	水喉	32.	motionless	不能動的
10.	Fire Brigade	消防隊	33.	swiftly	迅速地
11.	ambulance	救傷車	34.	handle	處理
12.	disaster/calamity	浩劫／災難	35.	gather	羣集
13.	residents	住客	36.	scream	大聲呼叫
14.	flames	火焰	37.	collapse	塌下
15.	kerosene cans	火水罐	38.	stiffen	變僵硬
16.	blackout	停電	39.	damage	毀壞
17.	fire extinguisher	滅火筒	40.	foam lorries	泡沫車
18.	roof-top	屋頂天台	41.	fire escape	太平梯
19.	police cars	警車	42.	industrial building	工業大廈
20.	property	財物	43.	Commission of Enquiry	調查委員會
21.	negligence	疏忽	44.	automatic alarm system	自動警報系統
22.	carelessness	不小心			
23.	ignorance	無知			

Gambling

Sentences

1. In Hong Kong, many people indulge in gambling.

   在香港，很多人沉迷於賭博。

2. Illegal gambling still exists.

   非法賭博仍然存在。

3. Gambling pollutes one's mind.

   賭博敗壞一個人的心。

4. A gambler not only loses his property but also wastes his time.

   一個賭徒不僅輸掉他的財產，而且浪費時間。

5. Gamblers eagerly pursue horse and greyhound race tips.

   賭徒們熱心地追尋賽馬及賽狗的貼士。

6. They are driven by a greedy mind.

   他們受貪念所驅使。

7. In the long run, they are sure to ruin their own future.

   長遠來說，他們肯定會摧毀自己的前途。

8. Gambling degrades a man's character.

   賭博降低一個人的品格。

9. It destroys his mental power.

   它破壞一個人的意志力。

10. It is usually connected with crime.

    它常與罪惡連在一起。

11. There is no guarantee that a man will win.

    我們不能保證一個人會贏錢。

12. The element of luck is sometimes brought into play.

    幸運的因素有時發揮它的作用。

13. In the end, gamblers often lose money.

    最終，賭徒往往是輸錢的。

14. When a person loses a lot of money, he may commit crime or even commit suicide.

    當一個人輸了很多錢的時候，他可能會去犯罪，甚至會自殺。

15. Moreover, gambling discourages the habit of hard work.

    此外，賭博改變了一個人勤勞工作的習慣。

16. Unfortunately, an increasing number of Hong Kong people have the "get-rich-quick" mentality.

不幸的是，愈來愈多的香港人有迅速致富的心態。

17. In a money-oriented society, wealth is regarded as a symbol of status.

在一個金錢掛帥的社會，財富被視為地位的象徵。

18. Many people fix their hope on successful gambling to amass fortune.

很多人寄望於賭博中贏錢，由此積聚財富。

19. To them, money enables the pursuit of material comfort.

對他們來說，有了金錢就可追求物質享受。

20. Gambling is particularly appealing to those who are bored with their work.

對於那些在工作上感到煩悶的人來說，賭博別具吸引力。

21. They place bets on horse races in the hope of securing a fortune through chance rather than hard work.

他們投注賭馬，希望借機致富，而非靠努力工作。

22. Sooner or later, they find themselves in financial trouble.

他們遲早會發覺自己陷於財政困難。

23. Indeed, gambling has wrecked many happy homes.

事實上，賭博破壞了很多快樂的家庭。

24. It often leads to various social problems.

它常常導致種種社會問題。

25. On the other hand, legal gambling in Hong Kong has brought in a lot of income for the Government.

另一方面，香港的合法賭博已為政府帶來大量的收入。

26. It has become one of the important sources of Government's recurrent revenue.

它已成為政府的經常性收入的主要來源之一。

27. However, legal gambling is still condemned by many local people.

然而，合法賭博仍然受到很多本地人的指責。

28. Gambling tax plays an important role in public welfare.

博彩稅在公共福利上擔任重要的角色。

29. Every year, the Hong Kong Jockey Club donates a large sum of money to help the development of social welfare, medical care, education as well as other social services.

每年，香港賽馬會都捐贈大量金錢以幫助社會福利、醫療衛生、教育和其他社會服務的發展。

30. On the whole, gambling is an unhealthy and restless excitement.

總的來說，賭博是一種不健康和無休止的刺激。

31. It often brings mishap to the whole family. 它常給整個家庭帶來不幸。

32. So, we should give serious consideration to the matter and refrain from becoming a gambling addict. 故此，我們應認真考慮這件事，以免成為賭徒。

 # Phrases

1.	a form of pastime	一種消遣的方式
2.	crime of violence	暴力罪行
3.	embezzlement of public funds	盜用公款
4.	miserable lot	不幸的命運
5.	to hit the jackpot	贏得彩金
6.	to stake on	下注
7.	to indulge in	沉迷於
8.	to place bets	投注
9.	to take bets	收取投注
10.	to crack down on	取締

 # Vocabulary

1.	casino	賭場	8.	Mark Six lottery	六合彩
2.	bankruptcy	破產	9.	chance	機會
3.	evil	邪惡	10.	probability	或然率
4.	tragedies	不幸	11.	cards	紙牌
5.	uncertainty	不確定	12.	poker	撲克
6.	off-course betting centre	外圍投注站	13.	horse races	賽馬
7.	Hong Kong Jockey Club	香港賽馬會	14.	theft	偷竊
			15.	temptations	引誘

16.	illusion	幻想	27. materialistic	物質主義的
17.	greed	貪念	28. popular	受歡迎的
18.	fate	命運	29. prevalent	流行的
19.	stakes	賭注	30. legalized	合法的
20.	Happy Valley	跑馬地	31. widespread	普遍的
21.	Shatin Race Course	沙田馬場	32. bet	下賭注
			33. wreck	破壞
22.	mahjong	麻將	34. ruin	毀滅
23.	gamblers	賭徒	35. windfall	橫財
24.	punters	投注者	36. blackjack	廿一點
25.	drawbacks	缺點	37. gambling dens	賭窟
26.	injurious/ detrimental	有害的	38. football bookmaking	足球博彩

37

Generation Gap

Sentences

1. Economic and social changes have affected people's thinking.

   經濟和社會的變動對人們的思想造成影響。

2. Hong Kong is influenced by Western culture, values and norms.

   香港受到西方的文化、價值和規範的影響。

3. Differences of opinion usually exist between the two generations.

   兩代往往有不同的意見。

4. They also have different attitudes towards life and society.

   他們對人生和社會的態度也不相同。

5. Ways to narrow the generation gap have to be found.

我們必須找尋縮小代溝的方法。

6. The old and the young should treat each other with concern and respect.

老年人及年青人應互相關懷及尊重。

7. Parents often have rich and useful experience.

父母常有豐富的和有用的經驗。

8. They may have a better view of the matter.

他們對事物會有較好的意見。

9. They often give us valuable advice which can be relied upon.

他們常給我們寶貴的、可以信賴的忠告。

10. Parents always show concern for their children's behaviour and academic achievement.

父母總是關注子女的行為及學業成績。

11. Parental guidance is extremely important.

父母的輔導是極之重要的。

12. Elders should set a good example.

長者應以身作則。

13. They should spend more time communicating with their children.

他們應利用更多時間與子女溝通。

14. Young people should show filial piety towards their parents and respect them.

年青人應孝順父母及尊敬他們。

15. Harmonious family relationships hinge on mutual understanding and effective communication between parents and children.

和諧的家庭關係依賴父母及子女間的了解及有效的溝通。

16. If we can bridge the gap between the old and the young, the quality of our life will be greatly improved.

如果我們能使老人與年青人互相溝通，我們的生活素質將大為改善。

17. People have different perceptions.

人們有不同的認識及領悟。

18. Many old people complain that very often their opinions are not respected.

很多老年人常抱怨他們的意見不被尊重。

19. There is a lack of mutual understanding between the two generations.

兩代間缺乏相互的了解。

20. Notions of personal freedom and individualism are new to traditional Chinese.

對傳統的中國人來說，個人自由及個人主義是新的觀念。

21. Most Hong Kong young people are brought up under the western educational system.

絕大部分的香港年青人都在西方的教育制度下成長。

22. Their behaviour and attitude are deeply influenced by the mass media.

他們的行為及態度深受大眾傳播媒介的影響。

23. They like doing their own thing.

他們喜歡做自己的事。

24. They may misinterpret freedom.

他們可能誤解自由。

25. Young people should show concern for and take good care of their parents.

年青人應對父母表示關心，以及好好地照顧他們。

26. We should take the initiative to communicate with others.

我們應主動與他人溝通。

27. It is important for the two generations to respect one another's social life.

兩代間互相尊重對方的社交生活是很重要的。

28. The Chinese in Hong Kong still place a very high value on family life.

香港的中國人仍然十分重視家庭生活。

29. We should appreciate the efforts our parents have made in raising us.

我們應感激父母在教養我們所付出的努力。

30. We should also extend more positive reinforcement to our parents.

我們也應給予父母更多正面的支援。

31. In Hong Kong, the number of extended families is decreasing.

在香港，多代同堂的家庭數目正在減少。

32. Respecting each other's personalities, needs and interests is conducive to bridging the generation gap.

兩代尊重對方的個性、需要及興趣對彼此的溝通有幫助。

33. They have to learn to accept one another and appreciate one another's strong and weak points with understanding and tolerance.

他們必須學習互相接受，並以體諒和容忍的態度去欣賞對方的長處及弱點。

34. The two generations often have different educational levels, mentality and state of mind.

兩代的人往往有不同的教育程度、智力及心態。

35. The young people are usually better educated but they lack experience.

年青人通常有較好的教育程度，但他們缺乏經驗。

36. They need advice and guidance from their parents.

他們需要父母的忠告及輔導。

37. At the same time, young people need to be understood.

同時，年青人需要別人的理解。

38. The world is changing all the time and the younger generation must be ready to accept the challenge.

世界時常變動，年青的一代必須準備接受挑戰。

39. The older generation often feels lonely.

年老的一代常常感到孤單寂寞。

40. We should put our love to effective action in our family.

我們應把愛心化為有效的行動，關懷家人。

41. To bring about good relationship between the two generations, the communication barriers must be eliminated.

為了兩代間能有良好的關係，我們必須消除溝通障礙。

 Phrases

1. scientific and technological advancement   科技上的進步

2. emotionally upset   情感上的困擾

3. fair treatment   公正的對待

4. hearing deficiency   聽覺上的缺陷

5. gradual loss of memory with age   隨年齡的增長而漸漸失去記憶力

6. embarrassing situations   窘迫的情況

7. from different points of view   從不同的觀點

8. a better view of   有較好的意見

9. interpersonal communication   人際間的溝通

10. emotionally secure   有安全感

11. sub-cultural difference   次文化上的分別

12. everyday home life   日常的家居生活

13. emotional stability   情緒上的穩定

14. social environment and personal upbringing   社會的環境及個人的教養

15. social interaction   社會上的交往

16. to object to　　　　　　　反對

17. wishful thinking　　　　一廂情願的想法

 ## Vocabulary

1.	impact	影響	24.	intractable	倔強的
2.	tradition	傳統	25.	thoughtful	體恤他人的
3.	attitude	態度	26.	fair	公平的
4.	prejudice	偏見	27.	resourceful	足智多謀的
5.	traits	特性	28.	obvious	顯而易見的
6.	virtue	德性	29.	annoying/ troublesome	煩擾的
7.	advice	忠告	30.	irrelevant	無關的
8.	barriers	障礙	31.	autocratic	專制的
9.	conflict	衝突	32.	over-active	過度活躍的
10.	conversation	談話	33.	impulsive	衝動的
11.	recommendation	推薦	34.	affective	感性的
12.	agitation	震動	35.	cognitive	智性的
13.	frustration	挫敗	36.	despite	儘管
14.	trend	趨勢	37.	adapt	適應
15.	feelings	感受	38.	distrust	不相信
16.	thoughts	思想	39.	neglect	忽視
17.	sympathetic	同情的	40.	curse	咒罵
18.	patient	有耐性的	41.	blame	譴責
19.	conservative	保守的	42.	impede	阻礙
20.	old-fashioned	舊式的	43.	refrain	抑制
21.	superstitious	迷信的	44.	consult	諮詢
22.	self-centred	自我中心的	45.	accept	接受
23.	demanding	要求高的			

46.	identify	認同	58. retirement	退休
47.	share	分享	59. nosey	愛管閒事的
48.	ignore	不理會	60. talkative	多言的
49.	isolate	隔離	61. obstinate	頑固的
50.	mistreat	虐待	62. dominating	霸道的
51.	misunderstand	誤解	63. considerate	為他人設想的
52.	enhance	增進	64. non-verbal communication	形態傳意
53.	maintain	維持		
54.	infirmity	衰弱	65. mental illness	精神病
55.	bent	佝僂	66. voluntary welfare agencies	志願福利機構
56.	furrow	皺紋		
57.	stoop	彎腰	67. homes for the aged	老人院

Happiness

Sentences

1. True happiness comes in not departing from nature.
   真正的快樂得自順應自然。

2. A happy person delights in what he has.
   知足常樂。

3. Happiness is an invaluable blessing.
   快樂是無價可估的祝福。

4. A happy man is one who is able to enjoy quietness of mind.
   能享受平靜的心境的人是一個快樂的人。

5. We should know the truth and learn from error.
   我們應認識真理及從錯誤中學習。

6. Many people attempt to search for happiness. 很多人嘗試找尋快樂。

7. Happiness takes many different forms, and people are happy for different reasons. 快樂有很多不同的形式，人們基於不同的理由而感到快樂。

8. Some people feel happy in the company of others. 有人作伴的時候，有些人便感到快樂。

9. A truly happy man will try to make other people happy and indeed care for their happiness. 一個真正快樂的人會嘗試使他人快樂，事實上他關心別人是否快樂。

10. Many people pursue success in a highly competitive society. 很多人在一個高度競爭的社會中追求成功。

11. To them, ingredients for happiness include a successful career, a high income and a good time. 對他們來說，快樂的要素包括成功的事業、優厚的薪酬及能盡情享受人生。

12. Helping others is the foundation of happiness. 助人為快樂之本。

13. Happiness exists in harmony with personal freedom. 快樂與個人的自由和諧地並存着。

14. Virtue should be preserved because it leads to happiness. 快樂之道在修德。

15. If we want to get eternal happiness, we must understand the set of rules for promoting health and physical well-being. 如果我們想得到永恆的快樂，必須明白養生之道。

16. Unselfish giving is a source of happiness. 無私的施與是快樂之源。

17. One who fervently loves his life and other people is a happy person. 一個熱愛生命和別人的人是個快樂的人。

18. A simple lifestyle is often a happy life. 樸素的生活常是快樂的生活。

19. Happiness is not a concrete thing. 快樂不是一件具體的東西。

20. Some people always aim at something higher. 有些人總是追求一個更崇高的目標。

21. Others go after material comforts and satisfaction. 另一些人熱衷於物質上的舒適及滿足。

22. There is no standard for happiness. 快樂是沒有標準的。

23. However, happiness should never be built on the agony of others. 然而，快樂永遠不應建築在他人的痛苦之上。

24. We may not succeed if we search for happiness intentionally.

假如我們刻意尋求快樂，我們不一定能夠成功。

25. A happy person can often appreciate life.

一個快樂的人通常能夠欣賞人生。

26. Friends are another source of happiness.

朋友是另一個快樂之源。

27. Our happiness will double if we share it with others.

同樂則樂倍之。

28. It is the sublimation of the supreme happiness.

這是至樂的昇華。

29. A happy person is always good to others.

一個快樂的人總是善待別人。

30. A broad-minded person often feels highly pleased.

一個心胸廣闊的人常感無上的喜悅。

31. Happiness does not come to us by accident.

快樂不是意外地降臨在我們身上的。

32. Some people may feel happy simply because they have no worries.

有些人只因他們沒有煩惱而感到快樂。

33. Others are happy because they wear robes or because they are applauded.

另一些人因身穿華服或受到讚揚而感快樂。

Phrases

1. a happy life 快樂的生活

2. a sound mind 健康的思想

3. a continual cheerfulness 無盡的喜樂

4. attitude to life 生活的態度

5. enjoyable activity 愉快的活動

6. a feeling of guilt 犯罪感

7. beyond the influence of fear or desire 不受恐懼或慾望的影響

8. young and strong 年青力壯

9. a happy family 快樂的家庭

10. peace of mind 心境的寧靜

11. without remorse or regret　　　　沒有悔恨或遺憾

12. stage of life　　　　人生的舞台

13. vain hopes　　　　虛幻的希望

14. idle fears　　　　無益的恐懼

15. troubled dreams of life　　　　令人煩惱的人生夢想

16. a noble cause　　　　崇高的目標

17. simple desire　　　　單純的願望

18. pleasive-seeking person　　　　追求享樂的人

19. to beam with satisfaction　　　　滿意地微笑着

20. to live in bliss　　　　生活得很幸福

Vocabulary

1. conditions 條件
2. advice 忠告
3. nature 自然
4. courage 勇氣
5. courtesy 禮貌
6. loneliness 孤單
7. wealth 財富
8. health 健康
9. power 權力
10. satisfaction 滿足
11. impulse 衝動
12. prestige 聲譽
13. obstacles 障礙
14. success 成功
15. intention 意向

16. discouragement 挫折
17. by-products 副產品
18. money 金錢
19. soul 心靈
20. eager 渴望
21. upright 正直的
22. steadfast 堅定不變的
23. lofty 崇高的
24. delightful/cheerful 令人愉快的
25. unselfish 不自私的
26. easy-going 隨和的
27. agreeable 適合的
28. egoistic 利己的
29. paramount/supreme 最高的

30.	open-minded	虛心的	37.	joy
31.	gratify	使滿意	38.	jubilant
32.	aspire	企望得到	39.	merry
33.	admire	羨慕	40.	entertainment
34.	share	分享	41.	rejoice
35.	seek	尋求	42.	pleasurable
36.	endure	忍受		

30. open-minded　虛心的
31. gratify　使滿意
32. aspire　企望得到
33. admire　羨慕
34. share　分享
35. seek　尋求
36. endure　忍受

37. joy　高興
38. jubilant　喜氣洋洋的
39. merry　快樂
40. entertainment　娛樂
41. rejoice　歡呼
42. pleasurable　令人愉快的

Hobbies and Pastimes

 Sentences

1. To prepare ourselves as useful citizens in the community, we must select our hobbies very carefully.

   我們為了成為社會上有用的公民作好準備，需要十分謹慎地選擇嗜好。

2. A good hobby can keep us occupied, thus giving no time for silly fantasy.

   一種良好的嗜好可使我們專心，由是無暇作可笑的幻想。

3. Suitable pastimes are good for maintaining a healthy body and a healthy mind.

   適當的消遣對我們的身心都有益處。

4. Healthy hobbies can broaden our knowledge and help to keep us in good physical condition.

   健康的嗜好能增長我們的知識，以及使我們健康情況良好。

5. Young people should make good use of their leisure time to cultivate a sound mind and a healthy body.

   年青人應善用餘暇以培養健全的思想及健康的體魄。

6. Work without rest is harmful to health.

   只有工作而沒有休息是對身體有害的。

7. We should select those leisure activities that suit our tastes, temperaments and pockets.

我們應該選擇一些適合我們的品味、性情與經濟情況的休閒活動。

8. A hobby is undertaken for its own sake.

人有我有，為嗜好而培養嗜好。

9. It is most desirable to cultivate an interest in reading.

培養閱讀興趣最好不過。

10. Reading is usually a life-long source of pleasure.

閱讀往往是人一生樂趣的來源。

11. Reading good books can increase our knowledge and enlarge our vocabulary.

閱讀良好的書籍可增加我們的知識及擴大我們的字彙。

12. Reading provides the knowledge we are unable to get from personal experience.

閱讀為我們提供一些個人經驗中所不能得到的知識。

13. It widens our ideas and outlook of life.

它擴闊我們的思想及人生觀。

14. It brings us pleasure and healthy recreation.

它為我們帶來樂趣及健康的消遣。

15. Reading is also a method of mental training.

閱讀也是一種訓練心智的方法。

16. From reading good books, we can cultivate high ideals and noble sentiments.

我們可從閱讀好書中培養崇高的理想與高貴的情操。

17. Reading is the second part of my life.

閱讀是我的第二生命。

18. Listening to music can stimulate our creative faculty and the development of our mind.

聽音樂可刺激我們的創造力及智力發展。

19. It enhances our artistic sense.

它提高我們的藝術意識。

20. Picnicking and hiking in the countryside enable us to enjoy the beauty of nature.

我們到郊野旅行及遠足，可欣賞到美麗的大自然。

21. Fishing can give us particular pleasure, especially when we are successful in hooking a fish.

垂釣能給我們特殊的樂趣，尤其是當我們成功地釣到一尾魚的時候。

22. Fishing is my best-loved pastime and I have a keen interest in it.

垂釣是我最喜歡的消遣，我對它有濃厚的興趣。

23. I fully enjoy the pleasure of fishing.

我十分享受垂釣的樂趣。

24. Taking a walk during leisure hours is a very good exercise.

閒時去散步是一項很好的運動。

25. It is indeed an enjoyable pastime.

它實在是一種怡情養性的消遣。

26. My favourite pastimes include collecting stamps, making model planes and playing chess.

我喜愛的消遣包括集郵、砌模型飛機及下棋。

27. It gives me great pleasure to engage in all these activities.

進行那些活動，使我非常愉快。

28. Some people are fond of collecting coins, postcards or specimens of plants.

有些人喜歡蒐集錢幣、明信片或植物標本。

29. Taking photographs appeals to some people very much.

對一些人而言，攝影是很具吸引力的。

30. They take both distance shots and close-ups.

他們既拍遠景，也拍近鏡。

31. Swimming is, beyond doubt, the most popular leisure activity of Hong Kong people in summer.

游泳無疑是最受香港人喜愛的夏日消閒活動。

32. They find it a lot of fun to soak in the cool, clean sea water and escape the heat.

他們浸在清涼的海水中避暑，樂趣無窮。

33. Another common pastime of Hong Kong people is to see films (or watch movies).

看電影是另一種香港人最普遍的消遣。

34. Many people like to read detective stories, sword-play stories or stories of romance.

很多人喜歡看偵探小說、武俠小說或愛情故事。

35. Watching television has become a very common indoor leisure activity in Hong Kong.

在香港，看電視已成為一種十分普遍的室內消閒活動。

36. Taking part in healthy social activities is good for us.

參加健康的社交活動對我們有好處。

37. Dancing is a good form of exercise and it can keep us fit.

跳舞是很好的運動，它能使我們身裁健美。

38. Everyone of us should cultivate a few interesting pursuits.

我們每一個人都應該培養一些有趣的消遣。

39. Keeping pets may not be within the reach of all.

飼養寵物不一定是每個人都能負擔得起的。

40. Many Hong Kong people like to play a game of mahjong when they have free time.

很多香港人喜歡在空餘打麻將。

41. It is most desirable to occupy ourselves with interests and recreation in our leisure hours.

以興趣和康樂活動作為消遣節目是最理想的。

42. Some people are devoted to a particular hobby.

有些人專注於一種特別的嗜好。

43. They often derive a sense of satisfaction and achievement from their pursuits.

他們往往能從消遣活動中得到滿足感和成就感。

44. In fact, there are many fully absorbing hobbies.

事實上有很多使人全情投入的嗜好。

45. Hobbies can relieve us from our daily drudgery.

嗜好能調劑我們日常的勞苦工作。

46. We should take the good hobbies and discard the bad ones.

我們對嗜好應擇佳而棄劣。

47. Some hobbies have bad effects on young minds.

有些嗜好對年青人有不良的影響。

48. They make it very difficult for students to settle down to study.

它們使學生很難靜心讀書。

49. To indulge in electronic games is one example.

沉迷於玩電子遊戲機是其中一個例子。

50. To go to a disco frequently is another.

時常上的士高是另一個例子。

51. All these activities merely excite our feelings and are detrimental to academic studies.

所有這些活動只是刺激我們的情感，而對學業是有害的。

52. Some people are crazy about gambling while others indulge in drinking.

有些人瘋狂賭博，有些人則酗酒。

53. They easily lose their temper.

他們很容易發脾氣。

54. These hobbies are often a waste of both time and money.

這些嗜好往往浪費時間和金錢。

55. The risk of cancer is often linked directly with cigarettes.

吸煙通常與癌症有直接關係。

56. Many smokers do not care about other people's feelings.

很多吸煙者不管別人的感受。

57. Smoking is not a healthy hobby.

吸煙不是一種健康的嗜好。

58. Smoking in public places often causes discomfort to other people.　在公共場所吸煙常常使其他人感到不舒服。

59. To many non-smokers, clouds of fumes are intolerable.　對很多不吸煙的人來說，香煙的氣味是不能容忍的。

60. Don't get into the bad habit of speaking foul language.　不要養成說粗言穢語的壞習慣。

 ## Phrases

1.	a carefree life	自由自在的生活
2.	a wide range of general knowledge	廣泛的常識
3.	most interesting	最引人入勝的
4.	funny moment	歡樂的時刻
5.	on special occasions	在特別的時刻
6.	rolls of films	膠片／軟片
7.	joy and excitement	歡樂及興奮
8.	my cup of tea	我的喜好
9.	doing yoga	練習瑜咖
10.	to get some exercises	做一些運動
11.	collecton of antiques	古董收藏
12.	flying kites	放風箏
13.	making models	砌模型
14.	flowering arrangement	插花

 ## Vocabulary

1.	interest	興趣	5.	fishing lines	釣魚絲
2.	leisure time	空餘	6.	hook	魚鈎
3.	fishing	垂釣	7.	bait	魚餌
4.	fishing rods	釣魚竿	8.	swimming	游泳

9.	sailing	風帆	35.	camping	露營
10.	water-skiing	滑水	36.	billiards	桌球
11.	windsurfing	滑浪	37.	Chinese billiards	康樂棋
12.	diving	潛水	38.	golf	哥爾夫球
13.	yachting	乘遊艇玩	39.	gardening	園藝
14.	ice-skating	溜冰	40.	specimens	標本
15.	ice rink	溜冰場	41.	philately	集郵
16.	roller-skate	溜冰鞋	42.	album	郵票簿
17.	aquarium	魚缸	43.	stamp catalogue	集郵指南
18.	pet	寵物	44.	model planes	模型飛機
19.	singing	唱歌	45.	travelling	旅遊
20.	hit-songs	流行歌曲	46.	reading	閱讀
21.	folksongs	民歌	47.	movies/films	電影
22.	guitar	結他	48.	photo-taking	攝影
23.	piano-playing	彈綱琴	49.	chess	棋
24.	dancing	舞蹈	50.	painting/ drawing	繪畫
25.	playing mahjong	打麻將	51.	wood-carving	木雕
26.	window-shopping	逛公司窗櫥	52.	dress-making	縫紉
27.	cookery	烹飪	53.	parachuting	跳傘
28.	knitting	織毛衣	54.	hot air ballooon	熱汽球
29.	cycling	騎自行車	55.	mountaineering	攀山
30.	ballet	芭蕾舞	56.	exploring	探險
31.	sports	運動	57.	oriqami	摺紙
32.	jogging	緩步跑	58.	pottery	陶藝
33.	hiking	遠足	69.	skiing	滑雪
34.	picnic	旅行	60.	floating	漂流

61.	sculpture	雕刻	84. moving	感人的
62.	musical instruments	樂器	85. imagine	想像
63.	comic books	漫畫書	86. engross	全神貫注於
64.	classical music	古典音樂	87. exchange	交換
65.	modern dance	現代舞	88. stroll	散步
66.	martial art	武術	89. slot machines	吃角子遊戲機
67.	indoor activities	戶內活動	90. karate	空手道
68.	outdoor activities	戶外活動	91. chit-chat	閒談
69.	pleasure cruising	遊船河	92. wander	漫步
70.	gambling	賭博	93. lingering	流連
71.	smoking	吸煙	94. relax	鬆弛
72.	nicotine	尼古丁	95. broaden	擴闊
73.	tar	焦油	96. cultivate	培養
74.	cancer	癌症	97. beneficial	有益
75.	electronic video games centre	電子遊戲機中心	98. promote	增廣
76.	crazy	狂熱的	99. regulate	調劑
77.	popular	流行的	100. enthusiastic	熱衷的
78.	favourite	喜愛的	101. enlighten	啟發
79.	monotonous	單調的	102. appreciate	欣賞
80.	enjoyable	怡情悅性的	103. stimulate	刺激
81.	meaningful	有意義的	104. well-balanced	平衡的
82.	thought-provoking	激發思考的	105. amateur	業餘的
83.	constructive	有建設性的	106. professional	職業的
			107. equipment	設備
			108. sportswear	運動服裝

Hong Kong by Night

Sentences

1. There are many fantastic sights and scenes in Hong Kong.

   香港有很多奇異的景象。

2. They give visitors an indelible impression.

   它們給遊客留下一個不能磨滅的印象。

3. Owing to its magnificent view at night, Hong Kong is often referred to as "the Pearl of the Orient".

   由於香港有華麗的夜景，所以她常被稱為「東方之珠」。

4. Imposing buildings line the waterfront.

   巨大的建築物在海岸兩旁排列着。

5. There are many towering skyscrapers on both Hong Kong Island and the Kowloon Peninsula.

   香港島和九龍半島都有很多摩天大廈。

6. Many magnificent edifices in the Mid-Levels overlook the harbour.

   在半山區有很多華廈俯瞰海港。

7. From the Peak, we can have an uninterrupted view of the beautiful harbour.

   在山頂，我們可以看到全無遮擋的、美麗的海港景色。

8. When night falls, the view is especially attractive.

   當夜幕低垂的時候，那景色尤其迷人。

9. Myriads of neon-lights twinkle and glimmer.

   無數的霓虹光管閃閃爍爍。

10. People move about in Star Avenue like a scribal of silver carp.

    晚上的星光大道，遊人如鯽。

11. At night in Causeway Bay and Mongkok, the lights are brilliant and it is boisterous there.

    在晚上，銅鑼灣及旺角燈光燦爛，非常熱鬧。

12. The prosperity in the main street in Yuen Long at night is no less than that on Hong Kong Island.

    晚上元朗區的大街一片繁榮，不下於港島鬧市。

13. The world-renowned splendour is expressed to the fullest extent.

蓋世的繁華，顯露無遺。

14. Hong Kong has made a name in the world.

香港是世界聞名的。

15. Hong Kong is a modern metropolis and the tempo of life is fast.

香港是一個現代化的大都會，而生活的節奏是急速的。

16. The Hongkong Bank Building in Central stretches its way into the sky, marking the achievements of Hong Kong.

中區的匯豐銀行大廈高聳入雲，標誌着香港的成就。

17. At night, millions of lights in different colours dot about the sea and the land.

入夜，數以百萬計的、不同顏色的燈光點綴大海和陸地。

18. They are like numerous sparkling diamonds spreading everywhere.

它們像是無數閃爍的鑽石散在各處。

19. Many famous buildings are decorated with coloured electric lights.

很多著名的建築物以繽紛的電燈裝飾着。

20. Numerous street lights wind their way in the darkness.

無數的街燈在黑暗中迂迴伸展。

21. Countless glittering electric lamps light up the sky.

無數明亮的電燈把天空照亮。

22. The lights are also reflected in the water.

燈光也反映在水面上。

23. The view is marvellous and breath-taking.

那景象是美妙的和非凡的。

24. Hong Kong is a well-known sight-seeing place and many tourists are caught by its beauty at night.

香港是一個人所熟知的觀光勝地，遊客們為她那美麗的夜景着迷。

25. Hong Kong is one of the three best natural harbours in the world.

香港是世界三大天然良港之一。

26. Many steam boats and ferries go across the sea, leaving behind them the ripple of silver lines in the water.

很多汽船和渡海小輪川流不息地在海上穿梭，在海面上畫出了一道道銀線。

27. Loud blasts of sirens can occasionally be heard.

我們有時可聽到汽笛的巨響。

28. Other small boats also ply their way along the watery surface.

其他小船也在水面上往來。

29. They throw up sprays of water.

它們濺起水花。

30. The picturesque landscape in Hong Kong has made it a famous tourist paradise.

香港那如畫的風景使她成為一個著名的遊客天堂。

 ## Phrases

1.	wonderful view	奇景
2.	incandescent lamps	明亮的燈
3.	rows of street lights	一排排的街燈
4.	an airy moonlit night	一個月白風清的晚上
5.	floating clouds and flimsy mist	浮雲薄霧
6.	bustling traffic	繁忙的交通
7.	tall buildings and big mansions	高樓大廈
8.	scenic beauty	美景
9.	prosperous and flourishing	繁盛
10.	the pride of Hong Kong	香港之光

Vocabulary

1.	night scenes	夜景	12.	peninsula	半島
2.	panorama	全景	13.	fluorescence	螢光
3.	skyscrapers	摩天大廈	14.	indistinct/vague	模糊不清
4.	harbour	海港	15.	tempting	吸引人的
5.	ferries	渡海小輪	16.	prosperous	繁榮的
6.	launches	小汽船	17.	crystal	晶瑩的
7	toot	號角聲	18.	magnificent	輝煌的
8.	oars	船槳	19.	lovely	可愛的
9.	waterfront	海岸	20.	especially	尤其是
10.	sight-seeing	觀光	21.	ashore	在岸上
11.	show-windows	商店櫥窗	22.	embellish	裝飾

23. ocean-going liners   遠洋輪船

24. meander   迂迴而行

25. glimmer   發出微光

26. signify   標誌着

41

Hong Kong Families

Sentences

1. Small families are prevalent in Hong Kong.   在香港，小家庭很普遍。

2. Many Hong Kong families spend a lot of money on rent.   很多香港家庭的租金支出龐大。

3. Home electrical appliances are widely used.   人們普遍使用家庭電器用品。

4. An increasing number of people can have a higher standard of living.   愈來愈多人的生活水準較高。

5. They enjoy a much better material life and comfort than before.   他們所享受到的物質和舒適生活較往日為佳。

6. The number of career women is rapidly increasing.   職業婦女的人數在迅速增加。

7. The young people are generally ambitious.   年青的一輩普遍有上進心。

8. They emphasize personal achievement.   他們重視個人的成就。

9. New ideas are emerging and the view on morality is changing.   新思想出現及道德觀念在轉變中。

10. Parents no longer enjoy their former supreme power.   父母不再享有他們昔日至高無上的權力。

11. The old and the young often have different criteria and concepts of value.   新舊兩代往往有不同的標準及價值觀。

12. Parents' attitude towards their children is also changing.

父母對子女的態度也在轉變中。

13. Economic and industrial boom has brought immense change to family life.

經濟和工業的興盛使家庭生活發生了巨大的改變。

14. It seems that the change is inevitable.

看來轉變是無可避免的。

15. Nuclear families go hand in hand with the modernization of family life.

核心家庭與家庭生活的現代化同時出現。

16. Many homes are furnished with modern furniture.

很多家庭陳設着現代化的傢具。

17. With the help of modern electrical appliances, household chores are no longer a problem.

藉着現代化的電器用品的幫助，家務已大為減少。

18. Some families keep pets.

有些家庭飼養寵物。

19. Family outings have become increasingly popular.

家庭旅行愈來愈普遍。

20. At night, many family members gather together to watch their favourite television programmes.

晚上，很多家庭成員聚在一起，欣賞他們喜愛的電視節目。

21. In a modern family, the spirit of co-operation is extremely important.

在一個現代化的家庭中，合作的精神是極其重要的。

22. Husband and wife are equal in importance.

丈夫及妻子同樣重要。

23. They should share happiness and sadness among themselves.

他們應分享快樂及分擔憂愁。

24. Every family member can enjoy basic human rights.

每個家庭成員都能享有基本的人權。

25. Women are no longer bound by the family.

婦女不再受家庭所束縛。

26. Nobody can deny that the family is a symbol of unity and harmony.

沒有人能否認家庭是一個統一及和諧的象徵。

27. It is the responsibility of every member to create a harmonious and comfortable atmosphere in the family.

每個家庭成員都有責任去創造一個和諧及舒適的氣氛。

Phrases

1.	a sense of responsibility	責任感
2.	the building of good character	良好品格的培養
3.	filial piety	孝順
4.	modern facilities	現代化的設備
5.	to contribute to	貢獻
6.	a red-letter day	一個值得紀念的高興日子

 ## Vocabulary

1.	sitting room	客廳
2.	dining room	飯廳
3.	bedrooms	睡房
4.	housewife	家庭主婦
5.	washing machines	洗衣機
6.	refrigerator	冰箱
7.	television set	電視機
8.	modernization	現代化
9.	freedom	自由
10.	family budget	家庭預算
11.	honours	榮譽
12.	tradition	傳統
13.	festival	節日
14.	reunion	團圓
15.	eve	前夕
16.	routine	慣常的
17.	lenient	仁慈的
18.	indulgent	縱容的
19.	harmonious	和諧的
20.	self-centred	自我中心的
21.	demanding	要求高的
22.	aloof	流離的
23.	unapproachable	不能接近的
24.	enterprising	有進取精神的
25.	revolutionary	富革命性的
26.	positive	積極的
27.	rejoicing	愉快的
28.	mutual	相互的
29.	appreciate	欣賞
30.	misunderstand	誤解
31.	celebrate	慶祝
32.	reinforce	加強
33.	extended families	多代同堂的家庭
34.	family albums	家庭相簿

Housing Problem

 Sentences

1. Hong Kong is particularly short of flat land for building purposes.

   香港特別缺乏建築用的平地。

2. Reasonably good housing accommodation within the means of the average Hong Kong people is often seriously lacking.

   香港人經常嚴重缺乏品質上佳而價格大眾化的居所。

3. Filthy and noisy living environment is quite common.

   污穢及嘈雜的居住環境頗為普遍。

4. Living space is often overcrowded.

   居住的地方常常是過度擠迫的。

5. The lack of overall city planning in the past has made the matter worse.

   過去政府缺乏通盤性的城市規劃，使情形更為嚴重。

6. Many Hong Kong people aspire to own a better home.

   很多香港人希望擁有一個較佳的居所。

7. It goes without saying that home ownership increases a sense of belonging to Hong Kong.

   不用說，如果市民能擁有居所，他們對香港的歸屬感必會增加。

8. It is the responsibility of the Government to provide the citizens with a convenient and agreeable living environment.

   為本港市民提供方便及適意的居住環境是政府的責任。

9. Because of the limited area, Hong Kong has to maximise the available living space.

   由於面積有限，香港必須充份利用所有的空間。

10. Owing to the scarcity of land and the large population, housing has often been a grave problem in Hong Kong.

    由於地小人多，居住往往是香港的一個嚴重的問題。

11. Small flats dominate in Hong Kong.

    香港的居所絕大部分是細小的單位。

12. Parks, playgrounds and sitting out areas are far from adequate.

公園、運動場及休憩地方十分不足。

13. There is indeed too little open space for the residents.

居民所享有的空曠地方委實過少。

14. Not all of them are eligible for public housing.

他們之中，不是人人都有資格入住公共屋邨。

15. Urban renewal and redevelopment programmes are in progress.

市區重建計劃正在進行。

16. The Government has developed many new towns and satellite towns in the New Territories with a view to solving the housing problem completely.

為了徹底解決房屋的問題，政府已在新界發展了多個新市鎮及衛星城市。

17. Indeed, many Hong Kong people yearn for a better living environment.

事實上，很多香港人渴望能得到一個較佳的居住環境。

18. With improved standards of living, a decent and comfortable home is no longer a luxury.

隨着生活水準的提高，合意及舒適的家已不是一項奢侈品了。

19. When the housing problem is solved, Hong Kong will surely become a more stable and prosperous city.

當房屋的問題獲得解決的時候，香港必定能夠成為一個更加安定繁榮的城市。

 **Phrases**

1.	financial considerations	財政上的考慮
2.	spiralling rent	不斷上升的租金
3.	unable to afford the high rent	不能負擔昂貴的租金
4.	rent control	租金管制
5.	to control over unauthorized structures	對非法建築的管制
6.	high interest burden	高利息的負擔
7.	to pay by instalments	分期付款
8.	supply of water and electricity	水電的供應
9.	poor sanitary and living facilities	惡劣的衛生及生活設施

10. basic facilities and amenities   基本設施及休閒去處

11. the minimum space standard of 5.5 square metres   每人至少 5.5 平方米的編配標準

12. rational allocation of public housing resources   公屋資源的合理分配

13. regular cleansing   定期清潔

14. resale restriction   轉售限制

15. sold at discounted prices   以優惠條件出售

16. concord designs   康和式設計

17. improving the living conditions   改善居住環境

18. furnishings and fittings   粉飾及裝修

19. determined by a ballot   以抽籤決定

20. being well received by tenants   大受住戶歡迎

21. in full swing   正全力進行

22. improving service standards   提高服務水準

23. illegal structures and extensions   違例搭建物和擴建物

24. to live in prosperity and contentment   安居樂業

25. more affordable prices   價格較為相宜

26. in prime location   位於黃金地段

27. to trade up their accommodation   換樓

28. units under construction   樓花

29. bank credit constraint   銀行收緊信貸

30. curb property speculation   抑壓炒賣房地產

Vocabulary

1.	tenants	住客	27.	temporary	臨時的
2.	landlord	業主	28.	residential	住宅用的
3.	priority	優先	29.	resettle	徙置
4.	sanitation	衛生	30.	construct	建造
5.	cubicle	斗室	31.	maintain	維持
6.	clearance	清拆	32.	aggravate	使惡化
7.	constraints	限制	33.	accelerate	加速
8.	efforts	努力	34.	re-build	重建
9.	solution	解決	35.	manage	管理
10.	slope	山坡	36.	refurbish	翻新
11.	pressure	壓力	37.	vacate	騰出空間
12.	developers	發展商	38.	soar	暴升
13.	property	地產	39.	well-furnished	設備齊全
14.	down-payment	首期供款	40.	Home Ownership Scheme	居者有其屋
15.	interest rate	利率			
16.	inflation	通貨膨脹	41.	low-cost housing	廉租屋
17.	speculation	投機			
18.	security	安全	42.	Housing Authority estates	房屋委員會轄下的公共屋邨
19.	bunk beds	碌架牀			
20.	over-crowded	過度擠迫的	43.	self-contained flats	自給自足的居住單位
21.	inconsiderate	不體諒別人的			
22.	permanent	永久的	44.	private buildings	私人樓宇
23.	inadequate	不足夠的			
24.	incredible	難以置信的	45.	sandwich class	夾心階層
25.	inconvenient	不方便的	46.	public housing tenants	公屋住戶
26.	limited	有限的			

47.	Harmony blocks	和諧式公屋	
48.	security upgrading programme	保安改善計劃	
49.	24-hour security guard service	24 小時護衛服務	

Illness

  Sentences

1. Where there is illness, there can be no happiness.

   身體有病，便不會快樂。

2. It is best to have a thorough medical check-up once a year.

   我們最好每年進行一次全面的身體檢查。

3. Under no circumstances should we risk injuring our health.

   在任何情況下，我們都不應冒損害健康的危險。

4. We should exercise regularly to keep fit.

   我們應經常做運動以保持身體健康。

5. Drinking plenty of water is good for one's health.

   多喝開水對健康有益。

6. The sooner you do something about it, the better.

   愈早治療愈好。

7. Doctors diagnose the patients and write out the prescriptions.

   醫生診斷病人，並開出藥方。

8. Sometimes our bodies may become hot.

   有時我們的身體會發熱。

9. We cannot work as usual if we get a headache.

   假如我們頭痛，便不能如常地工作。

10. When we fall ill, we usually stay in bed.

    當我們患病的時候，通常躺在牀上。

11. At that time, a doctor has to be called in to identify the cause of our illness.

在那時，我們需要請醫生看病，找出我們患病的原因。

12. Patients should follow the doctor's advice and take a good rest.

病人應遵照醫生的勸告，好好地休息。

13. It is better to take it easy.

我們最好不要太緊張。

14. Once I suffered from vomiting and my mother took good care of me.

有一次，我受嘔吐之苦，母親悉心地照顧我。

15. On that occasion, my mother's unselfish love was fully displayed.

那個時候，母親對我的無私之愛，顯露無遺。

16. The incident made a lasting impression on me.

那次事件給我留下永久的印象。

17. I got over the illness quickly.

我迅速復原。

18. We must be very careful about the food we eat, our personal hygiene and environmental health if we are to avoid transmittable diseases.

我們若要避免傳染病，就必須注意食物及個人與環境的衛生。

19. To many people, toothache is a frightening experience.

對很多人來說，牙痛是一個可怕的經驗。

20. The cavities need filling and the decayed teeth have to be extracted.

牙洞需要填補而蛀牙必須拔除。

21. Since we chew food with our teeth, oral hygiene is very important.

我們用牙齒咀嚼食物，所以口腔的衛生十分重要。

22. When we have a sore throat, we may take some effective medicine to relieve the pain.

我們喉痛的時候，可服食一些有效的藥物來止痛。

23. Usually, a patient does not feel like eating anything.

病人通常沒有食慾。

24. Sometimes, our nose is blocked up.

有時，我們會鼻塞。

25. We had better consult a doctor when we are unwell.

當我們身體不適的時候，最好去看醫生。

26. Doctors take the temperature of their patients.

醫生給病人量體溫。

27. If a person is seriously ill, he may have to be operated on.

如人患了重病，可能要動手術。

28. When the illness has cleared, the patient will be up and about.　　當疾病消除，病人便恢復健康。

 **Phrases**

1.	feeling chilly	身體發冷
2.	having a temperature	發熱
3.	no appetite	沒有食慾
4.	allergic to	對於某物有過敏性的反應
5.	inoculate against	預防性注射
6.	having an X-ray examination	做 X 光線檢查
7.	no panacea	沒有萬應靈丹
8.	preventable infectious diseases	可預防的傳染病
9.	providing counselling and medical consultation	提供輔導和診治
10.	traditional Chinese medicine	傳統中醫藥
11.	people with AIDS	愛滋病人
12.	stomach troubles	胃病
13.	seeking medical advice	延醫治理
14.	out of sorts	感不適
15.	immunize against	接受防疫注射
16.	health awareness	注重健康
17.	intensive care unit	深切治療
18.	intravenous drip	吊鹽水
19.	bile duct stones	膽結石
20.	sexually transmitted	性病
21.	tooth extraction	脫牙
22.	dental filling	補牙
23.	sore throat	喉嚨痛

Vocabulary

1.	headache	頭痛		26.	surgeon	外科醫生
2.	toothache	牙痛		27.	dentist	牙醫
3.	stomach-ache	胃痛		28.	treatment	治療
4.	fever	發高熱		29.	prescriptions	處方
5.	influenza	流行性感冒		30.	forehead	前額
6.	cough	咳嗽		31.	sickness/disease	疾病
7.	bronchitis	支氣管炎		32.	case	病例
8.	indigestion	消化不良		33.	reflection	反射
9.	diarrhoea	腹瀉		34.	operation	外科手術
10.	smallpox	天花		35.	bandage	繃帶
11.	pneumonia	肺炎		36.	blood pressure	血壓
12.	liver trouble	肝病		37.	vaccination	種痘
13.	tuberculosis	肺癆		38.	sick-leave	病假
14.	cholera	霍亂		39.	robust	強壯的
15.	cancer	癌症		40.	preventive	預防性的
16.	heart disease	心臟病		41.	immune	不受感染的
17.	measles	麻疹		42.	nervous	緊張的
18.	pains	痛苦		43.	unwell	不適
19.	crisis	危險時期		44.	numb	麻木的
20.	recover	痊癒		45.	pale	蒼白的
21.	tablets	藥丸		46.	swollen	腫脹的
22.	chest	胸部		47.	regular	有規律的
23.	lung	肺部		48.	console	安慰
24.	chemist shop	藥房		49.	advise	勸告
25.	physician	內科醫生		50.	rehabilitate	康復

51. examine	檢查	78. nephrolithiasis	腎石
52. detect	發現	79. cataract	白內障
53. perspire	出汗	80. chalazion	生眼挑針
54. ache	疼痛	81. sinusitis	鼻竇炎
55. relieve	解除	82. physiotherapist	物理治療師
56. sneeze	打噴嚏	83. pharmacist	藥劑師
57. vomit	嘔吐	84. prescription	配方
58. dizziness	頭暈	85. specialist	專科醫生
59. insomnia	失眠症	86. beriberi	腳氣病
60. enterovirus	腸病毒	87. prostatitis	前列腺炎
61. hepatitis	肝炎	88. back to normal	回復正常
62. caecitis	盲腸炎	89. community nursing service	社康護理服務
63. plague	鼠疫	90. acupuncture treatment	針刺療法
64. neuropathy	神經病	91. medical fees	醫藥費
65. nourishment	補品	92. mental illness	精神病
66. elixir	特效藥	93. occupational disease	職業病
67. cold pack	冷敷	94. medical treatment	醫療服務
68. cold medicine	感冒藥	95. red tide	紅潮
69. healthful	有益健康的	96. avian flu	禽流感
70. physiotherapy	物理治療	97. specialist clinics	專科診所
71. operation	手術	98. dental cavities	蛀牙
72. dementia	老人痴呆症	99. CT scan	電子掃描
73. endoscopy	內窺鏡	100. Parkinson's disease	柏金遜病
74. ostephytes	骨刺		
75. arthritis	關節炎		
76. osteoporosis	骨質疏鬆		
77. hyperlipidemia	膽固醇過高		

101.	rheumatoid arthritis	風濕	105.	orthodontics treatment	箍牙
102.	pleural effusion	肺積水	106.	otitis media	中耳炎
103.	periodontal disease	牙周病	107.	bone setter	跌打醫生
104.	diabetes mellitus	糖尿病	108.	Chinese medicine practitioner	中醫師

44

Juvenile Delinquency

Sentences

1. In a complex society like Hong Kong, teenagers easily go astray.

   在香港這個複雜的社會裏，青少年很容易誤入歧途。

2. Parents are too busy earning a living to take good care of their children.

   父母們忙於謀生而未能好好地照顧他們的子女。

3. Many teenagers have too much freedom and money to spend.

   很多青少年有過多的自由及可供使用的金錢。

4. Juvenile delinquency is a serious and urgent problem.

   青少年犯罪是一個嚴重及迫切的問題。

5. We must keep a watchful eye on the behaviour of the young people; otherwise they may end up in tragedy.

   我們必須留意青年人的行為，否則他們可能有可悲的結局。

6. Many young people go wrong partly because they lack suitable hobbies.

   很多年青人誤入歧途，部分原因是他們缺乏適當的嗜好。

7. Obscene films and pornographic literature have far-reaching influence on young minds.

   淫穢的電影及色情刊物對青少年的思想有深遠的影響。

8. Some juveniles are morally decadent because they often read comics of bad taste.

   一些少年道德低落，是由於他們時常閱讀趣味低劣的連環圖所致。

9. Many teenagers are interested in queer things and they want to do outstanding deeds.

很多青少年對奇異的事物感到興趣，他們想有突出的表現。

10. Since they are mentally immature, they are easily tempted by strange attractions.

由於他們心智尚未成熟，易受奇異的事物所誘惑。

11. We should look into the causes of juvenile delinquency and take preventive actions.

我們應探究青少年犯罪的原因並採取預防行動。

12. The Government must censor the press, television and films more strictly.

政府必須更嚴格審查報紙、電視及電影。

13. Films of violence and sex often pollute the minds of young people.

暴力及色情的電影往往腐蝕年青人的心智。

14. Heavier punishment must be imposed against offenders.

對犯罪者須嚴加處罰。

15. Some young people challenge tradition.

有些年青人挑戰傳統。

16. They are always ready to cast away old values and ideas.

他們隨時準備拋棄舊有的價值觀和理念。

17. The situation has reached a frightening stage.

情況已到達了可怕的階段。

18. Influenced by the mass media, many juveniles have developed a wrong concept of values.

很多青少年受到大眾傳播媒介的影響，產生一個錯誤的價值觀。

19. In a highly commercialized society, many people vigorously pursue material comfort and a luxurious life.

在一個高度商業化的社會裏，很多人拼命追求物質舒適及奢華的生活。

20. Juvenile delinquency is said to be a by-product of a rapidly developing economy.

有人說青少年犯罪問題是一個高速發展的經濟社會的副產品。

21. Families, schools and the authorities must join hands to deal with this serious social problem.

家庭、學校及政府當局必須攜手應付這個嚴重的社會問題。

22. Very often, parental love and concern are inadequate, and children lack appropriate guidance.

很多時候，父母對子女的愛護及關懷不足，而孩子們也缺乏適當的輔導。

23. In schools, there is a general lack of extra-curricular activities.

在學校，學生普遍缺乏課外活動。

24. The Government should administer effective punishment to deter young people from committing crimes.

政府應該執行有效的懲罰以阻止青年人犯罪。

25. We must make juveniles realize that crime does not pay.

我們必須使青少年明白到犯罪是不值得的。

26. The rapid increase in juvenile delinquency is causing serious concern in the community.

青少年犯罪的迅速增加正在引起社會人士高度的關注。

27. It is a headache for the authorities.

這是當局感到頭痛的問題。

28. Overcrowded living conditions are partly responsible for juvenile delinquency.

青少年的犯罪問題部分是由於擠迫的居住環境所造成的。

29. The changing mentality of young people is often overlooked.

青年人心態上的轉變常被忽視。

30. The problem of juvenile delinquency can be traced to the complicated social environment.

青少年犯罪的問題可追溯到複雜的社會環境。

31. Many teenagers are rebellious and they often psychologically resist the authorities.

很多青少年是具反叛性的,他們往往在心理上反抗權威。

32. A large number of them are unwilling to accept the advice of the elders.

他們之中,有很多不願意接受長輩的忠告。

33. In Hong Kong, there are many teddy boys and girls.

香港有很多阿飛型男女。

34. Many of them have been forced to join triad gangs.

他們之中,有很多已被迫加入三合會。

35. If juvenile delinquency cannot be contained, the life and property of citizens will be threatened.

如果青少年犯罪問題不能受到抑制,市民的生命財產將受到威脅。

36. Social stability will also be undermined and all economic activities hindered.

社會的穩定亦會被破壞,一切經濟活動也將受到妨礙。

37. It is the innocent citizens who suffer most.

受苦最大的將是無辜的市民。

38. Some young delinquents use threats to demand money from others.

有些年青的犯罪者以威嚇的手段向他人索取金錢。

39. They rob the passers-by of money and sometimes even brutally stab their poor victims.

他們行劫路人,甚至有時殘忍地把他們刺傷。

40. These youngsters must be properly educated.

這些年青人必須接受適當的教育。

41. It is no exaggeration to say that lenient laws have encouraged more juvenile delinquency.

仁慈的法律鼓勵更多的青少年犯罪，這種說法並沒有誇大。

42. Young people have to face the realities and stand on their own feet.

年青人需要面對現實並自立謀生。

43. However, we should not only put the blame on young people.

然而，我們不應只責怪年青人。

44. Other factors like unconcerned parents, the examination-oriented educational system and the extremely materialistic society should all be held responsible for the deteriorating juvenile delinquency.

青少年犯罪問題日趨惡化的其他因素有不關心子女的父母，以考試為主的教育制度，以及極端重視物質的社會。

45. If young people repeatedly commit crimes, they are to blame.

假如年青人再三地犯罪，他們應受到譴責。

46. Young people are vulnerable to triad influences.

年青人易受三合會的不良影響。

47. Heavy penalty is a powerful deterrent.

重罰是一個強大的阻嚇力量。

48. The Government may consider re-imposing the death penalty.

政府可以考慮恢復執行死刑。

49. The important thing is to reform and correct the young criminals so that they can also become contributing citizens of society.

最重要的還是改造及教導年青的犯罪者，使他們也能成為對社會有貢獻的市民。

Phrases

1. absence of parental control

沒有父母的管束

2. light punishment

較輕的處罰

3. a complete failure

徹底的失敗

4. no doubt

無疑地

5. poisonous elements

毒素

6. to turn to crime

開始犯罪

7. bad films

不良的電影

8. low-class entertainments   低級的娛樂

9. unconventional behaviour   不合禮節的行為

10. corrupting publications   腐化的出版物

11. for the sake of   為了⋯⋯的目的

12. conscious-stricken people   良心不安的人

13. degeneration of social morals   社會風氣的墮落

14. sense of citizenship   公民意識

15. Western ideas   西方的思想

16. by illegal means   以非法的方式

17. poor living environment   惡劣的居住環境

18. no proper channels   沒有正當的途徑

19. no sense of guilt   沒有犯罪感

20. susceptible to social environment   易受社會環境的影響

21. to identify with other peers   受其他同儕認同

22. to do things in their own way   為所欲為

23. a responsible attitude   負責任的態度

24. a hot bed of crimes   罪惡的溫牀

25. to play truant   逃學

26. small dancing halls   小舞廳

27. armed robbery   持械行劫

28. indecent assault   非禮

29. harmful effects   不良效應

30. being convicted of   犯有⋯⋯的罪

31. to make a deposition   錄口供

32. appalling crime   令人髮指的罪行

33. to give cause for concern   值得關注

34. to call for   呼籲

35. social justice   社會公義

36. crime prevention   防止罪案

37. to fight youth crime   撲滅青少年罪行

38. the involvement of young persons in drugs   參與毒品活動的青少年

39. public exhibitions   公開展覽

40. frame of mind   心態

41. pent-up frustration   抑壓着的挫敗感

 # Vocabulary

1. robbery	打劫	20. offenders	犯罪者
2. gang fight	集體打鬥	21. misunderstanding	誤解
3. hippies	嬉皮士	22. tragedy	悲劇
4. poverty	貧窮	23. recreation	康樂
5. slump areas	貧民區	24. enjoyment	享樂
6. teenagers	青少年	25. luxury	奢華
7. acquaintances	相識的人	26. temptation	引誘
8. conscience	良知	27. by-products	副產品
9. law court	法庭	28. curiosity	好奇心
10. criminals	罪犯	29. peer	同儕
11. gangsters	匪徒	30. self-identity	自我認同
12. guidance	輔導	31. mass media	大眾傳播媒介
13. crime rate	犯罪率	32. resistance	反抗
14. co-operation	合作	33. sex education	性教育
15. violence	暴力	34. family life education	家庭生活教育
16. measures	措施	35. assault	攻擊
17. bars	酒吧	36. undeniable	無可否認的
18. gambling	賭博	37. beast-like	禽獸的
19. drug addiction	吸毒		

38.	restless	不安靜的
39.	terrible	可怕的
40.	harmful	有害的
41.	wayward	頑強的
42.	adventurous	冒險的
43.	indecent	淫穢的
44.	rebellious	反叛的
45.	emotional	感情用事的
46.	pleasure-seeking	找尋歡樂的
47.	irresponsible	不負責任的
48.	improper	不正當的
49.	lenient	仁慈的
50.	meaningful	有意義的
51.	heinous	罪行極惡的
52.	ethical	倫理的
53.	spoil	摧毀
54.	bully	威嚇
55.	remedy	補救
56.	prosecute	控告
57.	disapprove	不贊同
58.	degenerate	墮落
59.	deter	阻止
60.	rape	強姦
61.	impose	施加

62.	safeguard	保障
63.	soar	上升
64.	reform	改造
65.	challenge	挑戰
66.	overlook	忽視
67.	arrest	拘捕
68.	correct	糾正
69.	culprit	罪魁禍首
70.	shop theft	店舖盜竊
71.	tattoos	紋身
72.	unruly	不守規矩的
73.	assault	毆打
74.	advocate	贊成
75.	anti-social behaviour	反社會行為
76.	anti-crime campaigns	反罪惡運動
77.	moral education	道德教育
78.	illegal immigrants	非法移民
79.	mobile reporting centres	流動報案中心
80.	triad society	三合會
81.	anti-crime message	反罪行信息

45

Music and the Performing Art

Sentences

1. Music is the art of organizing sounds.

音樂是組織音響的藝術。

2. It heightens our appreciation of beauty.

它加強我們對美的欣賞。

3. Listening to good music is a pleasure.

聽美好的音樂是一種樂趣。

4. Music has a wonderful effect on people's feelings.

音樂對人的情感有不能言喻的影響。

5. Many people have half an ear for music.

很多人都有點喜歡音樂。

6. Music is a universal language.

音樂是一種國際語言。

7. We find aesthetic pleasure in music.

我們從音樂中享受到美感的快樂。

8. Music conveys a beautiful feeling.

音樂傳達一種美感。

9. Soft music often cheers us up.

柔和的音樂常常使我們感到愉快。

10. Light music can calm our nerves.

輕音樂能使我們的神經平靜下來。

11. Music helps us to restore our former balance of mind.

音樂幫助我們回復心智上的平衡。

12. It has a soothing effect on our soul.

它有一種使我們心靈得到安靜的效果。

13. Music is the food of love.

音樂是愛的食糧。

14. It is also a means of communicating ideas.

它也是一種溝通思想的方法。

15. Music has a wide appeal.

音樂有廣泛的吸引力。

16. Music can touch the inner soul of people and therefore they are deeply moved by it.

音樂能觸動人們的靈魂深處，因而人們往往深受音樂所感染。

17. Many music appreciation programmes are presented by the Leisure and Cultural Services Department (LCSD).   很多音樂欣賞的節目是由康樂及文化事務處（康文處）主辦的。

18. Some talented students take music lessons in the Royal School of Music in London.   一些有才華的學生在倫敦皇家音樂學院學習音樂。

19. Every year, many Chinese and Western plays are staged in the Shouson Theatre at the Hong Kong Arts Centre.   在香港藝術中心的壽臣劇場，每年都有很多中西話劇上演。

20. The Hong Kong Dance Company promotes the art of traditional Chinese dance.   香港舞蹈團宏揚傳統中國舞蹈的藝術。

21. Demonstration performances of the Hong Kong Academy of Ballet have proved very popular among people of different ages.   香港芭蕾舞學校的示範表演深受不同年齡人士的歡迎。

22. Many Hong Kong people enjoy the performances of Chinese puppetry.   很多香港人欣賞中國木偶戲。

23. Comedies are suitable for people of all ages.   喜劇是老少咸宜的。

24. Every year, many internationally acclaimed artistes take part in the Festival of Asian Arts held in Hong Kong.   每年有很多國際知名的藝術家參加在香港舉行的亞洲藝術節的演出。

25. The Hong Kong International Film Festival is a highlight of local cultural life.   香港國際電影節是本地文化生活的精要部分。

Phrases

1. soft and sweet music   柔和美妙的音樂

2. lots of fun   趣味無窮

3. great musical masterpieces   偉大的音樂作品

4. the plot of a play   劇情

5. musical achievement   音樂上的成就

6. greeted with high acclaim   備受歡迎

7. to give five performances   表演五場

8. up-and-coming stars   明日之星

9. acting abilities 演技
10. carried away 看得如痴如醉
11. to stole the show 搶盡風頭
12. to somersault 翻觔斗
13. flying trapeze 空中飛人
14. pyramid building 疊羅漢
15. outfits and props 服裝與道具
16. inspiring music 動人的音樂
17. loud and clear 聲音嘹亮
18. without match 無與倫比
19. highlights from operas 折子戲

Vocabulary

1. melody 旋律
2. tones 音調
3. music hall 音樂廳
4. musician 音樂家
5. fun 樂趣
6. lullaby 催眠曲
7. pleasure 愉快
8. Beatles 披頭四
9. message 訊息
10. Beethoven Symphony 貝多芬交響樂
11. composer 作曲家
12. music lovers 音樂愛好者
13. jazz music 爵士音樂
14. tone-colour 音色
15. Music Office 音樂事務處
16. ballet 芭蕾舞
17. choreographers 編舞家
18. playwright 劇作家
19. drama house 劇社
20. Cantonese Opera Troupe 粵劇團
21. Hong Kong Arts Centre 香港藝術中心
22. opera 歌劇
23. Shakespeare 莎士比亞
24. Hong Kong Repertory Theatre 香港話劇團
25. performance 表演
26. folk dance 民族舞蹈

27.	harmonious	和諧的	54.	Hong Kong Chinese Orchestra	香港中樂團

27. harmonious	和諧的	
28. popular	受歡迎的	
29. rhythmic	有韻律的	
30. crazy	瘋狂的	
31. powerful	強而有力的	
32. amateur	業餘的	
33. inspire	觸發靈感	
34. appreciate	欣賞	
35. soothe	使平靜	
36. express	表現	
37. appeal	吸引	
38. admire	讚美	
39. highlight	精彩項目	
40. cello	大提琴	
41. spotlight	聚光燈	
42. floor show	夜總會表演	
43. recital	演奏	
44. solo	獨奏	
45. mezzo soprano	女中音	
46. accompaniment	伴奏	
47. prelude	前奏	
48. ensemble	合奏曲	
49. minuet	小步舞曲	
50. roundelay	圓舞曲	
51. fanfare	喧鬧序樂	
52. show piece	傑作	
53. Hong Kong Academy for Performing Arts	香港演藝學院	

54. Hong Kong Chinese Orchestra	香港中樂團	
55. professional	專業的	
56. modern drama	話劇	
57. Peking opera	京劇	
58. Kunqu opera	崑曲	
59. Yue opera	越劇	
60. Chiuchow opera	潮劇	
61. Huang Mei opera	黃梅調	
62. folk song	山歌／民歌	
63. folk dance	土風舞	
64. Waltz	華爾滋舞	
65. Latin	拉丁舞	
66. Tango	探戈舞	
67. Cha Cha	查查舞	
68. Jive	牛仔舞	
69. social dance	交際舞	
70. Break Dance	霹靂舞	
71. rock-and-roll music	搖滾樂	
72. soul	靈歌	
73. storytelling	說書	
74. stand up comedy	棟篤笑	
75. one-act play	獨幕劇	
76. popular songs	流行歌曲	
77. modern music	現代音樂	
78. classical music	古典音樂	

79.	pop music	流行音樂	83. modern dance	現代舞
80.	folk singing	民歌演唱	84. music scene	樂壇
81.	musical instruments	樂器	85. lyric songs	抒情歌曲
82.	fine arts	藝術	86. stunt show	特技表演
			87. stereo system	立體聲系統

Noise

Sentences

1. People generally become very irritated by noisy circumstances.

   嘈雜的環境通常令人焦躁不安。

2. Noises seriously affect our mental stability.

   噪音嚴重影響我們精神上的穩定。

3. In a noisy environment, our quality of life surely suffers.

   在一個噪雜的環境中，我們的生活素質必然受損。

4. We may easily lose our temper.

   我們很容易脾氣暴躁。

5. Noises impair our hearing capacity.

   噪音損害我們的聽覺。

6. The deafening sounds from construction sites get on our nerves.

   建築地盤所發出的震耳欲聾的聲音使我們神經緊張。

7. Noise pollution is often a cause of public concern.

   噪音污染常常是公眾關注的事。

8. The ill effects of noise are too obvious.

   噪音所產生的不良影響顯而易見。

9. Annoying sounds are usually intolerable.

   噪音的滋擾常令人難以忍受。

10. Indeed, most people cannot stand nerve-wrecking noises.

    實在大多數人都不能忍受那破壞神經的噪音。

11. Noise is a mental torture.

噪音是一種對心靈的折磨。

12. Busy traffic often results in a lot of noise.

繁忙的交通往往導致很多噪音。

13. The sound of horns can be heard all the time.

我們常常聽到汽車的喇叭聲。

14. Many people can hardly sleep beecause of the roaring sounds of jet planes.

噴射機的吼號使很多人難以入睡。

15. Sometimes, the noise of television can still be heard after mid-night.

有時，我們在午夜後仍能聽到電視機所發出的噪音。

16. Some people ignore the warning that, after eleven thirty at night, the volume of their television should be reduced.

有些人不理會「在晚上十一時三十分後應把電視機音量減低」的勸告。

17. Noises from hawkers are also disturbing when they shout at the top of their voice to attract customers.

小販那吸引顧客的高聲叫賣也是擾人的。

18. A lot of noise often comes from electric shops selling CD.

出售光碟的唱片店常發出很多噪音。

19. Another source of noise is the repairing of roads.

修路是噪音的另一來源。

20. It is a terrible torture to the residents nearby.

它對附近居民是一個很大的折磨。

21. Public outcry to reduce noises of various types can often be heard.

我們時常可以聽到公眾的大聲疾呼，請求減低各種噪音。

22. Laws have been enacted to bring noise pollution under control.

政府已制訂法律，管制噪音污染。

23. For example, the time at which powered mechanical equipment can be used has been stipulated.

例如，政府已規定可以使用電動機械設備的時間。

24. All of us hope to live in a quieter environment.

我們每個人都希望能在一個較寧靜的環境下生活。

Phrases

1. air-conditioning and ventilating system

冷氣及空氣調節系統

2. aircraft passing overhead

在頭上飛過的飛機

3. construction and industrial noise   建築及工業噪音

4. noise control   噪音的管制

5. noise abatement   噪音的減少

6. enactment of laws   制訂法律

7. noise emissioning from motor vehicles   車輛噪音

8. to help alleviate   有助減輕

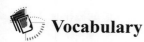 Vocabulary

1.	industrialization	工業化	20. annoying	滋擾的
2.	urbanization	城市化	21. irritating	使人憤怒的
3.	piling	打樁	22. nervous	神經緊張的
4.	construction site	建築地盤	23. grave	嚴重
5.	measures	措施	24. blare	發出喇叭聲
6.	uproar	喧囂	25. scream	大叫
7.	quarrel	爭吵	26. prohibit / ban	禁止
8.	complaint	投訴	27. prosecute	起訴
9.	investigation	調查	28. control	管制
10.	torture	折磨	29. contaminate	污染
11.	residents	居民	30. offenders	違例者
12.	offence	犯法	31. howl	怒吼
13.	regulations	規則	32. hoarse	嘶啞的
14.	legislation	立法	33. shrill	尖銳的
15.	tranquillity	安寧	34. high-pitched	聲調高的
16.	nuisance	討厭的事	35. applause	喝彩
17.	inevitable	無可避免的	36. thunderous	雷鳴般的
18.	disturbing	擾人的	37. laughter	笑聲
19.	intolerable	不能容忍的		

47

Online

Sentences

1. Many people send a personalized birthday card by e-mail.

   很多人用電郵發出個人生日卡。

2. Do you have your own website?

   你有沒有自己的網站？

3. This is the best after sales service on the web.

   這是網上最好的售後服務。

4. Our company provides instant delivery service regardless of the order size.

   不論訂單大小，本公司均提供即時送貨服務。

5. Surf the internet for the information you want.

   在互聯網上找尋你所需的資料。

6. Can I trust a computer programme to pay my bills?

   我可否信賴以電腦程式付款？

7. You can access your account anytime and anywhere through the internet.

   你可隨時隨地經由互聯網進入你的戶口。

8. Online bill payment is easy to use, but more and more banks offer the service free.

   網上付款容易使用，越來越多銀行提供免費服務。

9. For security reasons, please change your password periodically.

   基於保安理由，請定期更換你的密碼。

10. Please enter your personal information for verification.

    請輸入你的個人資料以便核對。

11. Upon upgrading our system, all services will be suspended temporarily.

    在進行系統提升期間，所有服務暫停。

12. Please click here to protect your online transaction.

    請按此保護你的網上交易。

13. Please do not login through hyperlink.

    請不要經超連結登入。

14. Our company will not ask customers for their personal information via e-mails.

    本公司不會經由電郵要求顧客提供他們的個人資料。

15. Customers should always be vigilant of fraudulent websites.

顧客須經常對欺詐網站保持警覺。

16. The web servers are protected by firewall systems to prevent unauthorized access.

網站伺服器設有防火牆，防止未經授權的人士進入。

17. Several consecutive login attempts with incorrect password will cause the online service to be suspended immediately.

連續數次輸入不正確的登入密碼，將引致網上服務即時被停止。

18. Simultaneous login of the same User ID via another computer is not allowed.

同一使用者不可透過另一部電腦同時登入。

19. Do not use easy-to-guess numbers or words as your password.

切勿使用容易被人猜中的號碼或文字作為你的密碼。

20. Download and install updates and patches for your operating systems and browsers regularly.

定期下載並按操作系統及瀏覽器更新程式。

21. Install anti-virus software on your personal computer.

你應為你的個人電腦安裝病毒偵測軟件。

22. Update the virus definition file and perform virus scanning regularly.

應定期更新病毒定義檔及進行病毒掃描。

23. Avoid downloading or installing programmes from unreliable sources.

應避免下載及安裝來歷不明的程式。

24. Avoid opening suspicious files or e-mails.

應避免開啟可疑的檔案或電子郵件。

25. New computer virus appears from time to time.

電腦病毒日新月異。

26. Virus, Trojan software and hacker programmes can be distributed via e-mails.

病毒、特洛伊軟件及黑客程式均可透過電子郵件傳播。

27. Turn off the power supply and disconnect from the wireless network after use.

使用無線網絡後，應關閉電源及中止連線。

28. Perform virus scanning before opening any file from insecure sources.

開啟任何外來的檔案前，先以防毒軟件進行掃描。

29. Do not save encrypted pages to disk.

不要把加密的畫面存到磁碟。

30. Click the "logout" button to exit from the system after you have finished all your online transactions.

完成網上交易後，必須按「登出」離開系統。

Phrases

1.	snap shots	快拍
2.	live web cast	網上直播
3.	text only	純文字
4.	What's new	新增項目
5.	computer crime	電腦罪案
6.	computer virus	電腦病毒
7.	double-click	雙按
8.	file compression	檔案壓縮
9.	grandfather-father-son technique	三代備份儲存法
10.	contact us	聯絡我們
11.	last updated	最後更新
12.	suspended temporarily	暫停
13.	fraudulent website	欺詐網站
14.	easy-to-guess number	容易被人猜中的號碼
15.	suspicious file	可疑檔案
16.	intellectual property right	知識產權
17.	low resolution graphics	低解像圖形
18.	plasma display	等離子顯示
19.	Point-to-Point Protocol	點對點協定
20.	pop-out menu	跳出式項目單
21.	power save mode	省電模式
22.	printer font	打印機字形
23.	random access	隨機存取
24.	syntax error	語法錯誤
25.	telephone jack	電話插口

26.	touch screen		觸式屏幕
27.	user-friendly		易學易用
28.	virus infection		病毒感染

 Vocabulary

1.	websites	網站		21.	motherboard	主機版
2.	hardware	硬件		22.	multimedia	多媒體
3.	software	軟件		23.	online	在線上
4.	search	搜尋		24.	resolution	解像度
5.	download	下載		25.	restart	重新啟動
6.	e-mail	電郵		26.	subtotal	小計
7.	website	網站		27.	template	範本
8.	internet	互聯網		28.	content page	主版網頁
9.	intranet	內聯網		29.	site map	網頁指南
10.	password	密碼		30.	traditional Chinese	繁體中文
11.	upgrade	提升		31.	simplified Chinese	簡體中文
12.	verification	核對				
13.	hyperlink	超連結		32.	bar code reader	條碼閱讀機
14.	virus	病毒		33.	boot disk	開機碟
15.	logout	登出		34.	Chinese character input	中文輸入法
16.	login	登入				
17.	browser	瀏覽器		35.	electronic pay system (EPS)	電子付款系統
18.	bookmark	標記				
19.	gigabyte	十億字節		36.	online shopping	網上購物
20.	megabyte (MB)	百萬字節		37.	computer programme	電腦程式

38.	online transaction	網上交易	47.	thermal printer	感熱打印機

38. online transaction　網上交易
39. hacker programme　黑客程式
40. inkjet printer　噴墨打印機
41. installation programme　安裝程式
42. sound card　聲效卡
43. sound synthesizer　(電子) 音響合成器
44. spreadsheet programme　試算長程式
45. system analyst　系統分析員
46. system engineer　系統工程師

47. thermal printer　感熱打印機
48. video compact disc (VCD)　視像光碟
49. web cam　網絡攝影機
50. web casting　網上廣播
51. word processor　文字處理器
52. electronic cash　電子現金
53. main memory　主記憶體
54. memory chip　記憶體晶片
55. injet print cartridge　噴墨打印墨盒
56. zip file　已壓縮檔

In the Park

Sentences

1. Parks are often called the green lungs of an urban area.　公園常被稱為市區的綠肺。

2. A walk in the park can calm our strained nerves.　在公園中散步能撫慰我們緊張的神經。

3. We can also enjoy the surrounding view.　我們也可欣賞周圍的景色。

4. The peaceful and beautiful environment is indeed enjoyable.　那和平及美麗的環境實在是令人愉快的。

5. In the morning sun, we can see a lot of people practising "Tai Chi".

在早晨的太陽下，我們可見到有很多人打太極拳。

6. They are all full of good spirits.

他們個個精神飽滿。

7. Some elderly people are exchanging their experiences of life.

一些老年人正在交換他們的人生經驗。

8. They are fond of sweet memories.

他們喜歡那甜蜜的回憶。

9. Parks are usually for people to take a rest.

公園通常是給人休息的地方。

10. We can often see some people sitting on a bench and reading a newspaper.

我們常常可以見到有些人坐在長椅上看報紙。

11. Some elderly people like to hang a birdcage onto the branch of a tree.

有些老年人喜歡把鳥籠掛在樹枝上。

12. Many people walk about the park in a leisurely manner.

很多人悠閒地在公園四周散步。

13. During holidays, nearly all the parks in Hong Kong are packed with people.

在假日，幾乎所有香港的公園都擠滿了人。

14. When the weather is fine, the whole family may spend an afternoon in a park.

假如天氣良好，一家大小可能在公園內渡過一個下午。

15. When they are in a park, they seem to forget all their worries.

他們在公園時，似乎忘卻所有煩惱的事。

16. They may take photographs with their cameras.

他們可以用相機拍照。

17. They can also enjoy looking at the various kinds of shrubs and plants or other visual appeals.

他們也可欣賞各種不同的灌木和植物，以及其他視覺上的吸引物。

18. In some large parks, we can see a lotus pond and a fountain.

在一些規模較大的公園裏，我們可以見到荷花池和噴泉。

19. Sometimes puppet shows are held in a park.

有時公園內舉行木偶表演。

20. People usually watch the show attentively.

人們通常留心地觀看表演。

21. In the games area, children are playing happily.

在遊戲區內，兒童高興地玩耍。

22. Some of them are playing exciting games like hide-and-seek.

有些兒童在玩刺激的遊戲，例如捉迷藏。

23. In the children's playground, some children are throwing quoits while others are enjoying skate rolling. 在兒童遊樂場內，有些兒童在玩投環遊戲，其他則愉快地玩滾軸溜冰。

24. In the open space, a group of people are doing some exercises. 在空曠的地方，一羣人正在做體操。

25. In the shade, two men are engrossed in a game of chess. 在樹蔭下，兩個男人正專注於下棋。

26. There is a small zoo in the park. 公園內有一個小動物園。

27. Some monkeys are kept in a cage. 一些猴子被關在籠內。

28. They jump through a ring. 牠們跳過一個鐵環。

29. Other animals are also fenced off. 其他動物也以欄柵隔開。

30. In a park, we should keep the place clean and be careful not to damage any public property. 在公園內，我們應保持地方清潔及不要毀壞任何公物。

 # Phrases

1. rows of trees 一行行的樹木

2. rich colours 繽紛的色彩

3. Cantonese opera performance 粵劇上演

4. to ride on a skateboard 踏在一塊滑板上

5. children's play area 兒童遊樂區

6. 300 species of birds 三百種鳥類

7. a revolving lantern 走馬燈

 # Vocabulary

1. Victoria Park 維多利亞公園

2. Hong Kong Zoological and Botanical Gardens 香港動植物公園

3. Hong Kong Park 香港公園

4. Peak Garden 山頂公園

5. Kowloon Park 九龍公園

6. Morse Park 摩士公園

7. Nan Lian Park 南蓮公園

8. Tuen Mun Park 屯門公園

9.	Walk Through Aviary	觀鳥園
10.	bench	長椅
11.	swing	鞦韆
12.	seesaw	蹺蹺板
13.	merry-go-round	旋轉木馬
14.	park-keeper	公園看守人
15.	flower-beds	花牀
16.	entrance	入口
17.	morning walk	晨運
18.	balloons	氣球
19.	breeze	微風
20.	tranquillity	平靜
21.	kiosk	小食亭
22.	food stalls	食物攤檔
23.	zoo	動物園
24.	stage	舞台
25.	magic show	魔術表演
26.	ice-cream	雪糕（冰淇淋）
27.	pool	池
28.	lawn	草地
29.	sandpit	沙地
30.	snacks	小食
31.	soft drinks	汽水
32.	Peak Lookout	太平山餐廳
33.	skateboard	滑板
34.	kite-flying	放風箏
35.	hoop	呼拉圈
36.	rope-skipping	跳繩
37.	drop-the-handkerchief game	掉手帕遊戲
38.	jumping-over	跳背
39.	pedal car	踏板小汽車
40.	toy cart	玩具車
41.	scooter	滑行車
42.	tricycle	兒童三輪車
43.	statue	人像
44.	open-air theatre	露天劇場
45.	railings	欄柵
46.	dustbin	垃圾箱
47.	Water Cascade	人工瀑布
48.	Amphi Theatre	露天劇場
49.	Garden Piazza	花園廣場
50.	azalea	杜鵑花
51.	shrubs	灌木
52.	foliage plants	觀葉植物
53.	jogging track	緩步跑小徑
54.	recreational grounds	康樂設施
55.	Chinese landscaped gardens	中國式的園林花園
56.	martial art	武術
57.	artificial lake	人工湖
58.	park rangers	公園管理員

Picnic

Sentences

1. Last Saturday, we went for a picnic.

   上星期六，我們去郊外野餐。

2. It was a fine day with a breeze blowing gently and the sun shining brightly.

   是日風和日麗。

3. The weather was warm and pleasant.

   天氣溫暖和煦。

4. The warm sun was hanging high in the blue sky.

   溫暖的太陽高掛在藍天上。

5. We gathered at the Star Ferry Pier.

   我們在天星碼頭集合。

6. We were all in high spirits.

   我們心情興奮。

7. We took advantage of the fine weather and the holiday to make an excursion.

   我們利用假日及天氣良好的機會去短途旅行。

8. We broke up into several groups and proceeded to the destination together.

   我們分成若干組，一同前往目的地去。

9. We queued up in front of No. 70 bus.

   我們在七十號巴士前排隊。

10. We took food with us and brought along other necessary things.

    我們帶了食物及其他必需品。

11. After about an hour's journey, we finally reached our destination.

    過了大約一小時的旅程，我們終於到達目的地。

12. We alighted from the bus.

    我們下了巴士。

13. We settled down quickly.

    我們很快安頓下來了。

14. Many classmates sat in the shade because it was cooler there.

    很多同學坐在樹蔭下，因為那兒比較涼快。

15. We all admired the surrounding picturesque view.

    我們欣賞四周圖畫似的風景。

16. Some classmates took a stroll around the destination. 有些同學在目的地四周散步。

17. Large stretches of green fields lay before our eyes. 大片綠色的田野呈現在我們的眼前。

18. It was indeed a thrilling scene. 這實在是一個使人驚喜的景象。

19. Other classmates sat on the bank of a river and played with the clear, sparkling water. 其他同學坐在河岸上，玩那澄清、閃亮的水。

20. The lucid water was so tempting! 清澈的河水是那麼誘人啊！

21. We could not help crying out loudly when we saw the splendid view. 當我們看到那壯麗的景色時，我們不禁大叫起來。

22. We went up the slopes and ventured inside the cave. 我們爬上斜坡，冒險深入洞中。

23. Some classmates tumbled and fell. 有些同學跌倒。

24. Sweat covered our brows, but we did not mind. 汗水佈滿我們的眉額，但我們不在乎。

25. The adventurous spirit of young people urged us on. 年青人冒險的精神在催促我們前進。

26. When we eventually reached the summit, we felt that the reward had been worth the effort. 我們漸漸抵達山頂，便感覺到付出這一番努力所得的回報是值得的。

27. The trees had thinned out as we approached the peak. 我們走近山頂時，樹木漸漸稀少。

28. The whole valley spread out before our eyes. 整個山谷展現在我們眼前。

29. We saw the whole town bathed in the soft rays of a setting sun. 我們看到整個市鎮沐浴在夕陽的柔和光輝中。

30. The panoramic view was marvellous. 那個全景是不可思議的。

31. To our left, the water of a stream was wriggling; in the distance, ranges of hills could be seen. 在我們的左邊，溪水蜿蜒而流；遠處則山巒起伏。

32. At that time, we were so cheered up. 在那時，我們的心情興奮起來。

33. We were thrilling with joy. 我們正激盪着歡樂之情。

34. There was suddenly an impulse within us.

突然間，我們心中起了一種激動。

35. We stumbled and dashed forward.

我們跌跌撞撞地前進。

36. When we saw the fantastic scenery, we felt refreshed.

當我們看到那奇異的風景時，我們精神為之一振。

37. Some classmates took many pictures of the landscape.

一些同學拍下很多風景照。

38. We enjoyed ourselves thoroughly.

我們盡情享樂。

39. On the whole, most of us played heartily and got a lot of fun and excitement.

總括而言，我們大多數人都愉快地玩耍，獲得很大的樂趣與刺激。

40. Feeling tired, we lay down on the green grass.

我們覺得疲倦了，便躺在綠草上。

41. The sun was already low in the sky when we started our descent.

當我們下山時，太陽已經降下天邊了。

42. The whole journey made us rejoice.

整個旅程使我們歡欣。

43. We felt the time pass quickly.

我們發覺時間很快地溜走。

44. We rested for a while, then packed our belongings and set out on our return journey.

我們休息了一會，然後收拾自己的東西動身回家。

45. We were still unwilling to leave.

我們仍不願回去。

46. The sky was cloudy and overcast, but later the weather turned fine.

初時天陰有雲，後來天氣轉佳。

47. It was cool and fresh when sunset approached.

接近日落的時候，天氣清新而涼快。

48. We turned to take a final glimpse.

我們回頭投下依戀的一瞥。

49. We recaptured the dreams of that time.

我們回味那時的幻夢。

50. We went home reluctantly, but with a delighted feeling.

我們不情願回家，不過情緒很愉快。

51. It was nightfall when we got back home.

我們回到家裏時，已是夜幕低垂了。

52. We felt it was a holiday well spent.

我們覺得自己好好地渡過了一個假日。

Phrases

1.	a bright sunny day	一個晴朗的日子
2.	later on	稍後的時間
3.	a happy crowd	一羣快樂的人
4.	on board a launch	在小汽船上
5.	radios going full blast	調校收音機的聲量至最大
6.	much fun and delight	很多趣味和愉悦
7.	on arrival	抵達時
8.	sitting down in a circle	圍圈而坐
9.	foaming waves	浪花
10.	shouts and yells	叫喊
11.	stretches of vegetable fields	一塊一塊的菜田

Vocabulary

1.	excursion	短途旅行	13.	landscape	景色
2.	trip	旅程	14.	summit	山頂
3.	bus terminus	巴士總站	15.	pavilion	涼亭
4.	railway station	火車站	16.	destination	目的地
5.	ferry pier	碼頭	17.	breeze	微風
6.	launch	小汽船	18.	slopes	斜坡
7.	voyage	航程	19.	valley	山谷
8.	refreshments	點心	20.	cove	小海灣
9.	sandwiches	三文治（三明治）	21.	torch	電筒
10.	soft drinks	汽水	22.	waterfall	瀑布
11.	fun	樂趣	23.	camp site	營地
12.	curiosity	好奇心	24.	holiday-makers	渡假者

25.	appetite	食慾	36. scenic	風景美麗的
26.	knapsack	背囊	37. charming	迷人的
27.	MacLehose Trail	麥理浩徑	38. exhausted	十分疲倦的
			39. memorable	值得回憶的
28.	Bride's Pool	新娘潭	40. rejoice	使喜悅
29.	firepits	燒烤爐	41. echo	發出回音
30.	footpath	小徑	42. hide-and-seek game	捉迷藏遊戲
31.	wildlife	野生動植物		
32.	compass	指南針	43. free time	自由時間
33.	enjoyable	愉快的	44. canned food	罐頭食品
34.	refreshing	令人振奮精神的	45. Outward Bound	外展訓練
35.	amazed	驚奇的		

Pollution

Sentences

1. The rapid increase in population and economic growth have brought about the problem of pollution.

   人口的迅速增加及經濟增長帶來了污染的問題。

2. Serious pollution spoils the quality of our life and threatens our very existence.

   嚴重的污染損害我們的生活素質及威脅我們的生存。

3. We must identify major sources of pollution and establish the factors affecting it.

   我們必須找出污染的主要來源及確定影響污染的因素。

4. Polluted air and poisonous gas are harmful to our health.

   受污染的空氣及有毒的氣體對我們的健康有害。

5. Black smoke often comes from the chimneys of factories and restaurants.

黑煙常由工廠和酒樓的煙囪中噴出來。

6. Exhaust fumes are also emitted from cars.

廢氣也由汽車噴出來。

7. It is the Government's responsibility to monitor atmospheric pollution levels with a view to controlling polluting emissions.

政府有責任觀察及測量空氣污染的程度以達監管廢氣污染的目的。

8. To improve the situation of air pollution, chimney height must be increased and cars frequently checked.

為了改善空氣污染的清況，煙囪的高度必須增加，而汽車也須經常進行檢查。

9. Agricultural waste caused by pigs and hens often gives off repulsive odours.

由豬隻及雞隻所造成的農業廢物常常發出令人討厭的氣味。

10. It should be collected and properly treated.

我們應收集及適當地處理這些廢物。

11. Litterbugs throw rubbish on the beach and other public places, and therefore they should be heavily punished.

垃圾蟲在海灘及其他公眾地方亂拋垃圾，因此他們應被重罰。

12. Water pollution is generally caused by the dumping of chemical waste and leakage from oil tankers.

排出的化學廢料及運油船內石油的溢出，通常造成海水污染。

13. Marine life, including fish, can hardly exist in seriously contaminated water.

包括魚類在內的海洋生物，難以在被嚴重污染的水中生存。

14. The Marine Department collects floating rubbish regularly.

海事處定期收集飄浮在水面的廢物。

15. The Government has built a sewage treatment works in Shatin.

政府已在沙田興建了一所污水處理廠。

16. To ensure a cleaner environment, effective precautionary measures must be taken and an overall environmental protection strategy formulated.

為了確保有一個較清潔的環境，政府必須採取有效的預防措施及制定一個全面的環境保護策略。

17. Through the mass media, we should educate the public on the sensible use of the environment.

我們應通過傳播媒介教育大眾明智地使用環境。

18. At the same time, the Government should rigorously enforce anti-pollution ordinances.

與此同時，政府應嚴厲執行反污染法例。

19. In recent years, the testing of nuclear bombs has also caused serious environmental pollution.

近年來，核子彈的試爆也造成了嚴重的環境污染。

20. Anti-pollution campaigns have been held in many countries.

很多國家曾舉行反污染運動。

21. The whole area of Hong Kong has been designated as a smoke control area.

整個香港已被指定為煙霧管制區。

22. It is the responsibility of every citizen to keep Hong Kong environmentally clean.

每一個市民都有責任保持香港環境的清潔。

23. In fact, the problem of pollution has been particularly acute in recent years.

事實上，近年的污染問題特別嚴重。

24. We must do our best to protect our environment if we are to enjoy a better quality of life.

假如我們要享受較好的生活素質，我們必須盡力保護我們的環境。

Phrases

1. toxic and dangerous waste — 有毒及危險的廢物

2. investigation work — 調查工作

3. proper control of — 適當的控制

4. to disperse polluting emissions — 驅散污染環境的廢氣

5. environmentally acceptable — 環境上可接受的

6. in an unsatisfactory state — 在不理想的狀況下

7. emissions from motor vehicles — 車輛廢氣

8. public nuisance — 公眾的滋擾

9. widespread malpractice — 普遍的不當行為

10. to pose a health risk to — 危害健康

11. in line with — 因應

12. to control dust emissions — 管制散逸的塵屑

13. refuse collection — 收集垃圾

14. licensing control — 牌照管制

15. to step up enforcement action   加強執法行動

16. environmental impact assessment   環境影響評估

17. the "polluter pays" principle   「污染者自付」原則

 # Vocabulary

1.	air pollution	空氣污染	21.	cement plants	水泥廠
2.	land pollution	陸地污染	22.	strategy	策略
3.	water pollution	海水污染	23.	data	資料
4.	industrial pollution	工業污染	24.	analysis	分析
5.	destruction	破壞	25.	experts	專家
6.	by-products	副產品	26.	tankers	運油船
7.	waste/rubbish/litter	廢物	27.	incinerator	垃圾焚化爐
8.	chemical waste	化學廢物	28.	survey	調查
9.	disease	疾病	29.	beach	海灘
10.	tuberculosis	肺病	30.	overcrowded	過度擠迫的
11.	bronchitis	支氣管炎	31.	selfish	自私的
12.	fines	罰款	32.	deteriorate	損壞
13.	smog	煙霧	33.	endanger	危害
14.	chimneys	煙囱	34.	generate	產生
15.	hazard/danger	危險	35.	diminish	減少
16.	installations	裝置	36.	air quality	空氣素質
17.	ordinance	法例	37.	diesel vehicles	柴油車輛
18.	regulations	規則	38.	sewage	污水
19.	sulphur dioxide	二氧化硫	39.	water quality	水質
20.	power stations	發電站	40.	Environmental Protection Department	環保署

41.	ozone	臭氧	46.	environmental protection ordinance 環境保護法例
42.	nuisance	滋擾		
43.	appropriate	適當的	47.	construction sites 建築地盤
44.	sustain	持續	48.	pollution index 污染指數
45.	recycle	循環再造	49.	noise pollution 噪音污染

At a Railway Station

Sentences

1. The train frequencies for trains moving between Shenzhen and Hong Kong are high. The train departs from both places at an interval of several minutes.

   行走深圳與香港間的火車班次頻密，兩地每隔幾分鐘就開出一班。

2. A journey by train is usually not long. We seldom see people cling together to say good-bye at the train station.

   乘坐火車出門，通常行程不長，所以在火車站上我們很少看到依依惜別的場面。

3. There are many automatic ticket machines in the concourse.

   火車站大堂設有很多自動售票機。

4. Most passengers use the Octopus cards.

   大部分乘客使用八達通卡。

5. Electrified trains have provided safety and comfort for the passengers.

   電氣化火車為乘客提供安全舒適的服務。

6. The concourse is well lit, clean and tidy.

   車站大堂光線充足，整齊清潔。

7. Many Hong Kong people like to take a pleasure trip to Mainland China by train during long holidays.

   很多香港人喜歡在長假期乘火車前往中國大陸旅遊。

8. Many China-bound passengers board the express train.

很多前往中國的旅客登上那列特別快車。

9. They carry a lot of luggage.

他們攜帶很多行李。

10. The train is full and passengers are packed like sardines.

那列火車全部客滿，乘客擠迫得像沙丁魚一樣。

11. In the pedestrian concourse, many people are seeing their relatives and friends off.

在火車站大堂內，很多人正向他們的親友送行。

12. It is indeed a crowded station.

這實在是一個擠塞的火車站。

13. Many passengers are catching a train.

很多乘客正在趕搭一班火車。

14. Some of them miss the train and they can only take the next train.

有些乘客未能趕上那班火車，他們只能乘搭下一班。

15. There is a long queue at the booking office.

售票處前有一條長龍。

16. Advance booking is accepted.

乘客可預訂車票。

17. A train is slowly pulling into the station.

一列火車正緩緩地駛進車站。

18. It arrives on time.

它準時抵達。

19. An old woman is alighting from the train.

一個老婦正在下火車。

20. A man is lending her a helping hand.

一個男人正幫助她下車。

21. Special facilities for use by the handicapped passengers have been set up at the station.

車站內有特別設施，方便傷殘人士使用。

22. There is a small cafe in the concourse at the terminus station.

火車總站大堂內，設有一家小型咖啡室。

23. Express through train services have become very popular with the passengers.

快速直通火車服務深受乘客歡迎。

24. The station has been expanded to cope with the ever increasing railway traffic.

為了應付日益繁忙的鐵路服務，這個車站已進行了擴建工程。

25. Daily operation at the railway station has been computerized.

火車站的日常操作已經電腦化。

26. Most passengers demand fast and frequent railway services.

大部分乘客要求快速及班次頻密的火車服務。

Phrases

1.	fast and frequent service	快速及班次頻密的服務
2.	double tracks	雙軌
3.	overhead footbridge	行人天橋
4.	ordinary train	普通火車
5.	hectic time	繁忙時間

Vocabulary

1.	journey	旅程
2.	locomotive	機車（火車頭）
3.	up trains	上行車（往新界）
4.	down trains	下行車（往市區）
5.	Lo Wu	羅湖
6.	Lok Ma Chau	落馬州
7.	terminus station	總站
8.	carriage	車廂
9.	platform	月台
10.	suitcase	小行囊
11.	booking office	售票處
12.	route	路線
13.	fence	欄柵
14.	seat	座位
15.	station master	站長
16.	month ticket	月票
17.	entrance	入口
18.	exit	出口
19.	night train	夜車
20.	freight train	貨物列車
21.	time-table	時間表
22.	baggage/ luggage	行李
23.	single ticket	單程票
24.	return ticket	雙程票
25.	engine driver	司機
26.	delay	誤點
27.	railway administration	鐵路局
28.	signal	訊號
29.	beacon	指示燈
30.	concourse	車站大堂
31.	parcel	包裹
32.	loud-speaker	擴音器
33.	kiosk	小賣部

34. railway cafe	鐵路餐廳	41. noise barriers	隔音屏障
35. clamorous	喧鬧的	42. immigration check point	過境關卡
36. first class	頭等		
37. automatic ticket machine	自動售票機	43. Guangzhou-Kowloon through train	港穗直通車
38. express through train	快速直通火車	44. train compartment	車卡
39. first train	頭班車		
40. last train	尾班車	45. electric train	電氣化火車

A Rainy Street

Sentences

1.	The sky was gloomy.	天空陰沉沉的。
2.	There were black clouds sailing on the dark sky.	烏雲在黑暗的天空飄浮着。
3.	A flash of lightning swept across the sky.	一道電光閃過天空。
4.	There is an intense heat in the air.	空氣十分酷熱。
5.	Soon, the rain poured heavily.	不久，大雨傾盆而下。
6.	Peals of thunder sounded every now and then.	有時天空響起雷聲。
7.	It was a deafening roar.	這是一陣震耳欲聾的吼聲。
8.	The merciless rain went on without pause.	無情的雨不停地下着。
9.	At its climax, the rain came down in sheets.	雨最大的時候，一大片一大片的傾下來。
10.	Some balconies and terraces were also affected by the heavy downpour.	一些陽台也受大雨所影響。

11. Many pedestrians dashed to shelters.	很多行人奔向避雨處。
12. Big drops spattered on their heads.	大滴的雨點灑在他們的頭上。
13. The rain drenched them thoroughly in no time.	雨水不久把他們淋得濕透。
14. They had the most dismal frame of mind imaginable.	他們有可以想像的最惡劣的心情。
15. Traffic was immediately held up.	頓時，路上發生交通擠塞。
16. There was serious chaos on the road.	路面上的情況異常混亂。
17. Both drivers and pedestrians had to be on the alert for conditions on the surface of the road.	司機及行人必須留意路面的情況。
18. People waded through the water.	人們涉水而過。
19. After an hour had passed, the street was nearly deserted.	一小時後，街道幾乎杳無一人。
20. The heavy rain continued to patter on the roof-tops and window-panes.	大雨繼續在屋頂及玻璃窗上滴嗒地響。
21. Many low-lying areas were flooded.	很多低窪地區遭受水浸。
22. The tingling sounds of dropping water could still be clearly heard.	水滴落下的滴嗒聲仍然清晰可聞。
23. Soon, the rain stopped and the sky was clear.	不久雨停了，天漸放晴了。
24. The air became cool.	天氣轉為清涼。

Phrases

1. torrents of rain	傾盆大雨
2. rains in drizzles	一縷縷的雨
3. breeze and drizzle	微風細雨
4. to drip down	滴下
5. to get all wet from head to toe	從頭到腳趾都被淋濕
6. drops of rain after a passing shower	驟雨後的雨點
7. flashes of lightning	閃電

8. miserable rain   惱人的雨

9. patter on   滴嗒地落在

10. wet through   濕透

11. two episodes of heavy rain   兩場暴雨

12. a trace of rainfall   輕微雨量

13. rain cats and dogs   下大雨

14. cause flooding in many places   引致多處地區水浸

Vocabulary

1.	shelter	避雨的地方	17. wet	濕的
2.	troubles	麻煩	18. waterproof	不透水的
3.	mud	污泥	19. unforgettable	難忘的
4.	thunder	雷	20. chaotic	混亂的
5.	thunderstorm	雷電暴風	21. alert	當心的
6.	raincoat	雨衣	22. flooded	遭水淹的
7.	umbrella	雨傘	23. foretell	預告
8.	traffic congestion	交通擠塞	24. soak	濕透
9.	smudge	污迹	25. block	阻塞
10.	sludge	泥濘	26. wade	涉水
11.	traffic lights	交通燈	27. rush	猛衝
12.	pavement	人行道	28. drizzle	毛毛雨
13.	motorists	駕駛人士	29. blizzard	暴風雨
14.	landslide	山泥傾瀉	30. occasional showers	間中驟雨
15.	rubbish	垃圾	31. Rainstorm Signals	暴雨警告訊號
16.	shelterless	沒有遮蔽		

Restaurants

Sentences

1. There are many big and comfortable restaurants in Hong Kong.

   香港有很多大型而舒適的酒樓。

2. They are usually situated in a good location.

   它們通常位於一個很好的地點。

3. They are beautifully decorated with chandeliers hanging from the ceiling.

   它們裝飾得美輪美奐，枝形吊燈懸掛在天花板上。

4. In order to attract more business, many restaurants serve their customers well.

   很多酒樓對客人招呼週到，藉以爭取較多的營業額。

5. In fact, some famous restaurants are very friendly.

   事實上，一些著名的酒樓服務都不錯。

6. Most Hong Kong people appreciate attentive and friendly service.

   很多香港人欣賞忠誠及友善的服務。

7. Many people take their lunch in a restaurant.

   很多人在酒樓內吃午飯。

8. Some people like being the host and treating their friends to dinner in a restaurant.

   有些人喜歡作東道，請他們的朋友在酒樓內吃晚飯。

9. Restaurants in Hong Kong are often crowded with customers.

   在香港，酒樓很多時都擠滿顧客。

10. On Sundays and public holidays, restaurants are often filled to capacity.

    在星期日與公眾假期，酒樓通常都坐滿了人。

11. Every table is occupied.

    每張桌子都有人坐。

12. Many late-comers wait patiently for seats in the morning.

    在早上，很多遲來者耐心地等候着座位。

13. People usually order dim sum or other favourite dishes.

    人們通常點一些點心或其他喜愛的菜。

14. Some restaurants serve food of superb quality. 　有些酒樓供應品質極佳的食物。

15. They provide a wide variety of food for customers to choose. 　它們提供多類食品供顧客選擇。

16. They usually recommend their special dishes. 　通常酒樓會介紹特別的菜式。

17. Some restaurants cater for customers' special tastes. 　有些酒樓迎合顧客的特別口味。

18. Their seats are usually filled by patrons. 　在座的多是常客。

19. Waiters usually take customers' orders on a note-pad. 　侍應通常把顧客所點的菜式記入單內。

20. In Hong Kong, people can enjoy the cuisine of various countries. 　在香港，人們可享受到各國的菜餚。

21. French and Italian cuisine, Japanese and Korean dishes, as well as Malay food, are all served in Hong Kong restaurants. 　香港餐廳供應法國菜、意大利菜、日本菜、韓國菜及馬來食品。

22. Most people in Hong Kong like Chinese cuisine. 　大多數香港人喜歡中國菜。

23. There is an extensive menu in the Chinese cuisine. 　中國菜式品種繁多。

24. Beijing roast ducks and Szechuan and Cantonese dishes are very popular in Hong Kong. 　北京烤鴨、四川菜及廣東菜都深受香港人歡迎。

25. In fact, the Chinese cuisine is world famous. 　事實上，中國菜是世界著名的。

 Phrases

1. magnificent interior decoration 　內部裝修華麗

2. the best service 　最好的服務

3. bad manners 　失儀

4. at a loss 　茫然失措

5. noodles in soup 　窩麵

6.	fried noodles with shredded pork	肉絲炒麵
7.	fried rice noodles with beef	乾炒牛河
8.	fried noodles in Shanghai Style	上海粗炒
9.	fried vermicelli in Singapore Style	星州炒米
10.	fried rice in Canton Style	揚州炒飯
11.	fried rice in Fujian Style	福建炒飯
12.	fried rice with tomato and cream sauce topping	鴛鴦炒飯
13.	trolley style noodles	車仔麵
14.	fish ball flat rice noodles	魚蛋粗麵
15.	hot and sour soup	酸辣湯
16.	glutinous rice in lotus leaf	珍珠雞
17.	instant-boiled seasonal vegetable	油菜
18.	sweet and sour pork	咕嚕肉／生炒排骨
19.	steam guifei chicken	貴妃雞
20.	sautéed diced chicken with cashew nuts	腰果雞丁
21.	roast Beijing duck	北京填鴨
22.	twice-cooked pork with chili pepper	回鍋肉
23.	sautéed broccoli with scallop	西蘭花炒帶子
24.	steam garoupa	清蒸石斑
25.	eggplant in hot pot	魚香茄子煲
26.	sautéed pea shoots	清炒豆苗
27.	bean curd with salty fish and diced chicken hot pot	鹹魚雞粒豆腐煲

Vocabulary

1.	customers	顧客	3.	gourmet	食家
2.	patrons	常客（熟客）	4.	menu	菜牌

5.	specialties	名菜	29.	fillet steak	牛柳
6.	dishes	菜餚	30.	Jasmine tea	普洱
7.	cuisine	烹飪術／菜餚	31.	Iron Buddha tea	香片
8.	dim sum	點心	32.	champagne	鐵觀音
9.	siu mai	燒賣	33.	Pu'er tea	香檳酒
10.	shrimp dumpling	蝦餃	34.	whiskey	威士忌
11.	steamed dumpling	小籠包	35.	brandy	拔蘭地
12.	wonton noodles	雲吞麵	36.	red wine	紅（葡萄）酒
13.	steamed flour roll	腸粉	37.	white wine	白（葡萄）酒
14.	port sticker	鍋貼	38.	beer	啤酒
15.	fried taro dumpling	芋角	39.	Maotai	茅台酒
16.	egg custard tart	蛋撻	40.	Shaoxing rice wine	紹興酒
17.	turnip/daikon radish cake	蘿蔔糕	41.	alcohol	酒類
18.	barbecued pork bun	叉燒包	42.	bill	賬單
19.	soup dumpling	灌湯餃	43.	tips	小賬
20.	shrimp dumpling	蝦餃	44.	reservations	訂座
21.	spring roll	春卷	45.	waiter	侍應
22.	Tan Tan noodles	担担麵	46.	change	零錢（找回的錢）
23.	porridge/congee	粥	47.	chef	主廚
24.	soup	湯	48.	trolley	食物車
25.	seafood	海鮮	49.	captain	部長
26.	lobster	龍蝦	50.	McDonald's	麥當勞
27.	oyster	蠔	51.	Spaghetti House	意粉屋
28.	garoupa balls	斑球	52.	Kentucky Chicken	肯德基雞
			53.	Pizza Hut	必勝客

54. fast food shops	快餐店	76. appetizer	頭盤
55. assorted BBQ meats	燒味拼盤	77. the main dish	主菜
56. jellyfish	海蜇	78. dessert	飯後甜品
57. abalone	鮑魚	79. à la cart	按菜單點菜
58. mushroom	冬菇	80. set lunch	午飯套餐
59. scallop	帶子	81. set dinner	晚飯套餐
60. vegetarian products	素食類	82. afternoon tea	下午茶
61. squid	魷魚	83. high tea	傍晚茶
62. cuttle fish	墨魚	84. French cuisine	法國菜
63. pork ribs	排骨	85. Italian cuisine	意大利菜
64. hairy crab	大閘蟹	86. Japanese cuisine	日本菜
65. geoduck clam	象拔蚌	87. Korean cuisine	韓國菜
66. sole	龍脷	88. Thai cuisine	泰國菜
67. sashimi	日本魚生	89. Vietnam cuisine	越南菜
68. shark's fin	魚翅	90. Indonesia cuisine	印尼菜
69. Vietnam rice noodles	越南粉	91. India cuisine	印度菜
70. Buddha's Delight	羅漢齋	92. Shanghai cuisine	上海菜
71. red bean sweet soup	紅豆沙	93. Sichuan cuisine	川菜
72. mango pudding	芒果布甸	94. luxurious	豪華的
73. sago pudding	西米布甸	95. magnificent	宏偉的
74. coconut milk with sago	椰汁西米露	96. hospitable	好客的
75. Malaysian sponge cake	馬拉糕	97. affluent	富裕的
		98. expensive	昂貴的
		99. popular	受歡迎的
		100. delicious	美味的
		101. order	點菜
		102. serve	接待

Robberies

 Sentences

1. Two robbers, armed with pistols, burst into a goldsmith's shop in Shanghai Street yesterday.

   兩個手持短鎗的劫匪昨天衝入上海街的一間金舖內。

2. They threatened the employees in the shop and ordered them to stand still.

   匪徒威嚇店員，命令他們站着不動。

3. The robbers were wearing blue denim jeans.

   匪徒當時穿着藍色牛仔褲。

4. One robber was of medium build while the other was of strong build.

   一個劫匪身材中等，而另一個則身體結實。

5. One of the robbers stood guard.

   其中一個劫匪把風。

6. Later, the robbers ordered the employees to squat.

   其後，匪徒命令店員蹲坐。

7. The robbers fired three shots, wounding two men.

   匪徒開了三鎗，擊傷了兩個男子。

8. One victim was hit by a bullet in the left shoulder.

   一位受害者的左肩被一發子彈擊中。

9. The robbers grabbed several trays of gold ornaments.

   匪徒攫取了數盤金飾。

10. They sped off in a getaway car.

    他們乘一輛偷來的車逃去。

11. The police are investigating the case.

    警方正調查該案。

12. The police appealed to the public to provide relevant information leading to the arrest of the robbers.

    警方呼籲公眾提供有關的資料以協助拘捕匪徒。

13. The injured were immediately admitted to Queen Elizabeth Hospital.

    傷者被立即送往伊利沙伯醫院。

14. In another robbery, a robber got away with watches worth more than $500,000.

在另一宗劫案中，一個匪徒搶走價值五十萬元的手錶。

15. It occurred at a shop selling watches in Tsim Sha Tsui.

這宗案件在尖沙嘴區的一間售賣手錶的商店發生。

16. The robber was wearing a pair of faded jeans and had a beard on his face.

匪徒身穿一條褪色的牛仔褲，面上有鬚。

17. He was also wearing a pair of sun-glasses.

他同時戴着一副太陽眼鏡。

18. Two shop assistants chased the robber after the incident.

事後兩位助理店員追趕劫匪。

19. The robber slipped once and fell on the road.

匪徒曾滑倒在路上。

20. The robber ran out of the shop hastily, holding a grey canvas bag.

匪徒匆匆拿着一個灰色的帆布袋走出商店。

21. He ran along Nathan Road towards Tsim Sha Tsui.

他沿着彌敦道走向尖沙嘴。

22. He disappeared at the junction of Nathan Road and Austin Road.

他在彌敦道與柯士甸道交界處消失。

23. The robber was wearing a mask.

匪徒戴上假面具。

24. No one was injured in the robbery.

劫案中無人受傷。

25. The third robbery took place on Hong Kong Island.

第三宗劫案在港島發生。

26. Two robbers robbed a bank in Central of six million dollars.

兩個匪徒在中區一間銀行劫走六百萬元。

27. The robbers pushed the customers against the wall.

劫匪把顧客推至牆邊。

28. They pointed a knife at the tellers.

他們用刀指向銀行櫃員。

29. The tellers were forced to hand over money and other valuables.

銀行櫃員被迫交出金錢及其他貴重物品。

30. One of the robbers had long hair which covered his ears and collars.

其中一個匪徒的頭髮長而直，遮蓋了他的耳朵及衣領。

31. The hair of another robber was parted in the middle and was quite short.

另一劫匪的頭髮較短，且中間分界。

32. The robbers held up the bank in broad daylight.	劫匪在光天化日下打劫銀行。
33. The guard of the bank disappeared at the time.	銀行的守衛員在那時候失了蹤。
34. All the customers in the main hall appeared to be scared.	大堂內所有的顧客都露出驚慌的神色。
35. The robbers were holding an airline bag.	匪徒當時手持一個航空公司的袋。
36. They escaped with one million dollars.	他們劫走一百萬元。
37. A fourth robbery happened in Sheung Shui in the New Territories.	第四宗劫案發生於新界上水。
38. An old woman was robbed of cash and other valuables to the total value of eight thousand dollars.	一個老婦被劫去總值八千元的現金及其他貴重物品。
39. The robber was a teenager.	劫匪是一個少年。
40. The old woman shouted for help after the incident.	事後那老婦高叫求助。
41. A policeman was patrolling there at the time.	時值一個警員在那處巡邏。
42. He rushed to the scene when he heard the old woman.	當他聽到老婦的聲音後便衝向肇事現場。
43. The policeman chased the robber and finally overtook him.	那警員追趕劫匪，最後追上了他。
44. The cash and valuables were immediately recovered.	那被劫去的現金及貴重物品即時被起回。
45. The teenager was taken to a police station for the investigation.	少年被帶往警署協助調查該案。
46. The old woman expressed her sincere thanks to the police constable.	老婦向那警員表示真摯的謝意。

Phrases

1. safety equipment	安全設備
2. armed robbery	持械行劫

3. "quick cash" crimes   迅速獲得現款的犯罪
4. law enforcement agencies   執法機關
5. statement from suspects   疑犯口供
6. photographic exhibits   照片證物
7. for presentation in court   作呈堂之用
8. current crime trends   最新的罪案趨勢
9. appeal to   呼籲
10. to detect crime   破案

 # Vocabulary

1.	cash	現金	16.	gunman	持鎗者
2.	ornaments	金飾	17.	goldsmith	金舖
3.	jewellery	珠寶	18.	bullet	子彈
4.	diamond necklace	鑽石項鍊	19.	ceiling	天花板
			20.	scout knife	童軍刀
5.	showcase	飾櫃	21.	hold-up	行劫
6.	counter	櫃位	22.	entrance	入口
7.	teller	櫃員	23.	pistol	手鎗
8.	witness	證人	24.	safe	夾萬
9.	robbers	劫匪	25.	glass pane	玻璃窗
10.	thug	匪徒	26.	victims	受害者
11.	burglary	入室偷盜罪	27.	alarm bell	警鐘
12.	detective constable	探員	28.	surveillance camera	防盜攝影機
13.	scene	現場	29.	scared	驚慌的
14.	T-shirt	T恤	30.	chase	追趕
15.	pavement	行人道	31.	struggle	糾纏

32.	report	報案	42.	crime information form	罪案資料郵束

32.	report	報案
33.	snatch	搶去
34.	flee	逃走
35.	raid	搜劫
36.	firearms	鎗械
37.	fingerprint	指模
38.	gang	匪幫
39.	video-tape	錄影帶
40.	re-enactments	案件重演／重組案情
41.	police telephone hotline	警方電話熱線

42.	crime information form	罪案資料郵束
43.	illegal	非法的
44.	law-abiding	奉公守法的
45.	identify	鑑證
46.	stand guard	守衛
47.	triangular file	三角鉎
48.	licensed number	車牌號碼

55

Scenic Spots in Hong Kong

Sentences

1.	Many local people and tourists visit the Ocean Park every year.	每年有很多本地人及遊客遊覽海洋公園。
2.	The Ocean Park is the world's largest oceanarium.	海洋公園是世界最大的海洋館。
3.	There are many varieties of marine life in the Ocean Park.	海洋公園內有種類繁多的海洋生物。
4.	Many visitors enjoy the dolphin show very much.	很多遊客非常欣賞海豚的表演。
5.	The dolphins perform acrobatic tricks to the delight of the spectators.	海豚表演奇藝，令觀眾看得十分開心。

6. Visitors also find it exciting to travel on the cable car.

遊客也對乘搭纜車感到十分刺激。

7. The wonderful sights of the Ocean Park will all come into view when a visitor takes a ride in a cable car.

遊客乘坐纜車時，海洋公園美妙的景色盡入眼簾。

8. The spectacular high diving performances often thrill the audience.

壯觀的跳水表演常令觀眾激動。

9. When special events take place, the Ocean Park will be especially crowded with visitors

當有特別表演項目的時候，海洋公園更見擠擁。

10. The Ocean Park plans to increase more facilities and attractions in the near future.

海洋公園計劃在不久的將來增設各種吸引遊客的設施及項目。

11. Visitors may get various pamphlets about the Ocean Park from the Information Centre.

遊客可以在諮詢中心獲得各種有關海洋公園的小冊子。

12. The Space Museum in Tsim Sha Tsui is another place worth visiting.

位於尖沙嘴的太空館是另一個值得遊覽的地方。

13. When visiting the Space Museum, people will have an opportunity to explore space.

當人們參觀太空館的時候，便有機會探索太空。

14. The Space Museum is equipped with solar telescopes and multi-lens planetarium projectors.

太空館內有太陽望遠鏡及多鏡星象投射器等設備。

15. The dome-shaped screen gives special effects to the films projected on it.

圓頂型的銀幕對所放射的電影有特別的效果。

16. The Space Museum provides visitors with information about life in the solar system.

太空館為觀眾提供了很多有關太陽系的生命的資料。

17. One of the aims of setting up the Space Museum is to arouse people's interest in solar science.

成立太空館目的之一是要引起人們對太空科學的興趣。

18. The exhibits in the exhibition hall are indeed very interesting and educational.

展覽館內的展品實在是十分有趣及富教育性。

19. The sky shows often attract a large audience.

太空表演常常吸引一大羣觀眾。

20. The Space Museum plays an important role in the study of astronomy in Hong Kong.

太空館在香港天文學的研究方面擔當一個重要的角色。

21. We can increase our knowledge and understanding about the universe by visiting the Space Museum.

我們通過參觀太空館，可以增加對宇宙的認識和了解。

22. The Victoria Peak commands a panoramic view of the whole city of Hong Kong.

從太平山頂可以看見整個香港市區的全貌。

23. The fine view of the Victoria Harbour has helped Hong Kong become a world famous tourist centre.

美麗的維多利亞港使香港成為一個世界知名的旅遊中心。

24. At Aberdeen, tourists can see many Chinese junks and sampans which constitute a very important part in the history of old Hong Kong.

在香港仔，遊客可見到中國式的帆船和舢板，它們構成了古老香港歷史的一個重要部分。

25. Tourists may also pay a visit to the Jumbo Floating Restaurant and taste the famous seafood there.

遊客也可到珍寶海鮮舫一遊，並且品嘗那裏著名的海鮮。

26. A sight-seeing cruise around Hong Kong Island is also recommended.

乘觀光船環繞香港島，也是值得推薦的。

27. There are not many places of historical interest in Hong Kong.

在香港，歷史古蹟不多。

28. Tourists may be interested in visiting the Imperial Terrace of the Sung Dynasty, the Lei Cheng Uk tomb and the Sun Yat-sen Historical Trail.

遊客可能會對參觀宋皇台、李鄭屋古墓及中山史蹟徑感到興趣。

29. The Tsim Sha Tsui Cultural Complex has become a centre of Hong Kong's cultural life.

尖沙嘴文化中心已成為香港文化生活的中心。

30. The Hong Kong Museum of History in Kowloon Park is also worth visiting.

九龍公園內的香港歷史博物館也值得參觀。

31. Many people visit the Buddhist Po Lin Monastery and the Ching Shan Monastery on holidays.

很多人在假日參觀佛教寶蓮寺及青山寺。

32. We can see many images of gods in these two places.

我們在這兩個地方可以看到很多佛像。

Phrases

1.	a breath-taking view	一個令人興奮的景象
2.	steep slope	峻峭的山坡
3.	Chinese paintings and calligraphy	中國畫及書法
4.	annual flower show	每年一次的花卉展覽
5.	a bird's eye view	鳥瞰
6.	to look at the scenery	瀏覽風景
7.	tourist resort area	旅遊勝地
8.	audio-visual devices	視聽器具
9.	marine life	海洋生物
10.	artificial waves	人造波浪
11.	suspended bridge	吊橋
12.	sun-bathing areas	日光浴地區
13.	Chinese landscaped gardens	中國式的園林花園
14.	martial art performance	武術表演
15.	white pagoda	白塔
16.	bronze statute of Buddha	銅佛像
17.	famous monuments	名勝古蹟
18.	an enchanting view	迷人的景致
19.	commemorative tablets	紀念碑
20.	world-class exhibition	世界級的展覽
21.	simulation experience	模擬經驗
22.	to take an exciting thrill ride	乘搭緊張刺激的快車

Vocabulary

1.	Ocean Park	海洋公園	4.	Ocean Theatre	海洋劇場
2.	oceanarium	海洋館	5.	dolphin show	海豚表演
3.	cable car	纜車	6.	sea seals	海豹

7.	sea lions	海獅	36.	film	電影
8.	penguins	企鵝	37.	model	模型
9.	killer whale	殺人鯨	38.	illustrations	圖片說明
10.	Wave Cove	浪濤館	39.	Ngong Ping Skyrail	昂平纜車
11.	Atoll Reef	珊瑚礁	40.	Wisdom Path	心經簡林
12.	aquarium	水族館	41.	Wetland Park	濕地公園
13.	novelties	新奇事物	42.	The Peak Tower	凌霄閣
14.	performance	表演	43.	Fung Ying Seen Koon	蓬瀛仙館
15.	spectators	觀眾	44.	Yuen Yuen Institution	圓玄學院
16.	auditorium	看台	45.	Stanley Market	赤柱市集
17.	Micky Mouse	米奇老鼠	46.	Ngong Ping Village	昂平市集
18.	Donald Duck	唐老鴨	47.	Chi Lin Nunnery	志蓮淨苑
19.	Disneyland	迪士尼樂園	48.	rockets	火箭
20.	Craft Village	工藝村	49.	satellite	衛星
21.	bumper cars	碰碰車	50.	planets	星球
22.	pendulum boat	搖擺船	51.	planetarium	星象廳
23.	puppet theatre	木偶劇場	52.	Tin Tan Buddha	天壇大佛
24.	Headland	山頂	53.	relics	歷史古蹟
25.	Space Museum	太空館	54.	images	肖像
26.	Space Theatre	太空劇場	55.	replicas	複製品
27.	exhibition hall	展覽廳	56.	antiquities	古物
28.	projector	放射器	57.	curios	古董
29.	telescope	望遠鏡	58.	costumes	民族服裝
30.	galaxy	銀河	59.	Waxworks Museum	蠟像館
31.	astronomy	天文學			
32.	universe	宇宙			
33.	space shuttle	太空穿梭機			
34.	astronaut	太空人			
35.	space suit	太空衣			

60.	ice rink	溜冰場	82. sight-seeing	觀光
61.	ice skating	溜冰	83. night stalls	夜攤
62.	Fool's Lookout	老襯亭	84. inshore	近岸的
63.	Arts Centre	藝術中心	85. sophisticated	精巧的
64.	Shouson Theatre	壽臣劇院	86. spectacular	壯觀的
			87. simulated	模擬的
65.	plays	話劇	88. fascinating	精彩的
66.	ballet	芭蕾舞	89. lively	栩栩如生的
67.	Aberdeen	香港仔	90. eye-catching	令人注目的
68.	seafood	海鮮	91. colourful	多姿多采的
69.	junk	帆船	92. applaud	喝采
70.	sampan	舢板	93. observe	觀察
71.	archaeology	考古學	94. display	陳列
72.	monument	紀念碑	95. depict	描述
73.	Kut Hing Village	吉慶圍	96. Tin Hau Temple	天后廟
74.	natives	當地人	97. Joss House Bay	大廟灣
75.	souvenir	紀念品	98. sights	風景
76.	Wong Tai Sin Temple	黃大仙廟	99. intriguing	引人入勝的
77.	Buddhist Po Lin Monastery	佛教寶蓮寺	100. Shark Aquarium	鯊魚館
78.	Ocean Terminal	海運大廈	101. Butterfly House	蝴蝶屋
79.	Lan Kwai Fong	蘭桂坊	102. thrill-ride	機動遊戲
80.	Discovery Bay	愉景灣	103. multi-sensory	多感官的
81.	holiday village	渡假村	104. unforgettable	難忘的

School Life

Sentences

1. A school is a society in miniature. 　學校是社會的縮影。

2. My school is like a big family. 　我的學校像是一個大家庭。

3. It is a very lively place. 　這是一個充滿生氣的地方。

4. The school is situated in Homantin. 　學校座落於何文田。

5. The transportation is convenient. 　交通方便。

6. The environment is very pleasant. 　環境十分優美。

7. It has a delightful campus. 　它有一個很可愛的校園。

8. The main building has five storeys and is able to hold over one thousand students. 　學校大樓有五層樓宇，可容納超過一千名學生。

9. Our school keeps academic and extra-curricular activities in balance. 　我校是學業與課外活動並行的。

10. We are encouraged to take part in more extra-curricular activities. 　學校鼓勵我們參加更多的課外活動。

11. There is a sufficient amount of books, magazines and scientific apparatuses and instruments to help our studies. 　學校有充足的圖書、雜誌及科學儀器幫助我們學習。

12. Many qualified and experienced teachers teach us. 　很多有豐富經驗的優良教師教導我們。

13. At school, we are educated to become a learned person. 　我們在學校接受教育，成為一個有學識的人。

14. The school cultivates us a clear and sound mind. 　學校培養我們有理智及健全的思想。

15. We are encouraged to develop more contacts with teachers and classmates. 　學校鼓勵我們多與老師及同學接觸。

16. Teachers and students are indeed closely related.

師生的關係十分密切。

17. We are fortunate enough to be nurtured by a group of dedicated teachers.

我們十分幸運，因為一羣獻身於教育的老師培育我們。

18. Teachers can shape our personality and temperament.

老師們能塑造我們的個性與性情。

19. Teachers are often referred to as the engineer of the human soul.

教師常被稱為人類靈魂的工程師。

20. They train students to think independently and adapt themselves to a changing society.

他們訓練學生獨立思考與適應社會轉變的能力。

21. At school, we learn many useful virtues which include punctuality, honesty, the best use of time, diligence, politeness and respect for others.

在學校，我們學習很多有用的美德，包括守時、誠實、善用時間、勤奮、禮貌及尊重別人。

22. The school provides training in leadership, co-operation, sports spirit and creativity.

學校給我們提供了領導能力、合作、體育精神及創造力等訓練。

23. It aims at cultivating all-round and well-balanced students.

它旨在培養全面及均衡發展的學生。

24. My school attaches a lot of importance to moral education.

我校對德育十分重視。

25. We are taught to accept challenges courageously.

學校教導我們要勇敢地接受挑戰。

26. We grasp the necessary skills for studies.

我們掌握學習所需要的技巧。

27. We develop knowledge and understanding of Hong Kong society.

我們認識及理解香港的社會。

28. We are taught to love others besides ourselves.

學校教導我們不但愛己而且愛人。

29. We learn to handle inter-personal relationships.

我們學習處理人際關係。

30. Teachers often tell us that a healthy mind lives in a healthy body.

老師常對我們說，健全的心智活在健康的身體裏。

31. We sometimes have an opportunity to render social service to the public.

我們有機會向公眾提供社會服務。

32. Our principal teaches us to stand for what is right and stick to the truth, even in times of temptation.

校長教導我們要堅守真理，抗拒誘惑。

33. On the whole, the influences of school life are healthy and good.

總的來說，學校生活的影響是健康及良好的。

34. Most of us look on our school life as a happy time.

我們大多數人都緬懷昔日在學校生活的歡樂時光。

35. We attend lessons regularly.

我們定時上課。

36. Some schoolmates take additional courses outside of school.

有些同學還在校外進修。

37. Our school holds a sports meeting annually.

我校每年舉行一次運動會。

38. We are very touched by the grand welcome ceremony.

我們被盛大的歡迎儀式所感動。

39. A wide variety of activities take place after classes.

種類繁多的活動在課餘時間舉行。

40. Many students are members of various school clubs and societies.

很多學生是學校各種學會的成員。

41. We have a school picnic each year and sometimes we visit factories and business organizations.

我們每年有一次學校大旅行，有時也參觀工廠和商業機構。

42. On the one hand, we are preparing for our future; on the other hand, we have a duty to the community.

一方面，我們為自己的前途作準備；另一方面，我們對於社會要盡責任。

43. The Speech Day is a very important day in the school calendar.

頒獎日是學校一個很重要的日子。

44. It is indeed a great privilege to receive a prize from the hands of the Guest of Honour.

從主禮嘉賓手上接受獎品實在是一件很榮幸的事。

45. Another important school function is the Open Day.

開放日是學校另一個重要的活動。

46. Teachers and students usually spend a long time preparing many articles for display at the Open Day.

師生通常要花很長時間預備很多的作業，以供開放日展覽之用。

47. We have a wide range of interests.

我們的興趣範圍很廣。

48. At school, we experience both happy and sad experiences.

在校內，我們經歷過愉快和痛苦的經驗。

49. Teachers disapprove of students' chatting during class.

老師不喜歡學生在上課時談話。

50. When recess comes, many schoolmates rush down the staircase.

小息時，很多同學急忙地衝下樓梯去。

51. Some students dash about the playground.

有些學生在操場上跑來跑去。

52. Occasionally, some classrooms of the lower forms are in a mess.

有時候，一些低年級的課室是一片混亂的。

53. Most students put great effort into studies.

大多數學生都盡力學習。

54. Many students in the lower forms find it difficult to learn through the medium of English.

很多低年級的學生對以英文作為學習的媒介感到困難。

55. School life is usually an unforgettable experience.

學校的生活常常是一個難忘的經驗。

56. It brings us many sweet memories.

它帶給我們很多甜蜜的回憶。

57. We hear a lot of laughter on the campus.

在校園內，我們可聽到很多歡笑聲。

58. A balanced education should include moral education, intellectual growth, physical education, social development and aesthetic education.

一個均衡的教育應包括德、智、體、羣、美五育。

59. Our school always places equal emphasis on each of these five aspects of education.

我校對這五育均同樣重視。

60. At school we benefit from a solid, general education.

學校的基礎通識教育使我們受益。

61. We can develop our ability to observe, analyse and integrate.

我們可以發展觀察、分析及綜合的能力。

62. Many students usually pay close attention to important current affairs.

很多學生常常密切留意目前社會發生的重大事件。

63. Some students do not understand the significance of self-discipline.

有些學生不明白自律的重要。

64. There is a lack of self-initiated learning among our schoolmates.

我校同學缺乏自發的學習精神。

65. Most schoolmates depend very much on the teachers to obtain academic knowledge.

在獲取學業上的知識方面，大多數同學都是十分依賴老師的。

66. The discipline in our school is quite strict.

我校的紀律頗為嚴厲。

67. Schoolmates will be punished for being late for school.

同學會因遲到上課而被罰。

68. Some classmates become intimate friends during their time at school.

一些同班同學在求學期間成為了知己朋友。

69. When examinations come, students have to work hard and pass the examinations; otherwise, they may not be promoted.

考試來臨時，學生必須勤加溫習以求考試合格；否則，他們不能升級。

70. Many students prefer a school life without examinations.

很多學生較喜歡一個沒有考試的學校生活。

71. However, it is impossible in Hong Kong.

然而，這在香港是不可能的。

72. When our schoolmates have any trouble, they can talk to the school social worker.

當我校同學有任何困難時，他們可與學校社會工作者傾談。

73. Student guidance and counselling work is being expanded in our school.

我校的學生輔導工作正在擴展中。

74. Our schoolmates are required to be familiar with and observe the school regulations.

學校要求同學熟悉及遵守校規。

75. If we always use our minds, we can make remarkable progress in our studies.

如果我們時常用腦思考，學業便能有顯著的進步。

76. Many schoolmates are often too lazy to use their minds.

很多同學常常懶於用腦筋思考事物。

77. During lunch hour, some schoolmates take their lunch at a nearby shop which sells Shanghainese food.

在午膳時間，有些同學到學校附近的一間上海食品店吃午餐。

78. Our school holds an annual bazaar on campus to raise funds for charity.

我校每年在校園舉行一次慈善賣物會。

79. Apart from the items for sale, there are usually some games stalls.

除了出售的物品，通常也有一些遊戲攤位。

80. Flying flags with bright colours make that day spectacular.

飄揚的彩旗使當天充滿了熱鬧的氣氛。

81. A variety show is often held before the Christmas holidays.   在聖誕假前，我校常舉行一個綜合遊藝大會。

82. The highlight is the plays presented by students.   最令人矚目的是學生的話劇表演。

83. The audience often exclaim, "What a show!"   觀眾常驚叫：「表演真精采！」

84. The Chinese dance performance also wins acclaim from the schoolmates.   中國舞蹈表演也贏得同學的喝采。

85. Many schoolmates do not want to miss all the excitement.   很多同學不願錯過這熱鬧的場面。

86. In these functions, many students gain experience in organizing extra-curricular activities.   在這些活動中，很多學生獲得了組織課外活動的經驗。

87. Some of them show leadership qualities.   其中有些同學表現出領導的才能。

88. On the whole, school life is enjoyable.   總括來說，學校生活是令人愉快的。

 Phrases

1. in comfort   舒適地

2. in high spirits   情緒高漲

3. in a great hurry   太匆忙

4. leave of absence   准假

5. to jeer at   恥笑

6. the most important characteristic   最重要的特點

7. stumbling block   障礙物

8. sense of responsibility   責任感

9. to manage a grin   強顏微笑

10. indomitable spirit   不屈不撓的精神

11. conducive to creation   有利於創作

12. to feel nostalgic   懷舊

13. to take the initiative   採取主動

14. to gain exposure   獲得接觸社會的機會

15. to try all out   全力以赴

16. to behave oneself   守規矩

17. to ask for leave   請假

18. to go to class   上課

19. to get out of class   下課

20. to continue improving   精益求精

21. with half the effort to achieve double results   事半功倍

 ## Vocabulary

1.	campus	校園	15. Discipline Master	訓導主任
2.	playground	運動場	16. Careers Master	職業輔導主任
3.	basketball court	籃球場	17. form-master/mistress	班主任
4.	football field	足球場	18. prefect	領袖生
5.	hall	禮堂	19. monitor/monitress	班長
6.	library	圖書館	20. schoolmates	同學
7.	tuck shop	小食部	21. graduates	畢業生
8.	canteen	食堂	22. Class Association	班會
9.	corridor	走廊	23. Students' Union	學生會
10.	laboratory	實驗室	24. house	社
11.	staff room	教員室	25. School Choir	合唱團
12.	Principal	校長	26. Drama Club	戲劇學會
13.	Vice Principal	副校長		
14.	Prefect of Studies	教務主任		

27. Bridge Club	橋牌學會	50. masquerade	化妝舞會
28. English Society	英文學會	51. celebrations	紀念活動
29. Science Society	科學學會	52. school picnic	學校旅行
30. school precepts	校訓	53. essay contest	作文比賽
31. school regulations	校規	54. penmanship contest	書法比賽
32. school spirit	學校精神	55. English debate	英語辯論
33. tradition	傳統	56. speech contest	演講比賽
34. school song	校歌	57. singing contest	歌唱比賽
35. school uniform	校服	58. drama competition	戲劇比賽
36. school emblem	校章	59. volleyball match	排球比賽
37. school magazine	校刊	60. tug-of-war	拔河
38. school newspaper	校報	61. proceeds	收益
39. Speech Day	頒獎日	62. graduation	畢業
40. Open Day	開放日	63. future	前途
41. extra-curricular activities	課外活動	64. drawer	抽屜
42. Sports Day	陸運會	65. mischief	惡作劇
43. Swimming Gala	水運會	66. bookworms	書獃子
44. charity bazaar	慈善賣物會	67. defect/ shortcoming	缺點
45. visit	參觀訪問	68. merit	優點
46. variety show	綜合表演	69. honours	榮譽
47. dance	舞蹈	70. homework	家課
48. play	話劇	71. features	特點
49. Games Day	遊戲日	72. alma mater	母校
		73. welfare	福利
		74. self-confidence	自信心

75.	reference books	參考書
76.	stage	舞台
77.	friendship	友誼
78.	co-operation	合作
79.	jokes	笑話
80.	laughter	笑聲
81.	rehearsal	彩排
82.	romance	浪漫史
83.	time-tunnel	時光隧道
84.	snackery	小食店
85.	snacks	點心
86.	lunch box	午餐盒
87.	syllabus	課程
88.	concepts	概念
89.	principles	原理
90.	examination	考試
91.	views/ideas	意見
92.	motion	辯論題目
93.	blood donation	捐血
94.	drive	魄力
95.	initiative	進取精神
96.	discipline	紀律
97.	detention	留堂
98.	sick leave	病假
99.	mischievous	頑皮的
100.	energetic	活潑的
101.	unselfish	不自私的
102.	honest	誠實的
103.	punctual	準時的
104.	studious	勤奮好學的
105.	competent	能幹的
106.	thought-provoking	激發思考的
107.	polite	有禮貌的
108.	participate	參加
109.	scold/reproach	責罵
110.	praise	讚賞
111.	stimulate	鼓勵
112.	motivate	激發
113.	acquire	掌握
114.	analyse	分析
115.	nourish	培育
116.	enlighten	啟發
117.	inattentive	不留心
118.	discouraged	氣餒
119.	make-up examination	補考
120.	co-educational school	男女校
121.	variety show	綜合表演
122.	fast food shop	快餐店
123.	co-operative society	合作社
124.	social service	社會服務
125.	school ethos	校風

Science: Its Benefits and Evils

 Sentences

1. Scientific invention has caused a great change in the mode of life of most people in the world.

    科學上的發明使世界大部分人的生活方式有巨大的改變。

2. Thanks to modern inventions, people's lifestyles have greatly improved.

    感謝近代的發明品，人類的生活已有很大的改善。

3. The application of scientific knowledge influences our daily life in many ways.

    科學知識的應用在很多方面影響我們的日常生活。

4. The progress of science has far-reaching consequences in all walks of life.

    科學的進步對各階層人士的生活都有深遠的影響。

5. It cannot be denied that technological advance has brought us a much better and easier life than we have ever dreamt of.

    無可否認，科技的進步已帶給我們較好的及舒適的生活，這些都是我們從未夢想到的。

6. Scientific advances greatly raise our standard of living and bring us material enjoyment.

    科學的進步大大提高我們的生活水準，帶給我們物質上的享受。

7. Science saves us a lot of trouble and time.

    科學給我們節省了很多麻煩與時間。

8. It also provides different kinds of amusement, enjoyment and luxury.

    它也提供了各種不同的娛樂、享受及奢華。

9. We should be grateful to medical advancement and invention for they have prevented the spread of diseases.

    我們應該感謝醫學上的進步與發明，因為它們防止了病菌的傳播。

10. Labour-saving and time-saving home appliances, like automatic washing and cooking machines, are products of science.

    省時省力的家庭電器用品如自動洗衣機及烹飪機器，都是科學的產物。

11. Agriculture also benefits from science as better methods have been devised for both cultivation and the controlling of diseases.

農業也從科學中受益，因為通過科學，人們改良耕種及控制病害的方法。

12. We have turned over a new leaf having entered the computer age.

進入電腦時代，使我們翻開新的一頁。

13. The invention of computers is a sign of scientific progress.

電腦的發明是科學進步的標誌。

14. The increasing use of computers and the constantly improved electronic data processing techniques have brought revolutionary changes to our daily life.

電腦應用的擴大及不斷改進的電子資料處理技術已給我們的日常生活帶來了革命性的改變。

15. The development of scientific knowledge enables us to understand and master nature for the benefit of man.

科學知識的發展使我們明白及主宰自然，為全人類帶來了利益。

16. Scientists often do research in an attempt to explain the world around us.

科學家常做研究工作，嘗試解釋環繞我們的世界。

17. Science in itself is innocent but, when it is wrongly used, its destructive power is uncontrollable and terrible.

科學本身是無罪的，但它被人用在錯誤的地方時，它的毀滅力量是難於控制和可怕的。

18. Atomic energy can be used to generate electricity.

原子能可用以發電。

19. At the same time, it can also destroy thousands of lives in a split second.

與此同時，它也可以在不及一秒的時間內，毀滅成千上萬的生命。

20. Scientific knowledge may also be applied to the mass production of other fatal weapons.

科學知識也可應用於大規模生產其他致命的武器上。

21. The armaments race among the superpowers has reached a critical stage.

超級大國間的軍備競賽已到了嚴重的階段。

22. The possibility of an outbreak of disastrous nuclear war cannot be ruled out.

我們不能排除發生災難性核子戰爭的可能性。

23. Many people are unaccustomed to the radical changes brought about by the advancement of science and technology.

很多人不習慣於科技進步所帶來的過激的改變。

24. They find themselves in a state of constant oppression both in mind and body.

他們發覺自己處於一個身心經常受到壓制的狀態。

25. In fact, living in an era of science, we are far from a natural placid life.

事實上，在科學的時代裏生活，我們遠離自然平靜的生活。

26. As a result, some people may suffer from mental illness or a nervous breakdown.

結果，一些人可能因此患上精神病或神經衰弱症。

27. Interpersonal relationships have not been given the attention they deserve.

人際關係並沒有受到應有的重視。

28. There is often a lack of communication and consultation between management and staff in the present scientific period.

在現今的科學時代裏，勞資雙方經常缺乏溝通與諮商。

29. When we weigh up the situation, however, we find that science has more advantages than disadvantages.

然而當我們考慮一切情形後，我們發覺科學利多於弊。

30. If progress in science is being used to serve good purposes, it can indeed be a great blessing to mankind.

假如科學的進步被用在好的方面，它實在是人類莫大之福。

Phrases

1. space exploration — 太空探險

2. scientific method — 科學的方法

3. to find the truth — 尋求真理

4. to draw a conclusion — 得出結論

5. destructive weapons — 破壞性的武器

6. mechanical instruments — 機械器具

7. electrical devices — 電器用品

8. household chores — 家庭雜務

9. electronic data interchange — 電子數據聯通

10. to curb the amount of paperwork — 減低商業文件數量

11. to improve efficiency — 提高工作效率

12. electronic trading — 電子貿易

13. disseminate information   傳播資訊

14. sensitive information   敏感資料

15. involving personal privacy   涉及個人私隱

16. satellite communication   衛星通訊

17. technological advancement   科技進步

18. personal communication services   個人通訊服務

19. instant photography   即影即有

20. technical know-how   專業技術

21. electronic data processing   電子數據處理

22. information superhighway   資訊超級公路

23. in line with   配合

24. to access to on-line information   取得聯機資料

25. user friendly   易於應用

26. to hook up to the internet   上網

27. to surf the internet   瀏覽互聯網

Vocabulary

1.	convenience	方便	11.	destruction	毀滅
2.	comfort	舒適	12.	motor cars	汽車
3.	speed	速度	13.	steamers	輪船
4.	efficiency	效率	14.	scientists	科學家
5.	communications	通訊	15.	Mass Transit Railway (MTR)	港鐵
6.	transport	運輸			
7.	telegraph	電報	16.	blessing	幸福
8.	computer	電腦	17.	facilities	設備
9.	medicine	醫藥	18.	benefits	利益
10.	diseases	疾病			

19.	evils	壞處
20.	stress	壓力
21.	mechanization	機械化
22.	automation	自動化
23.	missiles	導彈
24.	rockets	火箭
25.	anxiety	憂慮
26.	employment	就業
27.	entertainments	娛樂
28.	observation	觀察
29.	measurement	測量
30.	experiment	實驗
31.	survey	調查
32.	theory	理論
33.	devotion	專注
34.	regrettable	令人遺憾的
35.	fancy	想像
36.	realize	實現
37.	misuse	誤用
38.	adapt	適應
39.	encounter	遭遇
40.	homepage	網頁
41.	PC compatible	兼容機
42.	programme	程式
43.	word-processing	文字處理
44.	data base	數據庫

45.	on-line	聯機
46.	spread sheet	電子試算表
47.	random access memory (RAM)	隨機存取記憶體
48.	supersonic transport (SST)	運輸機
49.	intercom	對講機
50.	floppy disk	軟磁碟
51.	icons	小畫像
52.	cursor	游標
53.	printer	打印機
54.	code	代碼
55.	modem	調解器
56.	world wide web	全球資訊網
57.	teleshopping	電子購物
58.	information technology (IT)	資訊科技
59.	floppy drive	磁碟機
60.	CD ROM	電腦唯讀儲存器
61.	VCD player	影碟機
62.	DVD player	數碼影碟機
63.	Web TV	網路電視
64.	Video on demand	自選電視
65.	digital camera	數碼相機
66.	interactive	互動式的

67.	state-of-the-art	最先進的	76.	mobile telephone	流動電話
68.	liquid crystal display (LCD)	液晶顯示	77.	electronic mailbox (e-mail)	電子郵箱
69.	nuclear age	核子時代	78.	video-conferencing	視像會議
70.	atomic energy	原子能			
71.	atomic bombs	原子彈	79.	artificial intelligence	人工智能
72.	nuclear electricity plants	核子發電廠	80.	international direct dial (IDD)	國際直線電話
73.	environmental pollution	環境污染			
74.	man-made satellite	人造衛星	81.	automatic teller machine	自動出納機
75.	supersonic jets	超音速飛機	82.	web site	網址／網站

58

Shopping Mall

Sentences

1. Shopping centres are mostly opened in a big commercial complex.

   購物中心一般開設在大型商業大廈內。

2. Usually they occupy the ground floor and many other floors.

   購物中心通常連地下舖，並佔用多層樓面。

3. They are mostly located in districts with many people passing by.

   它們一般座落於行人眾多的地區。

4. The shops in the small shopping centres are usually small and there are shops of different kinds.

   在小型商場的店舖一般細小，各行各業都有。

5. Large shopping centres are spacious and the decoration is luxurious.

大型購物中心地方寬敞而裝修豪華。

6. Most shops sell products of famous brands.

店舖多銷售名牌產品。

7. There are many people in the shopping centre but the majority are just doing window shopping.

商場內有很多人，但絕大部分是看而不買的。

8. Window shopping in the shopping centre is one of the daily routine programmes.

逛商場廚窗是日常節目之一。

9. Shops in the big or small shopping centres sell boutiques and next ornaments.

店舖不論在大型或小型商場，以售買時裝佔最多，其次是裝飾品。

10. There are also shops selling food.

那裏也有賣食品的店舖。

11. For the sake of convenience of customers, there must be fast food shops and food courts of various kinds in the shopping centre.

為方便顧客休息及進食，商場內必有各類快餐店及食肆。

12. Shopping centres always organize cultural and entertainment activities to attract customers.

商場不時舉辦各種文娛活動，以吸引顧客。

13. They also organize commodities exhibition frequently.

商場亦常舉辦商品展覽。

14. The decoration of the new shopping centres is getting more and more luxurious.

新商場裝修日趨豪華。

15. That urges the old shopping centres to re-decorate so as not to be lagged behind.

這樣促使舊的商場亦重新裝修，以免落後。

16. The shopping centres welcome leases from famous brands, fast food shops and restaurants to enhance the fame of the centres.

商場歡迎名牌商店及食肆租用，以提高其知名度。

17. Well-known shops also wish to make use of the prime location and facilities of the centre to attract more customers to increase their occupancy rate of the market.

著名商號亦希望以租用商場的優勝位置與設施，吸引更多顧客，以擴大其市場佔有率。

Phrases

1.	pay by cheque	以支票付款
2.	pay by cash	以現金付款
3.	pay by credit card	以信用卡支付（碌卡）
4.	buy two get one free	買二送一
5.	duty free	免稅
6.	household utensils	家庭用具
7.	innovative design	創新設計
8.	in abundance	大量
9.	prompt delivery of goods	立即送貨
10.	luxurious decoration	豪華裝修
11.	to wear jewellery	戴珠寶
12.	crowds of people	人羣
13.	to line up	排隊
14.	for the sake of	為了
15.	to lag behind	落後
16.	king size	特大碼
17.	fashion model	時裝模特兒

Vocabulary

1.	durable	耐用	7.	souvenir	紀念品
2.	discount	折扣	8.	logo	專用標記
3.	sale	大減價	9.	boutique	時裝店
4.	size	尺碼	10.	cashier	收銀員
5.	coupon	贈券	11.	sofa	沙發
6.	gift	禮物	12.	rucksack	帆布背包

13. shoplifting	高買	38. salesman / saleswoman	售貨員
14. shopkeeper	店員	39. front-line staff	前線職員
15. promotion	推廣	40. Greater China Region	大中華區
16. invoice	發票	41. lucky draw	幸運抽獎
17. receipt	收據	42. shoppers' paradise	購物者天堂
18. escalator	自動扶梯	43. flagship store	旗艦店
19. refrigerator	冰箱	44. warranty card	保用卡
20. customers	顧客	45. food court	美食廣場
21. location	位置	46. air-conditioner	空調
22. majority	大部分	47. sports shoes	運動鞋
23. stationery	文具	48. commercial complex	商業大廈
24. pharmacy	藥房	49. washing machine	洗衣機
25. receptionist	接待	50. twin-bed	雙人牀
26. toys	玩具	51. single-bed	單人牀
27. bank	銀行	52. bedside table	牀側小几
28. bakery	麵包店	53. swimming costume	游泳衣
29. clinic	診所	54. digital camera	數碼相機
30. electronic apppliances	電器用品	55. entertainment	娛樂
31. men's wear	男裝	56. department store	百貨公司
32. women's wear	女裝	57. jewellery shop	珠寶首飾店
33. children's wear	童裝	58. book store	書店
34. trade mark	注冊商標	59. ice rink	溜冰場
35. security guard	保安人員	60. off-course betting centre	場外投注站
36. vacuum cleaner	真空吸塵機		
37. vacuum flask	熱水瓶		

59

Social Gathering

Sentences

1. Social gathering is a way of life.　　　　社交聚會是一種生活方式。

2. It is an occasion for making friends with others.　　　　它是一個交友的場合。

3. It further improves the relations among friends.　　　　它進一步改善朋友間的關係。

4. The happy atmosphere is conducive to mutual understanding among friends.　　　　歡樂的氣氛有助朋友間相互的了解。

5. Many business deals are concluded at social gatherings.　　　　很多商業交易在社交聚會中完成。

6. People gather together to have a friendly talk.　　　　人們聚集在一起友好地交談。

7. People attending a social gathering usually stand in groups chatting with their friends.　　　　出席社交聚會的人通常站在一小羣人中，與他們的朋友閒談。

8. Different kinds of drinks are often served at a social gathering.　　　　在一個社交聚會中，常常有不同種類的飲品供應。

9. People hold their glasses in their hands.　　　　人們拿着玻璃杯。

10. Some people thread their way amongst the crowd.　　　　有些人在人羣中穿插。

11. Social functions are suitable for people from all walks of life.　　　　社交活動適合各行各業的人。

12. A congenial atmosphere usually prevails at social gatherings.　　　　社交聚會通常充滿適意愉快的氣氛。

13. Many people get to know their friends on social occasions.　　　　很多人在社交場合中結識了朋友。

14. Many people are not willing to miss the chance of attending a social gathering.

很多人不願意錯過參加社交聚會的機會。

15. They may meet their future girl-friends at a social gathering.

他們可能在一個社交聚會中遇上將來的女友。

16. Wedding ceremonies usually take place at marriage registries.

結婚儀式通常在婚姻註冊署內舉行。

17. Wedding dinners are usually held at restaurants.

婚宴常在酒樓裏舉行。

18. A wedding dinner is sometimes a very lavish affair.

婚宴有時是一個十分鋪張的場面。

19. Many beautifully-dressed ladies attend a wedding dinner.

很多盛裝的女士出席一個婚宴。

20. The bride is particularly beautiful and charming at the time.

新娘在那時候特別顯得漂亮迷人。

21. Those attending the wedding dinner express their heartiest congratulations and best wishes to the bride and the bridegroom.

出席婚宴的人向新娘新郎表示他們最衷心的祝賀。

22. At a birthday party, guests usually wish the hostess a happy birthday.

在一個生日會上，客人通常祝賀女主人生辰快樂。

23. They all wish her many happy returns of the day.

他們恭祝她年年有今日，歲歲有今朝。

24. They express their warm congratulations to the hostess on the occasion.

他們對女主人的壽辰表示熱烈的祝賀。

25. They send her their greetings.

他們對她表示祝賀之意。

26. Social dancing is very popular at cocktail parties.

社交舞在雞尾酒會中是很受歡迎的。

27. A cocktail is usually made with a shaker.

雞尾酒一般是用調酒器調製的。

28. People toast their achievements at a cocktail party.

在雞尾酒會中，人們舉杯祝賀他們的成就。

29. Gentlemen usually fetch their female partners to attend a dancing party.

紳士常接他們的女伴去出席舞會。

30. At a tea party, the host extends a hearty welcome to his guests.

在茶會中，主人對客人致衷心的歡迎。

31. Guests are often asked to help themselves to the snacks and other food.

主人常請客人隨意吃點心和其他食品。

32. This is especially so on the occasion of a buffet dinner.

這在自助晚餐的場合中尤其如此。

33. The guests also thank the host for his invitation to the party when they leave.

客人臨走前，也對主人邀請其出席宴會表示謝意。

34. It is often true that courtesy costs nothing.

禮多人不怪，這往往是對的。

35. A farewell party is usually in honour of a person.

告別會通常是為某一個人而舉行的。

36. Sometimes, a farewell party leaves the participants with an unforgettable impression.

有時一個告別會給參加者留下難忘的印象。

37. People bid farewell to the person honoured by the party.

人們向告別宴會的主角告別。

38. Sometimes employers of leading companies may hold a dinner party and take the opportunity to thank their employees for their hard work and dedication to the organization.

有時大公司的僱主會舉行一個晚宴，藉此感謝僱員的辛勤工作及對公司的貢獻。

39. A social gathering is distinctive from a private meeting.

社交聚會不同於私人聚會。

40. At a social gathering, proprieties must be observed by all the participants.

在社交聚會中，所有的參加者必須遵守禮儀。

 **Phrases**

1. on that occasion 　　　　　　　在該場合

2. sincerest congratulations 　　　最真摯的祝賀

3. as a token of thanks 　　　　　聊表謝意

4. with great pleasure 　　　　　　非常樂意

5. personal achievement 　　　　　個人的成就

6. to make an appointment 　　　　約會

7. to say good-bye to 　　　　　　道別

8. to pay respect to a person 　　　向某人致意

9. to thank profoundly 表示衷心的謝忱

 Vocabulary

1.	cocktail party	雞尾酒會	23.	entertainments	餘興
2.	birthday party	生日會	24.	compliments	讚美
3.	tea party	茶會	25.	marriage	結婚
4.	dinner party	晚餐會	26.	recognition	賞識
5.	garden party	園遊會	27.	promotion	擢升
6.	Christmas party	聖誕聯歡會	28.	dignitaries	知名人士
7.	masquerade/ fancy ball	化妝舞會	29.	businessmen	商人
8.	farewell party	告別聚會	30.	professionals	專業人士
9.	banquet	晚宴	31.	casual	非正式的
10.	wedding dinner	婚宴	32.	sociable	善交際的
11.	host	主人	33.	delightful	愉快的
12.	guests	客人	34.	generous	慷慨的
13.	sofa	沙發	35.	unavoidable	不可避免的
14.	coffee tables	咖啡枱	36.	introduce	介紹
15.	trays	托盆	37.	congratulate	祝賀
16.	beer	啤酒	38.	deserve	應得
17.	champagne	香檳酒	39.	promote	促進
18.	presents	禮物	40.	social affairs/ social appointments	社交事務／應酬
19.	evening dress	晚禮服			
20.	cuisine	菜餚	41.	grand ceremony	盛會
21.	invitation card	邀請卡			
22.	engagement	約會	42.	Queen's English	標準英語

Sports and Games

Sentences

1. Physical exercise is necessary for health.	運動是健康所必需的。
2. It improves our general health.	它能增進我們身體的健康。
3. Swimming, for example, exercises all the muscles of the body.	例如游泳能運動全身肌肉。
4. Jogging and cycling are also good forms of exercise.	緩步跑及騎自行車也是良好的運動。
5. Physical exercise can strengthen our muscles and keep us fit.	運動可加強我們的肌肉，使我們身體健康強壯。
6. There are various types of sport.	運動有多種。
7. Outdoor sports include horse-racing, shooting and hunting.	戶外運動包括賽馬、射擊和打獵。
8. These sports require a lot of strength.	這些運動需要很多氣力。
9. Very often, poor physique is largely due to the lack of exercise.	很多時候，羸弱的體格主要是缺少運動所致。
10. Running and jumping are examples of athletic sports.	賽跑、跳高及跳遠是體育運動的例子。
11. Athletics can make us strong and energetic.	體育運動能使我們強壯而有力。
12. Through athletics, our physical potentials can be developed to the fullest extent.	通過體育運動，我們身體上的潛能可得到最大的發展。
13. Those taking part in sport should cultivate good sportsmanship.	參加運動者應培養良好體育精神。
14. The spirit of sport must be promoted.	必須提倡體育精神。

15. Winning a prize should not be the sole aim of participation in sport.

贏取一項獎品不應是參與運動會的唯一目標。

16. Athletes must appreciate the sporting spirit and avoid getting into a temper.

運動員須重視體育精神而避免鬧脾氣。

17. In recent years, the Government has attached much importance to athletic sport.

近年政府對體育運動十分重視。

18. Some modern and well-equipped stadiums have been built.

政府已興建了一些現代化及設施良好的體育館。

19. They include the Queen Elizabeth Stadium in Wan Chai, the Hung Hom Indoor Stadium and the Jubilee Sports Centre in Shatin.

它們包括灣仔伊利沙伯體育館、紅磡室內運動場及沙田銀禧體育中心。

20. The Inter-Schools Athletic Contest takes place in Hong Kong annually.

香港每年舉行一次學界陸運會。

21. There is a 400-metre all-weather running track.

那裏有一條四百米全天候跑道。

22. The field sport facilities are also up to world standards.

田賽運動方面的設備也達到世界水準。

23. Many records are broken every year.

每年都有很多紀錄被打破。

24. The cross-country race is a good test of perseverance.

越野賽是對毅力的一個很好的考驗。

25. The 100-metre sprint is very spectacular.

一百米短跑十分精彩。

26. Very often, it is a close match.

很多時候，這是一項雙方實力十分接近的比賽。

27. In the Marathon, some athletes may lead all the way.

在馬拉松長跑中，有些運動員可能一直領先。

28. Many athletes try their utmost to overtake their opponents.

很多運動員盡最大的努力去追及他們的對手。

29. Athletes usually do warm-up exercises before a match.

運動員通常在比賽前做熱身運動。

30. In the field, athletes throw a discus or javelin.

在田賽場上，運動員擲鐵餅或標槍。

31. All the spectators go into wide cheers when they see an athlete pass over the jumping-bar.

當目睹一個運動員越過橫桿時，所有觀眾都瘋狂地喝采。

32. When all the events are over, the presentation ceremony begins.

當所有項目完畢時，頒獎典禮便告開始。

33. Many winning athletes will receive their prizes from the honour platform.

優勝的運動員會在頒獎台上領獎。

34. Ball games teach us a sense of teamwork.

球類比賽教導我們團體精神的意義。

35. Football is one of the most popular games in Hong Kong.

足球是香港最受歡迎的球賽之一。

36. The World Cup Football Matches, which are broadcast live through man-made satellites, often receive tremendous enthusiasm from fans throughout the world.

用人造衛星直接現場傳播的世界盃賽事一直受到世界球迷的熱愛。

37. A match between two strong teams is often a tough struggle.

兩強相遇的賽事往往有一番惡鬥。

38. The spectators' stand is filled to capacity.

觀眾台上擠滿了人。

39. Not a vacant seat for an additional spectator exists.

觀眾席座無虛設。

40. When a match does not start on schedule, the audience will get restless.

比賽不依時開場，會引起觀眾鼓噪。

41. The footballers leave the field and take a rest after the first half.

半場賽事完畢，足球員離場休息。

42. A football team with sporting spirit will sincerely congratulate their triumphant opponent.

具體育精神的球隊會向獲勝的對方致以真誠的祝賀。

43. The match was played at Hong Kong Stadium.

比賽在香港大球場舉行。

44. South China opened the score first in the 21st minute.

開場二十一分鐘，南華首開紀錄。

45. That was a brilliant volley.

那是一個漂亮的射球。

46. Two footballers hugged each other.

兩位足球員互相擁抱。

47. The hero was held up.

球員把英雄抬起。

48. The South China supporters waved their flags and banners wildly.

南華的支持者瘋狂地搖着他們的旗幟和橫額。

49. After losing a score, Manchester United launched a series of counter-attacks.

曼聯失去了一球後，發動一連串的反攻。

50. Manchester United scored the equalizer in the last minute.

曼聯在最後一分鐘射入打成平手的一球。

51. A crowd of excited spectators cried out immediately.

一羣緊張的觀眾頓時高叫起來。

52. The referee blew the whistle and the match came to an end.

球證吹銀笛，球賽終結。

53. In a basketball match, the court is often filled with an atmosphere of suspense.

在一場籃球比賽中，球場通常充滿緊張的氣氛。

54. The players wear shorts for easy movement.

球員為了方便走動而穿着短褲。

55. They scramble for the ball.

他們互相爭球。

56. Accurate shooting is very important.

準確的射球是十分重要的。

57. The captain successfully scored a goal, to the delight of a cheering crowd.

隊長成功地射入漂亮的一球，球迷喜極歡呼。

58. Spectators often appreciate smart shots.

觀眾一向欣賞漂亮的射球。

59. All the players must observe the rules of a match.

球員必須遵守球賽的規則。

60. The electric signboard indicates the scores obtained by the two teams.

電子計分牌顯示兩隊入球的紀錄。

Phrases

1. vivid and interesting

生動有趣

2. grass soccer pitch

草地足球場

3. artificial turf

人工草地

4. international standards

國際水準

5. audience's reaction

觀眾的反應

6. spirit of sportsmanship

體育精神

7. a cut-and-thrust contest

激烈的比賽

8.	to make a clean sweep	大獲全勝
9.	many and varied	各式各樣的
10.	to organize training courses	舉辦訓練課程
11.	sporting competitions	體育比賽
12.	for people of all ages and abilities	為不同年齡及體能的人士
13.	additional resources	增加資源撥款
14.	regular practice	定期練習
15.	frequent competitions	經常比賽
16.	to encourage and promote sporting activities	鼓勵和推廣體育活動
17.	camping excursions	露營旅行
18.	through active participation	透過踴躍參與
19.	to develop the skill	發揮技能
20.	to share the fun	分享樂趣
21.	to appreciate human relationships	體察人際關係

 # Vocabulary

1.	gymnastics	健身操	10.	sprint	短跑
2.	gymnasium	體操場館	11.	100 metres dash	一百米賽跑
3.	physique	體格			
4.	trampolining	跳彈網	12.	4 x 100 metres relay	四乘一百米接力
5.	cycling	騎自行車（踩單車）	13.	track	跑道
6.	stadium	體育館	14.	distance run	長距離跑
7.	heats	初賽	15.	marathon (42.2 km)	馬拉松長跑（42.2 千米）
8.	semi-finals	準決賽	16.	starter	發令員
9.	finals	決賽	17.	pistol	鎗

18. shot put	推鉛球
19. discus throw	擲鐵餅
20. long-jump	跳遠
21. high-jump	跳高
22. pole-vaulting	持桿跳高
23. field events	田賽項目
24. track events	徑賽項目
25. boxing	拳擊
26. fencing	劍擊
27. judo	柔道
28. canoeing	獨木舟
29. archery	射箭
30. champion shield	冠軍盾
31. trophy	獎盃
32. medal	獎牌
33. overall championship	全場總冠軍
34. Olympic Games	奧林匹克運動會
35. arena	競技場
36. stands	看台
37. spectators	觀眾
38. friendship	友誼
39. participation	參與
40. honours	榮譽
41. fame	名聲
42. pluck	勇氣
43. self-control	自制

44. shorts	短褲
45. supporters	支持者
46. competitors/ opponents	競爭對手
47. swimming pool	泳池
48. footballer	足球員
49. goaler	守門員
50. substitutes	後備球員
51. referee	球證
52. fans	球迷
53. football announcer	足球評述員
54. gate receipts	入場收入
55. floodlights	夜明燈
56. basketball court	籃球場
57. scorer	射手
58. points	績分
59. coach	教練
60. volleyball court	排球場
61. table-tennis	乒乓球
62. bat	球拍
63. badminton	羽毛球
64. tennis court	網球場
65. racquet	網球拍
66. foot work	步法
67. squash court	壁球場
68. billiards	桌球

69.	cue	桌球棒	90.	fitness	健身
70.	team-mates	隊員	91.	tai chi	太極拳
71.	captain	隊長	92.	lawn bowls	草地滾球
72.	teams	球隊	93.	calisthenics	柔軟體操
73.	exciting	緊張刺激的	94.	sneaker	跑步鞋
74.	robust	強壯的	95.	karate	空手道
75.	professional	專業的	96.	exercise bike	健身自行車
76.	amateur	業餘的	97.	treadmill	健身跑步機
77.	accommodate	容納	98.	benefiting	受惠
78.	smash	凌空高壓網球	99.	physical drills	健身操
79.	Tuen Mun Golf Centre	屯門高爾夫球中心	100.	spiked shoes	釘鞋
80.	indoor stadium	室內體育館	101.	starting point	起點
81.	outdoor recreation centre	戶外康樂中心	102.	finishing-line	終點線
82.	summer youth programme	青少年暑期活動計劃	103.	forehand drive	正手抽擊
83.	rowing	划艇	104.	backhand drive	反手抽擊
84.	windsurfing	滑浪風帆	105.	soccer fans	足球迷
85.	holiday camps	渡假營	106.	penalty area	禁區
86.	rugby	欖球	107.	foul play	犯規
87.	fencer	劍擊手	108.	team spirit	團體精神
88.	taekwondo	跆拳道	109.	physical recreation	康樂活動
89.	water sports	水上活動	110.	penalty spot	十二碼罰球點

Spring

Sentences

1.	Spring is a season of freshness and greenness.	春天是一個新鮮與葱綠的季節。
2.	We can enjoy warm weather and fine days.	我們可享受到和暖晴朗的天氣。
3.	People like the bright and lovely sunshine.	人們喜歡那明媚可愛的陽光。
4.	Nature awakens from the long winter sleep.	大自然從漫長的冬眠中甦醒。
5.	All plants come to life again.	所有的植物重獲生命。
6.	They show new signs of life.	它們顯出了新生命的信息。
7.	The earth recovers its vitality.	大地恢復了生命力。
8.	The flowers bloom and are full of fresh fragrances.	百花盛開，充滿清新的香味。
9.	A wealth of grass is like a green carpet.	綠草如茵。
10.	Trees and grass grow luxuriantly.	草木生長繁茂。
11.	Hillsides are covered with fern.	山坡長滿羊齒類植物。
12.	Branches are swaying in a gentle breeze.	樹枝在柔和的微風中搖擺着。
13.	Willows are fresh and green.	柳樹清新而葱綠。
14.	The world is covered with rich earth.	世界為肥沃的土地所覆蓋。
15.	Swallows are flying to and fro.	燕子飛來飛去。
16.	Beautiful birds display their merry, sweet songs.	美麗的雀鳥一展牠們愉快及甜美的歌聲。
17.	They have an enjoyable time and sing cheerfully.	牠們享受時光，歡暢地高歌。

18. The surrounding beautiful, natural scenery spreads out before our eyes. 四周美麗的自然景色展現在我們的眼前。

19. It makes us refreshed. 它使我們心曠神怡。

20. People's spirits are cheered up. 人們的神情振奮起來。

21. Facing an air of unfathomable magnificence, we stand, mystified. 面對着無法形容的奇景，我們茫然地站立着。

22. We bathe in the soft mellow rays of an evening sun. 我們沐浴在夕陽的柔光中。

23. Millions of stars shine in the darkness. 數以百萬計的星兒在黑暗中閃爍着。

24. We live in a world of dreams. 我們生活在夢想的世界中。

25. Spring is the first season of the year; we should make good use of it and study hard. 春天是一年之始，我們應好好利用它來努力學習。

Phrases

1. mild weather   溫和的天氣

2. bloom with beautiful flowers   開滿着美麗的花朵

3. fragrant smell of wild flowers   野花的芳香

4. blue and cloudless sky   蔚藍而無雲的天空

5. make plans   作出計劃

6. verdant green   蒼翠

7. verdant and luxuriant   青葱茂盛

8. a carpet of green grass   如茵的綠草

9. in radiant bloom   鮮花盛放

10. here and there   錯落其中

11. soft breeze   微風

12. lovely scenery   景色怡人

13. refreshing air   清新空氣

Vocabulary

1.	season	季節	21.	gentle	溫柔的
2.	spring wind	春風	22.	lovely	可愛的
3.	shower	驟雨	23.	bewildered	迷惘的
4.	valley	山谷	24.	fascinating	迷人的
5.	horizon	水平線	25.	glittering	燦爛的
6.	ripple	微波	26.	regain	恢復
7.	willow	柳樹	27.	sparkle	閃爍
8.	bridge	小橋	28.	sway	搖擺
9.	bees	蜜蜂	29.	bloom	開花
10.	nectar	花蜜	30.	buzz	嗡嗡聲
11.	peach blossoms	桃花	31.	waken	喚醒
			32.	encourage	鼓勵
12.	scene	景色	33.	petal	花瓣
13.	hiking	遠足	34.	fair skies	藍天
14.	fishing	垂釣	35.	lawn	草地
15.	welcome	受歡迎的	36.	sow	播種
16.	glorious	燦爛的	37.	rainbow	彩虹
17.	carefree	自由自在的	38.	dew	露
18.	mild	溫和的	39.	mist	霧
19.	active	活躍的			
20.	charming	撫媚的			

Summer

Sentences

1.	Summer is the time for all things to develop prosperously.	夏天是萬物蓬勃滋長的時候。
2.	Plants flourish.	植物茂盛地生長。
3.	The air is bright and cheerful.	空氣明淨怡人。
4.	Summer looks more attractive and charming.	夏天似乎更具吸引力及迷人。
5.	The blue sky is covered with white clouds.	蔚藍的天空點綴着白雲。
6.	Everything appears promising.	一切都意味着新的希望。
7.	Farmers are busy sowing the seeds.	農夫正忙於播種。
8.	The sun looks like a great fiery ball.	太陽像一顆赤熱的大火球。
9.	Many people have to work under the fearful rays of the sun.	很多人須在可怕的烈日下工作。
10.	People change into light clothes.	人們轉換較薄的衣服。
11.	Students enjoy long summer holidays.	學生們享受悠長的暑假。
12.	The sunshine is much stronger than that of other seasons.	陽光遠較其他季節為強。
13.	Summer has the hottest weather and the greatest rainfall.	夏天有最熱的天氣及最多的雨水。
14.	Under the bright sunshine, flowers are in full bloom.	在晴朗的陽光下，花朵盛開。
15.	The clouds in the sky are as soft as fleece and as white as snow.	天空中的雲，其柔如毛，其白如雪。
16.	The sandy beach on the seaside is crowded with swimmers.	海濱的沙灘擠滿了弄潮兒。

17. They are enjoying a delightful time.   他們正享受着討人歡喜的時節。

18. They swim happily in the green waves.   他們在綠波中暢泳。

19. Farmers work under the blazing sun and the scorching heat.   農夫們在赤熱的驕陽下工作。

20. The fearful rays of the sun are often intolerable.   可怕的烈日常常令人難以忍受。

21. People are in their casual attire.   人們穿上便服。

22. Skies are sometimes overcast with heavy clouds.   天空有時烏雲密佈。

23. This may bring along heavy showers.   這種情形可能帶來大驟雨。

24. When a severe tropical storm is approaching, the typhoon signal No. 8 is hoisted by the Hong Kong Observatory.   當一股強烈的熱帶風暴接近本港時，天文台會懸掛八號強風訊號。

 Phrases

1.	early rising	早起
2.	hot waves	熱浪
3.	heavy rains	滂沱大雨
4.	storms with thunder	風雨雷電交加
5.	still water	靜止的水
6.	blistering heat	酷熱

 Vocabulary

1.	ice-cream	雪糕（冰淇淋）	6.	breeze	微風
2.	hue	色調	7.	dust	黃昏
3.	cicada	蟬	8.	seaside	海邊
4.	ray	光線	9.	brocade	織錦
5.	ripple	微波	10.	shade	樹蔭

11. swimming	游泳	25. agreeable	適意的
12. storm	暴風雨	26. magnificent	瑰麗的
13. typhoon	颱風	27. leisurely	逍遙的
14. lightning	閃電	28. suitable	適當的
15. thunderstorms	雷暴	29. crowded	擁擠的
16. landslides	山泥傾瀉	30. violent	劇烈的
17. flooding	水淹	31. reflect	反射
18. monsoon	季候風	32. cover	遮蔽
19. cyclones	旋風	33. sweat	出汗
20. standby	戒備	34. disappear	消失
21. scorching	灼熱的	35. threaten	威脅
22. stout	強壯的	36. sweltering	熱昏的
23. busy	忙碌的	37. heat stroke	中暑
24. diligent	勤奮的	38. cold drinks	冷飲

63

Supermarket

Sentences

1. Some supermarkets also sell traditional market foodstuff such like fresh meat, live fishes and vegetables.

有些超級市場兼售傳統街市的食物，如新鮮肉類、游水海鮮、蔬菜等。

2. These goods can be bought at will according to their weight. You can also buy those goods packed separately.

你可以隨意按重量購買這些貨品，亦可選取已包裝好的。

3. As for the prices, it may be slightly higher than those outside. Customers are happy to buy them because the shopping environment is comfortable and goods are fresh.

價錢方面，超級市場雖略貴於外邊，但由於購物環境舒適，貨品亦新鮮，所以顧客樂於購買。

4. Moreover, there are a variety cooked dishes and packed soup ingredients for the busy people.

更有已燒好的多款家常小菜及配好的湯料，方便忙碌的人煮食。

5. Goods can be delivered to the customer's home if the bill reaches the set amount.

購物滿限定金額，可以送貨。

6. Supermarkets also slash prices to attract customers.

超級市場亦以減價作為招徠。

7. Posters and written notes with goods at reduced prices will be stuck everywhere in its shop.

店內貼滿減價物品的海報及字條。

8. If the shopping bill reaches the set amount, stamps will be given. When a certain number of stamps are collected, they can be used to exchange free gifts.

購物到一定銀碼，他們會贈送印花。集齊若干數量，可以換取贈品。

9. In a supermarket, we can buy various daily necessities all under one roof.

我們可以在同一家超級市場購買各種日常必需品。

10. Supermarkets cater for different needs.

超級市場配合不同的需要。

11. Many housewives do shopping at a supermarket.

很多主婦到超級市場購物。

12. They can choose the goods at their own pace.

她們可以慢慢地選購貨品。

13. They select and purchase the goods they like.

她們選購喜愛的貨物。

14. Many customers have a buying tendency.

很多顧客有購買欲。

15. Very often, however, they buy on impulse.

然而他們很多時候是一時衝動而購買的。

16. Some shoppers prepare a list of things before they enter a supermarket.

有些購物者在進入超級市場前已備有一張購物的清單。

17. Supermarkets offer many advantages.

超級市場提供了很多好處。

18. There is a lavish display of goods.

那裏有豐富的陳列貨品。

19. The goods are nicely displayed on well-lit shelves.

貨品考究地陳列在光線充足的貨物架上。

20. They are attractively packaged and displayed.

它們包裝及陳設得極為吸引。

21. Some particular brands of goods are strategically placed.

一些特別牌子的商品被放置於重要的位置。

22. There is a wide choice of goods.

貨品種類繁多。

23. Customers are free to select the goods.

顧客可自由選購。

24. Supermarkets can offer their goods at competitive prices because of the large turnover.

由於銷售量很大，超級市場能夠以較低的價格出售貨品。

25. They usually maintain a lower rate of profit.

超市通常維持較低利潤。

26. To operate a supermarket successfully, stock control is very important.

存貨控制對成功地經營一間超級市場十分重要。

27. The study of consumer behaviour is instrumental in getting a larger turnover.

研究消費者的行為有助於銷售額的增加。

28. Operators of supermarkets should know something about human psychology in the respect of buying goods.

超級市場的經營者應對人類購物心理學有認識。

29. Shopping in the form of self service is now accepted by an increasing number of customers.

自助方式購物現已為愈來愈多的顧客所接受。

30. Supermarkets can satisfy the need for basic shopping.

超級市場能滿足基本的購物需要。

31. There are high standards of hygiene and a comfortable environment for shopping.

那裏有較高的衛生水準及舒適的購物環境。

32. Light background music is played throughout business hours in some leading supermarkets.

在一些規模較大的超級市場中，營業時間內會播放輕音樂。

33. Previously, patrons of supermarkets used to be foreigners or those who came from affluent families.

從前超級市場的常客多是外國人或來自富裕家庭的人士。

34. Now supermarkets have become very popular among ordinary shoppers.

現在超級市場深受一般購物者的歡迎。

35. More and more supermarkets are being opened every year in the urban areas as well as in new towns in the New Territories.

每年愈來愈多的超級市場在市區及新界新市鎮中開設。

36. It has become a way of life to do shopping in a supermarket.

在超級市場內購物已成為了一種生活的方式。

37. Many supermarkets install electronic devices to minimise shop-lifting.

很多超級市場裝置有電子儀器，藉以把盜竊貨物減至最低限度。

38. In spite of the popularity of supermarkets, some grocery stores can still exist because of the personal services they offer to their customers.

雖然超級市場受歡迎，但一些雜貨店仍能生存，這由於它們向顧客提供個人化的服務。

39. Very often, supermarkets are testing grounds for new products.

很多時候，超級市場是新產品的試驗場所。

 Phrases

1.	a long freezer	一個長長的凍櫃
2.	to snap up	搶購
3.	best buy	抵買
4.	super value	超值
5.	buy two get one free	買二送一
6.	pay by Octopus	以八達通卡付款
7.	cheques are not accepted	不接受支票
8.	cash only	只收現金
9.	to use less plastic bags	減少使用膠袋

 Vocabulary

1.	chocolate	朱古力（巧克力）	3.	candies/sweets	糖果
2.	biscuits	餅乾	4.	basket	籃
			5.	trolley	手推車

6.	housewives	主婦	28. cheap	便宜的
7.	cashier	收銀員	29. eye-catching	顯眼的
8.	cash-register	收銀機	30. detect	偵查
9.	turnstile	旋轉柵門	31. display	陳列
10.	entrance	入口	32. tempt	誘使
11.	sundries	雜項用品	33. appeal	吸引
12.	wine	餐酒	34. circulate	流動
13.	liquor	烈酒	35. accept	接受
14.	articles/items	商品	36. analyse	分析
15.	shoplifting	店舖盜竊	37. predict	預測
16.	aisles	通路	38. bargains	便宜貨／特價品
17.	availability	獲得	39. barcode	條碼
18.	customers/shoppers	顧客	40. promotion	促銷
19.	shop assistants	售貨員	41. frozen meat	凍肉
20.	shelves/stacks	貨物架	42. frozen food	冷藏食品
21.	colour	顏色	43. canned food	罐頭食品
22.	shape	形狀	44. chewing gum	香口膠
23.	cigarettes	香煙	45. point of sale (POS) system	終端銷售系統
24.	convenient	方便的	46. special offer	特別推薦
25.	clean	清潔的	47. food label	食物標籤
26.	spacious	寬闊的	48. environmental protection bag	環保袋
27.	enjoyable	愉快的		

Television

 Sentences

1. Television is a very effective medium for mass communication.

電視是十分有效的大眾傳播媒介。

2. It is one of the most wonderful inventions of modem times.

它是現代最奇妙的發明品之一。

3. Watching television is a very popular form of recreation nowadays.

看電視是今日十分普遍的消遣。

4. It has become part of the local people's way of living.

它已成為本地人生活的一部分。

5. Television is undoubtedly an influential factor in society.

電視影響社會很大。

6. It is a very good medium for socializing.

它是一個絕佳的社會化媒介。

7. Through television, information, ideas, values and beliefs are widely spread.

透過電視，資訊、觀念、價值及信念被廣泛地散佈。

8. Television tells us the most up-to-date news more vividly by giving us a picture of a situation.

由於電視給我們影片圖象，它更生動地把最新的消息告訴我們。

9. It brings before our eyes the event which happens thousands of miles away.

它能把數千里外發生的事帶到我們的眼前。

10. We can see various kinds of activities live on the screen.

我們可以看見各種不同的活動生動地在電視熒光幕上出現。

11. Therefore, we have a closer touch with reality.

因此我們與現實有較近的接觸。

12. Watching television can widen our knowledge and experience.

看電視能擴闊我們的知識與經驗。

13. It is both educational and entertaining.

它既富娛樂性，也具教育性。

14. Television provides a vast encyclopedia of knowledge.

電視提供了一部龐大的知識百科全書。

15. It is also an amusement enjoyed in a family setting.

它也是全家可以欣賞的娛樂。

16. Thanks to television, there is a widespread increase in general knowledge among children.

兒童常識普遍增加，這是拜電視所賜。

17. Television is no longer a luxury.

電視已不再是一種奢侈品。

18. Watching television is a means of passing time and brings joy to all.

看電視是一種消遣，它為所有人帶來歡樂。

19. People can sit before the screen and enjoy rich programmes in comfort.

人們可以坐在熒光幕前舒適地欣賞豐富的節目。

20. Watching favourite television programmes is good for relaxing the mind.

觀看喜歡的電視節目使我們的精神鬆弛。

21. Television caters for various tastes and interests.

電視迎合各種不同的口味及興趣。

22. Watching television refreshes our minds.

看電視使我們怡神。

23. Television enriches the life of people.

電視使人們的生活更多姿多彩。

24. It functions to fuse the gap between the two generations.

它有把兩代融合在一起的功能。

25. It helps to keep children off the streets, thus minimising accidents.

它使兒童少在街上流連，減低意外發生。

26. Some scenes are filmed outside.

一些景是在外面拍攝的。

27. Some programmes are broadcast live.

有些節目是現場直播的。

28. It cannot be denied that many television programmes are very attractive.

無可否認，很多電視節目是十分吸引的。

29. People find it hard to resist the temptation of watching programmes on the screen.

人們不易抗拒電視的吸引力。

30. Television can change our attitudes towards life and beliefs.

電視能改變我們的人生態度及信念。

31. Some drama serials advocate incorrect social values and corrupted goals.

有些電視劇集提倡不正確的社會價值及墮落的人生目標。

32. Many television advertisements convey a bad sense.

很多電視廣告有不良的意識。

33. The social and cultural values implied in these programmes and commercials are incorrect.

這些節目及廣告所蘊涵的社會及文化價值是不正確的。

34. There is often a remarkable display and exaggerated presentation of wealth and luxury on the screen.

電視熒光幕常常凸顯出及誇張地展示財富和奢侈品。

35. It is mainly due to the influence of television that many people have developed wrong goals and attitudes towards life.

很多人主要受電視的影響，有錯誤的人生目標及態度。

36. Making money, consuming luxurious goods, pursuing material comforts and enjoying life have become the sole goal in life for many Hong Kong citizens.

賺取金錢、消費奢侈品、追求物質上的舒適與及享受人生已成為很多香港市民唯一的人生目標。

37. The traditional virtues of diligence and thrift are long forgotten.

勤奮工作及節儉的傳統美德早已被遺忘。

38. At the same time, the unhealthy sense of television is being spread far and wide in the community.

與此同時，電視的不良意識正在社會上廣泛地流傳着。

39. Some programmes have unsound themes.

有些節目含有不健康的主題。

40. Abusive language and triad terms can often be heard in these programmes.

在這些節目中，我們常可聽到穢言惡語及三合會暗語。

41. The adverse effect is that vulgar language has become many people's daily language.

它帶來了不良的後果 —— 粗俗的語言成了很多人的日常用語。

42. Sex and violence are often exaggerated on the screen.

性及暴力常在電視熒光幕上被過份的渲染。

43. Adolescents often imitate indiscriminately the characters portrayed in the drama serials.

青少年常常不加選擇地模仿電視劇集中所描述的人物。

44. Television often reflects and stresses the evil side of life.

電視常反映及強調人性罪惡的一面。

45. Programmes with positive values and significance are lacking.

電視缺乏具有正面價值及意義的節目。

46. This makes young people feel bewildered and they doubt the real meaning of life.

這使青年人迷惑及懷疑生命的真正意義。

47. Undesirable television programmes are one of the major causes that has led to an increase in juvenile delinquency.

不良的電視節目是導致青少年犯罪增加的主要原因之一。

48. Many bad programmes may corrupt children's minds.

很多不良的節目會腐化兒童的思想。

49. They make children misunderstand sex and blindly resort to violence.

它們使兒童對性產生誤解及盲目依賴暴力。

50. Many children are absorbed in the programmes, thus neglecting their studies.

很多兒童沉迷於電視節目，疏忽了功課。

51. Many students can hardly concentrate on their studies because of television.

由於電視的影響，很多學生難以集中精神讀書。

52. Many children stay up late watching television and this is very harmful to their health.

很多兒童看電視到夜深，對他們的健康很有害。

53. Watching television for a long time will also harm their eyesight.

長時間看電視也損害他們的視力。

54. Television often distracts children from their studies.

電視會分散孩子們在學業上的專注力。

55. Watching television is a passive form of entertainment and therefore children are deprived of the opportunity of independent thinking.

看電視是一種被動的娛樂，兒童會因而喪失獨立思考的機會。

56. To some extent, television controls people's thinking and stifles their imagination.

在一定程度上，電視控制了人的思想，並抑壓了他們的想像力。

57. People usually accept passively what they see without considering whether it is right or wrong.

人們通常被動地接受他們所看到的東西，而沒有考慮是與非的問題。

58. Most television viewers lack the ability to judge and do not have a critical mind.

大多數電視觀眾都缺乏判斷力及批判性的思想。

59. Moreover, they are easily influenced by the commercials.

而且他們很易受電視廣告所影響。

60. Very often, time seems to be regulated by television programmes.

很多時候，時間似乎是受電視節目所管制的。

61. Occasionally, there are quarrels over the choice of channel.

有時人們在選台方面發生爭執。

62. We must exercise strict self-control and not indulge in watching television excessively.

我們必須有嚴格的自我控制，不可耽溺於看電視。

63. We had better make good use of the educational programmes.

我們最好利用教育電視節目。

64. The authorities concerned should exercise strict censorship on television programmes and commercials.

有關當局應對電視節目及廣告進行嚴格的檢查。

65. The conclusion is that television can be beneficial to most people provided that they can use it wisely and properly.

結論是若人們能明智及適當地使用電視，它可以給大多數人帶來好處。

Phrases

1.	knowledge and skills	知識與技能
2.	dramatic effect	戲劇的效果
3.	suspense-detective series	懸疑偵探劇集
4.	violence and bloodshed	暴力及屠殺
5.	teddy boys and girls	阿飛型男女
6.	evil behaviour	邪惡行為
7.	ill effects	不良的影響
8.	plenty of talking topics	很多話題
9.	socially approved	社會上所贊同的
10.	a method of education	一種教育的方式
11.	transmission of information	消息的傳播
12.	a fountain of knowledge	知識之泉
13.	prime-time broadcast	黃金時段的廣播
14.	profound effect	深遠的後果

15. not suitable for children	兒童不宜的
16. serialised dramas	連續劇
17. animated cartoon show	卡通片集
18. fund-raising charity shows	慈善籌款盛會
19. most popular	最受歡迎的
20. topics of interest	感到興趣的題材
21. fine manner	風采
22. a feature film	故事片
23. blue jokes	色情笑話
24. to project an atmosphere of joy	營造歡樂氣氛
25. to catch on	流行起來
26. becoming household words	家傳戶曉

Vocabulary

1. mass media	大眾傳播媒介	12. artist	藝員
2. mass entertainment	大眾娛樂	13. programme	節目
		14. over-viewing	看電視過多
3. screen	熒光幕	15. audience	觀眾
4. television channels	電視台	16. cast	演員
5. criticism	批評	17. impact	影響
6. drawback	缺點	18. setting	情況
7. dispute	爭論	19. attitude	態度
8. attractions	吸引物	20. satellite	人造衛星
9. producer	監製	21. theme	主題
10. director	導演	22. trend	趨勢
11. host	節目主持人	23. comedies	喜劇
		24. City Forum	城市論壇

25.	side-effects	附帶產生的影響	49.	disturb	騷擾

25. side-effects　附帶產生的影響

26. background music　背景音樂

27. studio　錄影室

28. production assistants　節目製作助理

29. shots　拍攝

30. costumes　服裝

31. make-up　化妝

32. cameramen　攝影師

33. characters　劇中人物

34. close-up　近鏡

35. home viewers　家庭觀眾

36. commercials　電視廣告

37. enjoyable　怡情悅性的

38. educational　教育性的

39. entertaining　娛樂性的

40. informative　提供有用信息的

41. impulsive　衝動的

42. fantastic　奇異的

43. potent　強而有力的

44. rewarding　有益的

45. beneficial　有利的

46. inevitable　不可避免的

47. miss　錯過

48. pervade　普及

49. disturb　騷擾

50. hamper/hinder　妨礙

51. encourage　鼓勵

52. exaggerate　誇張

53. select　選擇

54. edit　剪輯

55. watch　觀看

56. imitate　模仿

57. publicize　宣揚

58. TVB Jade　無線電視翡翠台

59. Star TV　衛星電視

60. Phoenix Chinese Channel　鳳凰衛視中文台

61. sword-play serials　武俠劇集

62. sitcom　喜劇片集

63. news presenter　新聞報導員

64. well received　大受歡迎的

65. eye-opener　令人大開眼界的經歷

66. star-studded　星光熠熠的

67. nonsensical　胡鬧的

68. documentary films　紀錄片

69. educational television　教育電視

70. theme songs　主題曲

71.	television viewers	電視觀眾	74.	consumers' rights	消費者權益
72.	television channels	電視頻道	75.	soap opera	肥皂劇
73.	entertainment magazine	娛樂雜誌式節目	76.	digital TV	高清廣播（數碼電視）

Traffic Problem

 Sentences

1. The traffic problem is a serious problem that has existed for a long time. | 交通問題是一個長期存在的嚴重問題。

2. This is partly due to Hong Kong's geographical factor. | 這部分由於香港地理因素所造成的。

3. There is a serious shortage of flat land in Hong Kong. | 香港缺少平坦的土地。

4. There is an enormous number of private cars in Hong Kong and this number is increasing rapidly. | 香港的私家車數目龐大，而這數目正迅速地增加。

5. The increase in road space always lags far behind the increase in the number of vehicles. | 路面面積的增加總是遠遠落後於車輛數量的增加。

6. It is a common scene that both cars and pedestrians scramble for the road. | 人車爭路是常見的景象。

7. Passengers are often caught in traffic jams. | 乘客常被困於交通擠塞之中。

8. During rush hours, traffic congestion is especially serious. | 在繁忙時間，交通擠塞尤其嚴重。

9. Traffic is often held up. | 車輛常因交通擠塞而不能前進。

10. There are indeed too many people and cars in Hong Kong.

香港實在有太多人和汽車了。

11. Crossing a busy road is often a trying experience.

橫過一條繁忙的馬路常是一個令人痛苦的經驗。

12. Careless drivers are a menace to other road users.

不小心駕駛的人士對其他的道路使用者造成威脅。

13. Hong Kong has a very high density of population and traffic.

香港的人口及交通密度非常高。

14. Long queues of vehicles often completely block the roads and cause delays.

長長的車龍往往完全阻塞了道路，造成延誤。

15. The congestion is further aggravated at weekends and during holidays when many people go out to enjoy their holidays.

周末及假日，很多人外出享受假期，使擠塞的情形更為嚴重。

16. Many people rush across the roads without paying heed to the traffic signals.

很多人不注意交通燈號而衝過馬路。

17. In doing this, they risk their own lives.

他們這樣做是妄顧生命危險的。

18. There must be long-term transport planning to keep pace with the rapid development.

為了配合迅速的發展，長遠的運輸計劃是必需的。

19. In view of the serious traffic problem, the Government has published a White Paper on transport policies.

鑑於交通問題的嚴重，政府已公佈了一個關於交通政策的白皮書。

20. The Government plans to improve the road system and make more economical use of the roads.

政府計劃改善道路系統及較經濟地使用道路。

21. Another policy measure is to expand and improve public transport.

另一個政策是擴大及改善公共交通。

22. To cope with the steadily intensifying transport pressures, the transport system must be adjusted accordingly.

為了應付日漸增加的交通壓力，運輸系統必須作出配合性的調整。

23. To keep pace with the rapid traffic development, alternative means of transport have to be devised.

為了配合交通的迅速發展，我們必須設計其他的運輸方式。

24. The Mass Transit Railway (MTR) began operating in 1979.

地下鐵路在一九七九年開始通車。

25. The opening of the MTR has a noticeable effect on Hong Kong's traffic patterns.

地下鐵路的通車對香港的交通形式有顯著的影響。

26. It provides a smooth flow of traffic.

它提供了流暢的交通。

27. At the same time, it helps to ease the movement of traffic on the road surface.

與此同時，它幫助疏導路面上的交通。

28. The Kowloon-Canton Railway was double-tracked and electrified in the early 1980s.

八十年代初期，九廣鐵路鋪設雙軌，並推行電氣化服務。

29. The Light Rail Transit system mainly serves residents of the north-western New Territories.

輕便鐵路主要為新界西北部居民提供服務。

30. The Airport Express provides a fast passenger link to the airport.

機場快線提供連接機場的快速客運服務。

31. The Tsing Ma Bridge is the world's longest suspension bridge carrying both road and rail traffic.

青馬大橋是世界上最長的公路及鐵路吊橋。

32. The Western Harbour Crossing helps to relieve congestion at the two existing cross-harbour tunnels.

西區海底隧道有助紓緩目前兩條海底隧道的擠塞情況。

33. Public light buses provide supplementary services.

公共小型巴士提供輔助性的服務。

34. Public transport is / becomes the dominant mode of transport.

公共交通成為一個重要的交通形式。

35. The use of private cars will be discouraged.

政府會勸喻市民盡量減少使用私家車輛。

36. The Government has planned to curb the rapid increase in private cars through heavy taxation.

政府已計劃以加重徵稅的方式減低私家車的增加。

37. To cut down the growth rate of private vehicles, the first registration duties have been greatly increased.

為了減低私家車輛的增加率，政府已大幅度增加私家車輛的首次登記稅。

38. Also substantially increased are the tax on imported cars, petrol duties, licence fees and parking fees.

汽車進口稅、汽油稅、牌費及停車收費也有大幅增加。

39. The Government thinks that the most effective way of solving the traffic problem is to restrict the rate of increase in private cars.

政府認為解決交通問題最有效的方法是限制私家車輛的增長率。

40. This car restraint policy has aroused opposition and protest from many car-owners.

這項抑制車輛的政策已引起很多車主的反對和抗議。

41. In order to smoothen the flow of traffic, more new roads will be built and the existing narrow roads widened.

為了使交通暢順，政府將興建更多的新路及擴闊現有的狹窄的道路。

42. The Government hopes to reduce traffic congestion to a minimum.

政府希望把交通擠塞減至最低限度。

43. The development of new towns and satellite towns in the New Territories can help alleviate the traffic pressures in the urban areas.

在新界發展新市鎮及衛星城市能幫助減輕市區所承受的交通壓力。

44. The Tuen Mun Highway linking the major new towns of Tuen Mun and Tsuen Wan offers six-lane traffic.

連接屯門及荃灣兩個主要新市鎮的屯門公路提供了六線行車的交通服務。

45. Traffic accident is nearly a daily phenomenon in Hong Kong.

在香港，交通意外幾乎是每日常見。

46. This problem is particularly acute in the busy urban areas.

這個問題在繁忙的市區中特別嚴重。

47. The Government has conducted research into the underlying causes of Hong Kong's traffic accidents.

政府已研究香港交通意外的基本原因。

48. Road safety publicity campaigns have been launched by various organizations.

各團體已發起宣傳交通安全的運動。

49. Pedestrians are educated on the correct use of the roads.

他們教育行人正確地使用道路。

50. Drivers must drive safely and their cars must undergo regular maintenance checks.

駕駛人士必須安全地駕駛車輛，並為他們的車輛進行定期的維修檢查。

51. Careless driving often gives rise to accidents and therefore it should be heavily punished.

不小心駕駛常導致意外，這種行為應被重罰。

52. Carelessness on the part of pedestrians also partly accounts for some of the tragic accidents.

行人的不小心也造成悲慘的意外。

53. Road manners and courtesy should be promoted.

使用道路的禮貌應予提倡。

54. Both drivers and pedestrians should always be on the alert when using the road.

當司機及行人使用道路時，都應該時刻保持警覺。

55. They must realize that accidents wreck lives.

他們必須明白意外足以致命。

56. So they should always exercise patience and maintain courtesy.

故此，他們應時常忍讓及保持禮貌。

57. To separate pedestrians from the busy traffic, a covered footrbidge system has been installed in Central.

為了隔開行人及繁忙的交通，一個有蓋的行人天橋系統已在中區裝置。

58. The Government has made it compulsory for car-owners to undergo regular vehicle inspection.

政府規定車主必須定期進行車輛檢查。

59. Parking spaces are seriously lacking in Hong Kong.

香港嚴重缺乏泊車位。

60. The penalties for parking contraventions have been greatly increased.

違例泊車的罰款已大為增加。

 **Phrases**

1. engine disorder 機器故障

2. on-street parking 街上停車

3. traffic management 交通管理

4. conventional mode of transport 慣用的交通形式

5. at the crossroads 在十字路口處

6. widespread propaganda 廣泛的宣傳

7. deaths and injuries 傷亡

8.	dangerous bends	危險的彎道
9.	a menace to pedestrians	對行人的威脅
10.	drunken driving	醉酒駕駛
11.	red light camera	衝紅燈攝影機
12.	serious congestion problem	嚴重的擠塞問題
13.	to maintain traffic flow	維持交通暢順
14.	emergency situation	緊急情況
15.	contingency plans	應變計劃
16.	the access road	通路
17.	uninterrupted flow	川流不息
18.	compulsory fitting and wearing of seat belts	強制安裝及佩戴安全帶

 Vocabulary

1.	traffic congestion	交通擠塞	12.	fines	罰款
2.	annoyance	煩惱	13.	traffic police	交通警察
3.	traffic accidents	交通意外	14.	driving licence	駕駛執照
4.	traffic diversion	交通改道	15.	traffic regulations	交通規則
5.	bottleneck	瓶頸地帶	16.	flyovers	天橋
6.	junction	十字路口	17.	pedestrian footbridge	行人天橋
7.	parking meters	停車收費錶	18.	collision	相撞
8.	speed limits	車速限制	19.	waterfront	海旁
9.	zebra-crossing	斑馬線	20.	roadworks	道路工程
10.	traffic lights	交通燈	21.	traffic safety	交通安全
11.	publicity posters	宣傳海報	22.	pavement	行人道

23. Mass Transit Railway (MTR)	港鐵	48. urge	敦促
		49. ensure	確保
24. jay walkers	橫衝直撞的行人	50. avert/avoid	避免
25. commuter	經常來往的搭客	51. endanger	危及
		52. reinforce	加強
26. modernization	現代化	53. promote	提倡
27. efficiency	效率	54. relieve	解除
28. over-loading	超載	55. ring road	回環路
29. priority	優先	56. expressway	高速公路
30. bus-only lane	巴士專線	57. Road Safety Campaign	交通安全運動
31. feeder route	輔助路線		
32. public light bus	公共小型巴士	58. franchised buses	專利巴士
33. taxi	的士	59. multi-storey car parks	多層停車場
34. traffic legislation	交通立法	60. traffic black-spot	交通黑點
35. negligence	疏忽		
36. pedestrian subway	行人隧道	61. pedestrians' precinct	行人專用區
37. chaotic	混亂的	62. Transport Advisory Committee	交通諮詢委員會
38. inconvenient	不方便的		
39. delay	延遲	63. close circuit television	閉路電視
40. complain	抱怨		
41. solve	解決	64. enquiry hotline	查詢熱線
42. reduce	減少	65. sales and customer service hotline	營業及客戶服務熱線
43. punish	處罰		
44. co-operate	合作		
45. ban	禁止	66. complaints hotline	投訴熱線
46. implement	施行		
47. accelerate	加速		

Typhoon

Sentences

1. The stillness in the atmosphere may be the sign of an approaching typhoon.

    靜止的空氣可能是颱風將至的徵兆。

2. People begin to pay full attention to radio broadcasts.

    人們開始密切留意電台廣播。

3. As a typhoon approaches Hong Kong, everybody hurries home.

    當颱風接近香港的時候，人人都趕回家去。

4. Public vehicles and ferries are crowded with passengers.

    各種公共交通工具及渡海小輪都擠滿了乘客。

5. Most offices and shops are closed.

    大部分寫字樓及商店關上了門。

6. Schools break up.

    學校停課。

7. Many functions, meetings and appointments have to be postponed or cancelled.

    很多活動、聚會與約會須延期或取消。

8. School-children enjoy an extra holiday.

    學童享受一日額外的假期。

9. There may be a heavy downpour.

    天空可能下大雨。

10. At first the No. I stand-by signal is hoisted by the Hong Kong Observatory.

    最初天文台懸掛一號戒備訊號。

11. This is a warning signal.

    這是一個警告訊號。

12. Sometimes, the sky is full of heavy clouds.

    有時天空中滿佈密雲。

13. When a typhoon comes close to Hong Kong, the No. 3 typhoon signal will be hoisted.

    當颱風接近香港時，天文台三號颱風訊號。

14. For safety's sake, all the windows have to be barred.

    所有窗戶必須加上橫木，以策安全。

15. The air pressure is usually low.

    氣壓通常較低。

16. Sometimes, typhoons can bring a lot of rain. 有時颱風能帶來大量的雨水。

17. Some streets in low-lying areas may be flooded with water. 一些低窪地區的街道可能遭受水淹。

18. Some people have to wade through the streets. 有些人需要涉水走過街道。

19. When the wind becomes fierce, typhoon signals No. 8, No. 9 or No. 10 will be hoisted by the Hong Kong Observatory. 當風力達到烈風程度時,天文台將懸掛八號、九號或十號颱風訊號。

20. In that case, the typhoon will attack Hong Kong directly. 在這種情況下,颱風將正面吹襲香港。

21. Citizens are advised to take every possible precaution against the typhoon. 天文台勸喻市民採取所有可能的防風措施。

22. People listen to repeated broadcasts of the progress of the typhoon. 人們聆聽重複的颱風進展報導。

23. Red flags are hoisted on all beaches to warn swimmers against the danger of the typhoon. 所有海灘都掛起紅旗,警告泳客注意颱風的危險。

24. Rough and huge waves can be seen in the sea. 在海上我們可看到狂暴的巨浪。

25. We can hear the howling whistle of the fierce wind. 我們可以聽到強風的怒叫。

26. The big waves toss the small boats high up in the air. 巨浪把細小的船隻拋到高高的空中。

27. Some big ships may run aground. 一些大船可能擱淺。

28. Ferry services are suspended. 渡輪服務中斷。

29. Buses and trams give limited services. 巴士及電車提供有限度的服務。

30. The suspension of services at any moment is announced. 它們宣佈公共交通工具隨時停駛。

31. If the typhoon continues to rage, great losses of lives and property will be caused. 假如颱風繼續肆虐,將造成人命及財物的巨大損失。

32. Many scaffoldings on buildings under construction may fall. 在地盤內,很多建築物的棚架可能塌下。

33. They will block the thoroughfare.

它們將阻塞大道。

34. Typhoons will also cause extensive damage to crops in the New Territories.

颱風將對新界農作物造成廣泛的破壞。

35. It is due to the typhoon that the price of vegetables will increase sharply.

由於颱風的關係，蔬菜的價格將大幅度上升。

36. Supermarkets and stores are flooded with customers and are doing a roaring business.

超級市場及士多擠滿了顧客，生意滔滔。

37. Radio stations provide emergency information services.

電台提供緊急報告的服務。

38. Some people have to report for duty.

有些人須報到當值。

39. Ambulances and fire engines have to stand-by.

救傷車及消防車須候命出發。

40. Trees are swaying in the wind.

樹木在大風中搖擺着。

41. A few people may be fighting their way against the wind.

少數人可能在大風中奮力前進。

42. Their umbrellas are either blown over or blown inside out.

他們的雨傘被吹倒或吹翻。

43. Many signboards are swinging dangerously.

很多廣告招牌正在危險地搖擺着。

44. Deserted streets present a scene of desolation.

沒有人的街道呈現一片蕭條的景象。

45. When a typhoon has died down, streets are scattered with broken glass and piles of rubbish waiting to be cleared up.

當颱風停息時，街道上佈滿破碎的玻璃與大堆垃圾，等待人們清理。

46. The typhoon leaves behind a trail of destruction.

颱風留下一道道破壞的痕跡。

47. Many boats enter the typhoon shelter.

很多船進入避風塘。

48. People of Hong Kong have become accustomed to typhoons.

香港人已經習慣了颱風的來臨。

49. During a typhoon, many people go to see a film or play a game of mahjong at home.

颱風肆虐期間，很多人去看電影或在家中打麻將。

Phrases

1.	an awful sight	一個可怕的景象
2.	the fury of winds and waves	狂暴的風浪
3.	white surf	白色浪花
4.	roll upon roll of big billows	滾滾巨浪
5.	to suffer hardships	吃苦頭
6.	deaths and injuries	傷亡
7.	warnings of hazardous weather	惡劣天氣警報
8.	advice on the necessary precautions to take	提醒市民採取適當的預防措施
9.	a colour-coded rainstorm warning system	一套以顏色標示的暴雨警告系統
10.	traffic disruption	交通擠塞
11.	strong monsoon	強烈季候風
12.	to set up a home page on the Internet	在國際電腦網絡設立網頁
13.	around the clock	二十四小時（不分晝夜）
14.	serious road flooding	路面嚴重水淹

Vocabulary

1.	temperature	氣溫	9.	waterfront	海旁
2.	signs	象徵	10.	pier	碼頭
3.	typhoon signal	颱風訊號	11.	destruction	破壞
4.	Hong Kong Observatory	香港天文台	12.	gale	強風
5.	signboards	廣告招牌	13.	typhoon shelter	避風塘
6.	pedestrians	行人	14.	window panes	玻璃窗
7.	warning	勸告	15.	storm	狂風暴雨
8.	cinema	電影院	16.	disaster	大災難

17.	preparation	準備	29. block	阻塞
18.	typhoon season	颱風季節	30. collapse	塌下
19.	landslide	山泥傾瀉	31. evacuate	撤離
20.	litter-bin	廢紙箱	32. capsize	翻轉
21.	wind speed	風速	33. devastate	蹂躪
22.	knots	海哩	34. strand	擱淺
23.	scaffolding	棚架	35. disseminate	發布
24.	frightened	害怕	36. thunderstorm	雷暴
25.	horrible	可怕的	37. weather forecast	天氣預告
26.	violent	強烈的	38. tropical cyclone	熱帶氣旋
27.	missing	失踪		
28.	fasten	繫緊		

67

A Visit to a Hospital

Sentences

1. My aunt Polly was taken ill last week.
   我的姨母波莉上星期患了病。

2. She stayed at the Queen Elizabeth Hospital in Kowloon.
   她在九龍伊利沙伯醫院留醫。

3. Last Saturday I paid her a visit at the hospital and asked after her health.
   上星期六，我前往醫院探望她，並問候她。

4. I took some fruit and a bunch of flowers.
   我帶了一些水果及一束鮮花前往探病。

5. The flowers brightened up the ward.
   那些鮮花使病房充滿色彩。

6. Before I entered the ward where my aunt stayed, I had to walk through a long corridor.

我進入姨母病房前，必須走過一條很長的走廊。

7. I walked with a heavy heart.

我懷着凝重的心情走着。

8. A strong smell of medicine nearly made me choke.

一股強烈的藥水氣味幾乎使我窒息。

9. In the ward, many patients looked pale.

在病房內，很多病人臉色顯得蒼白。

10. I tried to squeeze a smile.

我嘗試擠出笑容。

11. A patient was in a wheelchair.

一個病人正坐在輪椅上。

12. Her terrible expression gave me a great shock.

她那可怕的表情使我感到極大的震驚。

13. A doctor and two nurses were on duty.

一位醫生及兩位護士正在當值。

14. They took good care of the patients.

他們小心照料病人。

15. My aunt had just received a simple operation.

我的姨母剛剛接受一個簡單的外科手術。

16. I said hello to her.

我向她問好。

17. She felt a little better that day.

那天她感到好一點。

18. A nurse was taking my aunt's temperature.

一位護士正為我的姨母量體溫。

19. The nurse said my aunt's fever had come down.

那位護士說我的姨母已退熱。

20. My aunt was expected to have a speedy recovery.

醫院方面預期我的姨母可迅速復元。

21. She was very glad to see me.

她很高興見到我。

22. She talked energetically with me.

她起勁地與我傾談。

23. A doctor came and felt her pulse.

一個醫生進來並聆聽她的心跳。

24. He recorded her condition.

他紀錄她的情況。

25. The records were for the doctor's reference.

那些紀錄是備醫生參考的。

26. The doctor said if things went smoothly, my aunt would require no further treatment.

醫生說，如果事情順利的話，我的姨母不需要接受進一步的治療。

27. Later, my aunt took a spoonful of medicine.

不久，姨母服食一湯匙藥水。

28. A white cloth was hanging from her neck.

一塊白布懸掛在她的頸項上。

29. My aunt could not move about at the time.

那時我的姨母不能走動。

30. She would be discharged from hospital in a week's time.

一星期後她可以出院。

31. I did wish she would get well soon.

我真希望她能早日康復。

32. After an hour, I kissed her good-bye.

過了一小時，我向她吻別。

33. Although I was tired when I left, I was pleased.

雖然我離開的時候很疲倦，但卻心情愉快。

Phrases

1.	medical services	醫療服務
2.	thorough examination	詳細的檢查
3.	a heart of sorrow	傷心
4.	a minor case	輕微的個案
5.	to recover from an illness	恢復健康
6.	to keep quiet	保持肅靜
7.	to have a slight cold	有點感冒
8.	a crowded situation	擠迫的情況
9.	to heave a sigh	嘆氣

Vocabulary

1.	hospital ward	醫院病房	3.	patient	病人
2.	casualty ward	急症室	4.	nurse	護士

5. trolley	手推車	25. spacious	寬敞的
6. tray	托盤	26. slight	輕微的
7. doctor	醫生	27. insufficient	不足夠的
8. file	檔案	28. anxious	擔心的
9. stethoscope	聽診器	29. dizzy	暈眩的
10. chart	紀錄表	30. comfort/console	安慰
11. X-ray	X 光	31. recover	復元
12. pain	苦楚	32. tuberculosis	肺病
13. medicine	藥水	33. heartfelt	衷心的
14. tablets	藥片	34. affordable	廉宜的
15. injection	注射	35. fever	發熱
16. bandage	繃帶	36. operation theatre	手術室
17. thermometer	體溫計	37. isolation ward	隔離病房
18. temperature	體溫	38. out patient	門診病人
19. blanket	毛氈	39. diagnose	診斷
20. relatives	親人	40. discharged	出院
21. flowers	鮮花	41. treatment	治療
22. fruit	水果	42. potted plants	盆栽
23. tonic	滋補品	43. primary health care	基本醫療服務
24. health certificate	健康證明書		

Window-Shopping

 Sentences

1. Window-shopping is a popular pastime among women.	逛公司櫥窗是很受婦女歡迎的一種消閒活動。
2. Some people always like to look at goods displayed in shop-windows without any intention of buying anything.	有些人只喜歡瀏覽商店櫥窗陳列的貨品，而沒有購買任何東西的意欲。
3. To many Hong Kong people, window-shopping is part of life.	對很多香港人來説，逛公司櫥窗是他們生活的一部分。
4. They think that, on the one hand, window-shopping can kill their spare time; on the other hand, it is very enjoyable.	他們認為逛公司櫥窗一方面可以消磨空閒的時間，而另一方面，這是一件十分愉快的事。
5. Clever businessmen make good use of their shop-windows to attract many potential customers.	聰明的商人會善用櫥窗，以吸引眾多未來的顧客。
6. Shop-window design is a commercial art.	櫥窗設計是一種商業藝術。
7. Exquisite designs of shop-windows appeal to our visual sense.	一個優美的櫥窗設計能吸引我們的視線。
8. These shop-windows arrest the attention of passers-by.	這些櫥窗往往吸引路人的注意力。
9. The decoration of shop-windows conveys the message of a department store.	櫥窗的裝飾傳達了一間百貨公司的訊息。
10. By looking at shop-windows, people get the feel of a festive atmosphere.	只要看一看櫥窗，人們即可感受到節日的氣氛。
11. Shop-windows can also be used to publicize a big bargain sale.	公司的櫥窗也可用來宣傳大減價。
12. Many people go window-shopping on Sundays.	很多人在星期日去逛公司櫥窗。

13. Well-stocked shopping centres are packed with window-shoppers.

貨色齊備的購物中心擠滿了逛公司櫥窗的人。

14. These window-shoppers are potential customers for the shops.

這些逛公司櫥窗的人可能成為商店的顧客。

15. They are attracted by the numerous goods on display in different sections.

他們被各部門陳列的大量商品所吸引。

16. Many goods of excellent quality are available for sale.

這裏有很多品質上乘的貨品發售。

17. Some goods are on sale at greatly reduced prices.

一些商品割價出售。

18. Many people may make good bargains.

很多人可能購得價廉物美的貨品。

19. Some women go window-shopping until their legs begin to ache.

很多婦女去逛公司櫥窗，直至她們開始感到雙腳疼痛為止。

20. Most girls are fond of looking at boutiques.

大多數女孩子喜歡看時裝店。

21. They usually pay attention to the style and design of clothes.

她們通常注意服裝的款式及設計。

22. Some clothes are very expensive and may be regarded as luxuries.

有些時裝十分昂貴，被視為奢侈品。

23. Some window-shoppers may be interested in other goods such as jewellery, cosmetics, ornaments and toys.

一些逛公司的人會對其他貨品感到興趣，例如珠寶、化妝品、裝飾品及玩具。

24. If the merchandise is of good quality and reasonably priced, there could be a lot of buyers.

假如貨物的品質好而訂價合理，通常會有很多人購買。

Phrases

1. window display

櫥窗陳設

2. a bargain sale

大減價

3. embroidered table cloth

繡花枱布

4. strings of pearls

珠串

5. beautifully designed

設計得美輪美奐

Vocabulary

1.	shop-windows	商店櫥窗	22.	high-heeled shoes	高跟鞋	
2.	department stores	百貨公司	23.	ornaments	飾物	
3.	boutique	時裝店	24.	toys	玩具	
4.	taste	愛好	25.	sportsware	體育用品	
5.	design	設計	26.	furniture	傢具	
6.	packaging	包裝	27.	counter	櫃台	
7.	ribbon	絲帶	28.	shelf	架子	
8.	present/gift	禮品	29.	carpet	地氈	
9.	cosmetics	化妝品	30.	Chinaware	瓷器	
10.	salesladies	女售貨員	31.	porcelain	瓷製品	
11.	discount	折扣	32.	parcels	包裹	
12.	arcades	商場	33.	price-tag	標價牌	
13.	shopping centres	購物中心	34.	expensive	昂貴的	
14.	luxuries	奢侈品	35.	fascinating	迷人的	
15.	styles	款式	36.	exquisite	極美的	
16.	customers	顧客	37.	display	陳列	
17.	jewellery	珠寶	38.	appreciate	欣賞	
18.	handicrafts	手工藝品	39.	electric goods	電器用品	
19.	perfume	香水	40.	electronic games	電子遊戲	
20.	handbags	手袋	41.	carved ivory	象牙雕刻品	
21.	suit	套裝				

Winter

Sentences

1. Winter is the coldest season of the year.   冬季是一年中最冷的季節。

2. The weather is cold and dry.   天氣寒冷而乾燥。

3. At higher elevations in the New Territories, temperature can drop below 0˚C.   在新界較高的地方，氣溫可能降至攝氏零度以下。

4. Occasional spells of cold wind may be too cold and comfortable.   偶然的一陣冷風，可能冷得使人感到不舒適。

5. In Hong Kong, winter does not last for a long period of time.   在香港，冬季並沒有持續一段很長的時間。

6. Minimum temperature below 5˚C is not common in Hong Kong.   最低溫度在攝氏五度以下並不常見。

7. It is extremely rare to see a snow scene in Hong Kong.   在香港極少有機會見到雪景。

8. It is mainly due to Hong Kong's being situated in the sub-tropical region of the world.   這主要由於香港在世界上位於亞熱帶地區所致。

9. In winter, the north wind is dreadful.   冬天的時候，北風可怕地怒號。

10. The severe cold drives many people out of the streets.   嚴寒的天氣使很多人不上街。

11. The earth looks dull and motionless.   大地看似沉悶而沒有生氣。

12. Most trees have lost their leaves.   樹木多已落葉。

13. The movement of the leaves makes a rustling sound.   樹葉的移動沙沙作響。

14. People prefer staying at home.   人們喜歡逗留在家中。

15. They wear cotton-padded clothes.

他們穿上棉襖。

16. The poor beggars are exposed to the cold dry northerly wind.

可憐的乞丐暴露於乾冷的北風之中。

17. They shake with cold.

他們冷得發抖。

18. Very often, people have to endure an intense cold front.

很多時候，人們須忍受一股強烈的冷鋒。

19. Children cuddle up under the blankets.

孩子們擁睡在毯子下面。

20. The morning is quiet and the garden is desolate.

早晨是寂靜的，園子是荒涼的。

21. The songs of the birds disappear completely.

雀鳥的歌聲消失得無影無蹤。

22. Many trees are stripped of their leaves.

很多樹木的葉子落下了。

23. Because of the coldness, people have to put on thicker clothes.

由於寒冷的緣故，人們不得不穿上較厚的衣服。

24. Winter is also a festive season.

冬季也是一個節日的季節。

25. In Hong Kong, both Christmas and the Winter Solstice are in winter.

在香港，聖誕節及冬至都在冬季。

26. Cold weather can also do harm to agricultural products.

寒冷的天氣也會對農作物造成損害。

27. The flower-growers in the New Territories will suffer great losses if the winter is extremely cold.

假如天氣十分寒冷，新界的花農將遭受重大的損失。

28. Owing to the dry weather, fires can easily occur in winter.

由於天氣乾燥，火災很容易在冬天發生。

29. Numerous trees will be destroyed in a disastrous fire.

一場大火會燒毀無數樹木。

30. We should therefore often pay heed to fire danger warnings in winter.

因此我們應該常常留意在冬季發出的火災危險警告。

Phrases

1.	bright and cold weather	晴朗而寒冷的天氣
2.	a silver world	一個銀色的世界
3.	to shiver in the cold	在寒冷中顫抖
4.	dreary weather	陰沉的天氣
5.	peaceful surroundings	寧靜的環境
6.	the bleakest day of winter	最凜冽的冬日

Vocabulary

1.	fire-place	壁爐	17.	widespread	流佈甚廣的
2.	frost	霜	18.	dry	乾燥的
3.	ice	冰	19.	dull	沉悶的
4.	mist	霧	20.	desolate	荒涼的
5.	temperature	氣溫	21.	mild	溫和的
6.	fur	皮草	22.	intense	強烈的
7.	pond	池塘	23.	hardly	幾乎沒有
8.	outline	輪廓	24.	wither	枯萎
9.	seagulls	海鷗	25.	skate	溜冰
10.	Winter Solstice	冬至	26.	persist	持續
11.	peaceful	寧靜的	27.	shiver	震慄
12.	grey	灰色的	28.	resist	抵抗
13.	bleak	蒼涼的	29.	freeze	結冰
14.	poor	可憐的	30.	plum flowers	梅花
15.	miserable	可悲的	31.	winter fire	冬天發生的火災
16.	mysterious	神秘的